Solar Energy, Technology Policy, and Institutional Values

Energy policies that promote new technologies and energy sources are policies for the future. They influence the shape of emergent technological systems and condition our social, political, and economic lives. *Solar Energy, Technology Policy, and Institutional Values* demonstrates the difficulties that individuals in and out of government encounter when they try to instigate a reconsideration of these broader properties of technological systems and the policies that support them. This historical case study analyzes U.S. renewable energy policy from the end of World War II through the energy crisis of the 1970s. The book illuminates the ways in which beliefs and values come to dominate official problem frames and get entrenched in institutions. In doing so it also explains why advocates of renewable energy have often faced ideological opposition, and why policy makers failed to take them seriously.

Frank N. Laird is Associate Professor of Technology and Public Policy at the Graduate School of International Studies, University of Denver. He has received grants from the National Science Foundation and the GTE Foundation, and he has published in such journals as *Policy Currents*, *The American Prospect*, and *Science, Technology and Human Values*.

T0370846

Solar Energy, Technology Policy, and Institutional Values

FRANK N. LAIRD

University of Denver

CAMBRIDGE
UNIVERSITY PRESS

CAMBRIDGE UNIVERSITY PRESS
Cambridge, New York, Melbourne, Madrid, Cape Town, Singapore, São Paulo

Cambridge University Press
The Edinburgh Building, Cambridge CB2 2RU, UK

Published in the United States of America by Cambridge University Press, New York

www.cambridge.org
Information on this title: www.cambridge.org/9780521782470

First published 2001
This digitally printed first paperback version 2006

A catalogue record for this publication is available from the British Library

Library of Congress Cataloguing in Publication data

Laird, Frank N.
Solar energy, technology policy, and institutional values / Frank N. Laird.
p.   cm.
ISBN 0-521-78247-3
1. Solar energy.   2. Energy policy.   I. Title.
TJ810.L32.2001   333.792´3 – dc21   00-064190

ISBN-13 978-0-521-78247-0 hardback
ISBN-10 0-521-78247-3 hardback

ISBN-13 978-0-521-03429-6 paperback
ISBN-10 0-521-03429-9 paperback

To my mother and late father, Mary F. and Frank E. Laird

Contents

Preface

Why do governments take seriously some policies and not others? Indeed, what does it mean to say that a government takes a policy "seriously"? What distinguishes fringe policies from their mainstream counterparts, and how can policies move from one to the other? This study addresses these questions through an analysis of U.S. renewable energy policy. The result is a longitudinal case study of energy policy change that explains what has been taken seriously and what has not, and why.

As other authors have noted, although we discuss energy systems in the language of BTUs and barrels of oil, they are so pervasive and important that arguments about them are, in many instances, arguments about the kind of society that people desire. This concept helps us to understand how much was at stake in energy policy decisions between the end of World War II and the postoil embargo period in the United States – the period that this study examines. This feature of energy policy makes it a prime example of what I call policies for the future. In the coming decades public policy, among other influences, will shape emerging technological systems. Those systems will, in turn, condition and constrain important political and social decisions. That fact makes it imperative that we better understand and deliberate over such policies.

Recent studies of politics and policy have emphasized the importance of ideas in shaping the political world, and this work builds on that literature. Ideas interact in complex ways with interests and institutions, all three shaping each other in the process. Ideas also form the basis for the problem frame through which policy makers view policy problems and solutions. Energy policies are powerfully affected by such ideas.

This book is primarily for those who are concerned with energy and environmental policy in particular and broader questions of public policy more generally – anyone working in the areas of policy studies; political science; history of technology; and science, technology, and society, as well as professional policy analysts, policy advocates, and policy makers. Anyone who seeks to influence policy making, especially as it concerns energy policy and other technology policies, will, I hope, find lessons in this study. I show that effective policy arguments must address issues as they are understood by the officially accepted problem frame. If particular policy arguments cannot do that, their advocates must work on changing the problem frame to change policy.

During the period that I examine here, solar energy advocates, both prominent individuals and organized groups, tried to influence energy policy. Solar energy was then an umbrella term, often referring to what we now call renewable sources of energy, including such things as wind and biomass. Solar advocates enjoyed only modest success. Solar energy failed to become a strong option for meeting U.S. energy needs during this period, not for simple reasons of untested technology or economic cost, but for complex reasons that include a failure to institutionalize new ideas about the energy problem at the top executive levels of government. To support this position, I take a longer historical view of solar energy policy than is typical to analyze the special dynamics of creating public policy around emerging technologies.

The introduction lays out the terms and theoretical frameworks that help us to distinguish the strands of complex ideas that shape national energy policy. It provides the tools for analyzing the ways in which particular ideas come to dominate the official definition of a problem; the conceptualization of its possible solutions; and the rules, norms, and operating procedures of particular institutions.

The chapters in Part I concentrate on U.S. energy policy between World War II and the 1970s' energy crisis. They examine the ways that the federal government and private groups sought to develop solar energy and how various interested parties framed its potential.

Part II applies the same interpretive tools to the energy crisis and its aftermath. The crisis gave energy policy much greater saliency, raising its profile among the public and policy makers alike. The crisis caused many people to express doubts about both American international hegemony and, coming along with the rise of the environmental movement, the viability of the modern industrial way of life. People involved in energy policy increasingly perceived that energy technology choices entailed political and social consequences of the first order, and that perception engendered extensive and bitter conflict.

Examining the interactions of ideas, interests, and institutions surrounding solar energy policy from the postwar to the postembargo period can help us to discover why we have the overall energy policies that we do. It also helps us to understand why changing such deeply embedded policies as those about energy is so difficult. Ultimately, a better understanding of this interaction may help to show how policy can be made better, especially when policy makers are confronted with difficult long-term emergent technological issues.

Acknowledgments

It never ceases to amaze me how indebted I am to so many people for what I keep referring to as "my book." Unlike most debts, these are a joy to have and a pleasure to acknowledge here.

Many friends helped to form my professional community. They are a source of ideas and advice, to be sure, but just as importantly they provide the support and sense of belonging that is such an important part of intellectual life. In particular I want to thank Evelyn Brodkin, Penelope Canan, David Guston, Patrick Hamlett, Bruce Hutton, Sheila Jasanoff, W. D. Kay, David Levine, Dianne Rahm, Richard Sclove, and Ned Woodhouse.

People have contributed to my research for this book in wonderfully diverse ways. The staffs at seven presidential archives helped to guide me through their voluminous holdings. I want to express my gratitude to the archivists at the Harry S. Truman Library, Independnece, MO; the Dwight D. Eisenhower Library, Abilene, KS; the John F. Kennedy Library, Boston, MA; the Lyndon B. Johnson Library, Austin, TX; the National Libraries Nixon Project, part of the National Archives now in College Park, MD; the Gerald R. Ford Library, Ann Arbor, MI; and the Jimmy Carter Library, Atlanta, GA. These materials, a gold mine for scholars and a crucial resource for our history, are so extensive that I felt lost when first confronting them. The archivists patiently helped me to make sense of the bewildering collections and find what I needed. The people and the materials are both national treasures.

I also benefited greatly from the use of the library at the National Renewable Energy Laboratory, Golden, CO. The librarians there guided me to their historical collection, which contains materials found no-where else.

Colleen Dunlavy found the privately printed biography of Farrington Daniels at a yard sale and sent it to me. I never would have found it on my own, and it helped me in more ways than even its appearance in the endnotes would indicate. Al Teich, who knows a great deal about 1970s energy policy, gave me all of his files on solar energy, including some little-known studies that greatly aided my research. It pays to let your friends know what you're working on.

Many people helped to shape my approach to technology policy. Attending Langdon Winner's courses more than twenty years ago, reading his work, and talking to him ever since has opened my eyes to a whole range of approaches to the subject. When I sometimes got lost in the theoretical and empirical minutiae of the work, Langdon's ideas helped me to stay focused on the important political issues. Ted Greenwood and Gene Skolnikoff, in addition to guiding me through graduate school and tolerating my incessant challenges to almost everything that they tried to teach me, also provided examples of academics deeply committed to being part of the policy process. Sheila Jasanoff and Ned Woodhouse both spent more time talking to me about this project than they probably care to remember, particularly at a time when I was struggling with it. The book is much better for their labors. My intellectual debts to Deborah Stone are only partly revealed by her frequent appearance in my endnotes. As both a teacher and a scholar, Deborah has been a model for me with her joyful and serious commitment to a life of ideas and political change.

The Gerald R. Ford Library provided me with a travel grant that enabled me to work in their archive. I am also deeply grateful for crucial financial support from the National Science Foundation, grant SBER 9023010. I got wonderful help from Vivian Weil and Rachelle Hollander in guiding me through the process of applying to the NSF. The views expressed in this book are strictly my own, and do not reflect in any way on the NSF or its employees.

The NSF grant made it possible for me to hire wonderful research assistants – Jack Boynton, Enrique Zaldua, and, especially, Meade Love Thomas Penn. They greatly amplified my ability to do research.

Gail Reitenbach provided developmental editing for the entire manuscript at a crucial point in its evolution, improving its organization and coherence. Two anonymous reviewers for Cambridge University Press also provided insightful comments on the manuscript. They helped me greatly in improving it. Alex Holzman, Alissa Morris, Lewis Bateman, and Elise Oranges of the Press guided my manuscript through every stage of the publication process, and did so ably.

My parents have always supported me, with no strings attached, in whatever direction I have chosen to take in life, including stressing that I should get the best education of which I am capable. As I have gotten older I have come to realize what a rare gift they gave me, which is why I dedicate this book to my mother and late father.

I am at a loss to think about how I can adequately express my gratitude to my wife, Pamela. A remarkable scholar in her own right, she has been involved in this book from day one – talking over concepts, helping to structure my research, reading numerous drafts of numerous chapters, and helping me do research in some of the archives. As an accomplished historian, she was invaluable in teaching this nonhistorian some of her craft. But all of these things still understate her contribution to my work. She kept me going when I was discouraged, and made it possible for me to recover from setbacks. She has given me a home, a place of grace, from which I can face the tasks ahead and enjoy the accomplishments of the past. I marvel at my good fortune to have a love such as that.

Needless to say, all of these good people are absolved from whatever inadequacies lie within. For those I must, alas, claim sole responsibility.

Note on Sources and Archival Abbreviations

The primary sources for much of this work come from the archives of Presidential Libraries and from the vertical files of the library of the National Renewable Energy Laboratory. This last collection is not in a strict sense an archive, but they have a very wide range of newsletters and obscure journals, many now defunct, that are unavailable almost anywhere else. I use the following abbreviations in the endnotes for brevity.

DDEL   Dwight D. Eisenhower Presidential Library, Abilene, KS
GRFL   Gerald R. Ford Presidential Library, Ann Arbor, MI
HSTL   Harry S. Truman Presidential Library, Independence, MO
JCL   Jimmy Carter Presidential Library, Atlanta, GA
JFKL   John F. Kennedy Presidential Library, Boston, MA
LBJL   Lyndon Baines Johnson Presidential Library, Austin, TX
NLNP   National Libraries Nixon Project, an annex of the National Archives, Alexandria, VA
NREL   Vertical Files, Library, National Renewable Energy Laboratory, Golden, CO
WHCF   White House Central Files, a major collection in most presidential libraries

Introduction
Solar Energy, Ideas, and Public Policy

On June 20, 1979, President Jimmy Carter dedicated the solar hot water heating system newly installed in the West Wing of the White House. A "Who's Who" of solar energy advocates joined him at that ceremony. Although they provided part of the White House's hot water needs, the solar collectors served more importantly as a symbol of Carter's commitment to promoting solar energy to meet the nation's energy needs. This ceremony marked the symbolic height for solar energy within the executive branch. Not only did the president announce new policy initiatives, he did so while publicly associating himself with the activists and government officials who had been pushing for them, and all of this against the backdrop of solar collectors on the White House roof. No activist could ask for a better scene and set of props. The event was not only a symbolic peak but a policy peak as well, for solar had never before been treated by the federal government with such generosity or seriousness.[1]

Yet, as in any theater, scenes and symbols can mislead as well as inform. The White House ceremony conveyed the impression of solar advocates' great success as President Carter announced policies for which they had been fighting for years. Since many of these very same people had pushed successfully for new environmental laws and institutions, one could conclude that a new movement and its leaders had acquired the resources and skills to influence government policy decisively. Yet such a conclusion would be mistaken. Solar advocates' successes largely evaporated when Ronald Reagan assumed the presidency eighteen months later. But even while Jimmy Carter was president, their influence in the executive branch eroded severely, beginning only weeks after this ceremony. Moreover, the activists were well aware of the limits of their influence and of President Carter's commitment to their cause. Even at the White House ceremony, they complained to reporters that Carter's policy initiatives were inadequate – barely the minimum that the solar

1

community would accept.[2] How could their success be so illusory and ephemeral?

To understand the development of solar energy policy we need to analyze a historical chain of events over a period of decades, paying close attention to the dynamic interrelationships of ideas, interests, and institutions, both in solar energy policy and in energy policy more generally. The conceptual framework for this analysis, and part of its contribution to understanding technology policies more broadly, is a long-term longitudinal case study that analyzes how key ideas, both technical and normative, enabled actors to frame problems and understand their interests, and how such ideas got embedded in institutions.

IDEAS IN PUBLIC POLICY

In the last decade numerous scholars have argued for the importance of ideas in shaping public policy. They have each conceptualized ideas slightly differently, calling them beliefs, knowledge, values, ideology, and so on, and have analyzed an assortment of ways in which those ideas enter and influence the policy process. Central to all of these analyses, despite their differences, is the notion that either normative or technical ideas, or a combination of both, play a role in setting and changing policy, a role that is not simply a derivative of other more traditional influences on policy, such as interests or institutional structures.

For example, Peter Haas argues that consensual scientific and technological knowledge can be embodied in transnational scientific entities called epistemic communities. Such communities can play crucial roles in international policy making, particularly in facilitating cooperation among states, by helping governments to understand the nature of transnational problems and their feasible solutions. Epistemic communities are bound together by both shared scientific knowledge and shared normative notions about the importance of the problems under study. This combination of normative and technical ideas can influence policy because it can present decision makers with consensual interpretations of uncertain events and provide legitimation to policy decisions, particularly when members of the epistemic community become officials in government ministries. Epistemic communities can help decision makers understand what their interests are in uncertain environments.

In Haas's analysis, ideas gain their force from their acceptance and promotion by a transnational community of experts, and that community's importance derives from its relationship to various governing institutions. Haas does not overplay the importance of epistemic communities, noting that government policy makers sometimes elect to ignore expert recommendations. He argues that the power of the ideas depends on whether the community members are able to garner bureaucratic power.[3] The field of solar energy had a group of experts that comprised an epistemic community. However, just at the time that it began to achieve some bureaucratic power it also began to unravel in terms of its technical and normative cohesion.

John Kingdon, in his study of agenda setting and public policy, argues that ideas are more important in promoting policy than many analysts of politics and policy think. Interest group pressures certainly affect policy, but the substantive content of policies also influences their success, in particular the coherence and persuasiveness of policy advocates' arguments. At any given time numerous policy ideas float around policy systems, and the important question is why some of them take hold and others do not. Policy communities, groups of technical specialists in and out of government, champion various policy ideas. Policy communities resemble Haas's epistemic communities, except that a policy community may or may not share a consensus about the most desirable ideas for some particular policy. Ideas influence policy in Kingdon's analysis because organized institutional forces champion them and so use them in the policy system.[4]

Deborah Stone argues persuasively that ideas about public policy are both the instruments that partisans fight with and, just as importantly, the goals that they fight for:

Ideas are a medium of exchange and a mode of influence even more powerful than money and votes and guns. Shared meanings motivate people to action and meld individual striving into collective action. Ideas are at the center of all political conflict. Policy making, in turn, is a constant struggle over the criteria for classification, the boundaries of categories, and the definition of ideals that guide the way people behave.

Stone develops an analysis of how ideas play out in setting policy goals, framing problems, and evaluating solutions. She shows that groups and individuals fight over and negotiate the detailed meanings of ideas like equity and liberty in the context of particular policy controversies, and that such meanings can change over time as well as across issues.[5] Stone has much in common with Haas and Kingdon, although she gives a higher priority to the processes of developing shared meanings of normative ideas and less to the use of technical knowledge as a political resource. She also provides numerous tools to analyze the ideas that partisans express in their policy analyses and pronouncements.

Donald Schön and Martin Rein discuss the ways in which ideas coalesce into frames, which they describe as the "underlying structures of belief, perception, and appreciation" through which people make sense of and understand their world, particularly in the cases of difficult, intractable policy controversies. Frames can be either quite specific to a particular policy problem or broadly shared cultural understandings. Disputants in policy controversies usually employ different frames, which makes communication between them difficult and the controversies hard to resolve.[6]

These authors and others share several key notions about the role of ideas in public policy, despite their many differences of emphasis and conceptualization. First, they stress the importance of ideas in policy making, claiming that such importance is often overlooked. They also stress that ideas, whether normative or technical, enable people to make sense of the world, to understand the circumstances of their lives and what courses of action will serve them best. Finally, they argue that a shared understanding of ideas can provide the means to collective action. Of course, ideas do not determine policy exclusively. They interact dynamically with other, more traditional policy variables, such as interests and institutions. As Hugh Heclo has argued, one should analyze the interactions of ideas, interests, and institutions, instead of assuming a priori the importance of one over the other two.[7]

Ideas, interests, and institutions interact in a variety of ways. For example, interests are not simply things that we have which were given to us in some mysterious way. Ernst Haas argues that we need knowledge (a form of ideas) to understand what our interests are. Identifying something as "in our interest" means that we have normative ideas that shape our concept of what is good for us and technical ideas that some course of action will move us toward that good situation and so benefit us. In addition, new knowledge or new technological opportunities may cause us to change what we perceive to be our interests.[8] This and other analyses make a persuasive case that what we think of as interests are in fact influenced by the ideas that we and others hold. Of course, this interpretation does not exclude the other relationship – that the ideas we hold are related to our interests. The point is to ensure that we do not reduce ideas to some cynical derivative of interests, since ideas are actually constitutive of interests.

One difficulty in the analysis of ideas in policy derives from the blurry distinction between normative ideas (values) and positive ideas (facts and empirical concepts). Actors base their positions on both types of ideas, and often one cannot cleanly separate the facts from the values in a policy argument.[9] Even more important in this analysis, partisans in a policy dispute will argue over just where that boundary is, wanting to put as much of their argument in the "facts" category and as much of their opponents' argument in the "values" category as possible. Sheila

Jasanoff analyzes this boundary work when scientific advisory committees try to assert what constitutes a scientific consensus in contentious technical issues. She concludes that successful boundary work establishes the boundary in a broadly accepted way and so stakes out part of the issue as the province of scientists and engineers, and that this sort of firm boundary is necessary for closure on some issues. Partisans in energy policy disputes often do contest such boundaries as a way of trying to influence a policy debate and a firm boundary is one barrier to contesting and reopening the way in which an issue is framed and conceptualized.[10]

Energy policy advocates are motivated by the meanings they attach to the technologies they advocate. Trevor Pinch and Wiebe Bijker delineate social groups that are relevant to some technology because they all accept a shared meaning for the technology. The technology is not merely some good that they produce or consume, but has a more complex set of meanings associated with it. Pinch and Bijker explain that technologies have interpretive flexibility in that different groups may design them differently and attach different meanings to them.[11] If we are interested in policy conflicts, we need to understand the political and social meanings that different energy technologies have to participants in the policy debates.

Analyses of technology-based policies need a framework that links particular technological choices with different sets of ideas. If ideas, with their complex mixture of normative and technical components, influence people's choices of energy technology, how can we make inferences that connect the choices with the ideas and attendant meanings? Langdon Winner provides a concept that we can use as an interpretive scheme: technology as legislation. Winner argues that certain technological ensembles – large systems that produce major goods and services such as food, energy, transportation, and communications – are more than mere tools. They are constitutive parts of modern life. This concept does not imply any notion of technological determinism but instead suggests that in making large-scale technological choices we are choosing systems that will encourage some forms of political and social life and discourage others. *"Different ideas of social and political life entail different technologies for their realization."*[12] Winner intended this concept as a way of analyzing extant technological systems. I am using it differently, as an interpretive tool for understanding the meanings that drive people to favor certain choices of technological systems over others.

Partisans in the debate over emergent energy technologies clearly associated their preferred technologies with their larger visions of a desirable way of life. These political and social visions were most overtly tied to energy technology choices during the 1970s, but they were still present, although more implicitly, in the writings of energy advocates throughout the period of this study. It follows that analyzing debates over government policies about future energy technologies must take into account various actors' views of the good polity and society, that is, their normative political and social ideas. It does not matter for my analysis whether or not partisans were correct in thinking that certain energy technologies would in fact lead to their desired society. What does matter is that partisans *thought* that certain technological choices would lead to political and social goals and that a shared meaning of the technology, correct or not, drove their advocacy. Therefore, the notion of technology as legislation provides a framework for helping us to extract partisans' normative and technical ideas from their policy arguments, providing an explanation for why certain energy policies dominated decision making. This framework will facilitate analysis of the way in which actors in the policy process perceived energy policy problems and solutions. In sum, my framework has two different parts: It analyzes the dynamic interplay of ideas, interests, and institutions; and it uses the concept of technology as legislation to understand and interpret that interplay in the case of solar energy policy. The framework also can readily apply to other significant emergent technologies.

POLICY FOR THE FUTURE

While ideas are important in virtually all policy issues, they are especially important in a certain class of policies – those that deal heavily with the future and its attendant uncertainty – and so for which we can make few confident predictions. While all policies involve uncertainty, these issues are particularly burdened by it, and the uncertainty is so deep that it may approach simple ignorance. Policies concerned with developments, both social and technological, ten or twenty years hence must confront the various and widely divergent paths that those developments can take. The specific consequences of such developments may be as unpredictable as the developments themselves. For example, it is impossible to predict what percentage of our electricity will come from renewable sources in thirty years and what percentage from the traditional sources of coal, oil, and natural gas. In addition, it is hard to say which renewable technologies will be used the most heavily and in what manner. Furthermore, it is not always possible to predict the differential impacts of using various energy technologies, even if relative directions are clear. Yet those technological developments will influence what we pay for the electricity, how it affects the environment, how much oil we have to import, the structure of the utility industry, the ways in which that industry is regulated, and a host of other social and political questions. Moreover, policies that we implement now – including resources for research and development, regulations on existing utilities, subsidies for renewable energy, and the advent of competition in the utility industry – will strongly influence which technologies look the most attractive in thirty years, so that we are, in part, creating our future, despite its uncertainty. Under such immense technical uncertainly, people's ideas about what constitutes a good political and social order, and which institutional and technological arrangements they think will further that order, come to dominate policy-making debates, since long-term interests are hard to identify and predict and institutions may be embryonic or nonexistent.

Numerous technology policy issues, including some parts of energy policy, fall into this uncertain-future category, and so they require far better understanding. Solar (often used interchangeably for the broader category of renewable) energy policy in the decades since World War II presents important conceptual and pragmatic questions for policy scholars. It calls for refining conceptual tools for understanding policy change and development, as well as the incorporation of recent work on the politics and sociology of technology. Pragmatically, it is an important substantive issue in itself, and, as an emergent technology, is also part of this broader set of future-oriented, highly uncertain policies for which governments need to be better prepared. An analysis that stresses the role of ideas and their interaction with interests and institutions offers several strengths. It provides a more nuanced account of the process of policy making itself, both for the case in question and more generally. It also helps us discover why it is that we have the solar energy policy that we do. More importantly, such an integrated approach also enables us to determine how policy can be made better in the context of a democracy struggling with difficult long-term technological issues. An analysis of the dynamics of policy making suggests the dimensions along which we might seek improvement. What policy should we have for solar energy, and how could we imagine getting it?

Edward J. Woodhouse, David Collingridge, and a few other scholars have begun to articulate a set of criteria and an analytical framework through which we can make such evaluations. They argue that, for technology policies plagued with uncertainty, policy makers should seek to tap the intelligence of democracy by incorporating views from a wide variety of possible participants, avoid large mistakes, maintain their flexibility, and use feedback to learn about and improve the policies.[13] This prescription means that better energy policy making would include the views of a more diverse array of people and fulfill the substantive criteria of flexibility and feedback.[14] The question immediately arises of how to improve policy making so that policies better fulfill these criteria. In the case of solar energy, in many instances various actors did try to increase the range of voices speaking to policy makers, but those efforts had negligible, or in one case limited, success. This case study demonstrates why is it so hard to make these sorts of improvements in policy. It is not enough for more voices to speak to policy makers. They must speak in a way that is consistent with the dominant problem definition or frame, or seek to change it.

An understanding of the *dynamics* of the policy-making process gives us a better idea of how to change it to make better solar policy and better technology policies more generally. Given the importance of ideas in policy making and the way they shape interests and interact with institutions, concerns for democracy suggest that key institutions and actors be more open to ideas that challenge conventional views of the world, and that policy debate within those institutions be structured so as to provide critical reflection on the ideas that underlie policy and often go unchallenged. In short, the policy-making process should be made more democratic by opening it up to include better debate about the normative goals that we seek with our technological policies. Others have made this suggestion, but the analysis presented here makes it clear that conventional pluralist methods of participation fall far short of this goal, given the often subtle ways that ideas influence policy. Pluralist notions of democracy depict participation as the actions of organized groups in gaining access to and trying to influence decision makers. Given the fragmented and allegedly permeable nature of the American state, groups can choose among many routes into policy making.[15] In this view, groups are limited only by their political resources and skill in using them, assuming a fair policy process in which all groups so inclined have the opportunity to make their voices heard. This framework has much to commend it, but it misses some crucial parts of the policy process, and I will show that even a process that is explicitly designed to open up policy making to alternative conceptions of values, problems, and solutions can fail to do so by failing to address the problem of the institutionalization of ideas explored here.

PROBLEM FRAMES

If ideas are important in public policy, then we must analyze how they enter into and affect the policy process. To understand how ideas interact with interests and institutions and why those interactions affect outcomes, we need to look in detail at how ideas give us a particular depiction of a problem, often called problem definition or problem framing, and how they influence decision makers' evaluations of potential solutions to the problem. Problem frames do not determine policy outcomes in any simple sense, but they do have immense influence on them. Donald Schön and Martin Rein show that frames enable us to construct stories about our policy problems that make the "normative leap" from analyzing a problem to saying what one ought to do about it. If that story is well-constructed, the final normative leap will seem like the natural outcome, the only reasonable one.[16]

At the most specific level this analysis asks, how did advocates and policy makers between 1946 and 1981 frame solar energy technology? How did they conceptualize its then present status and future potential? How did they conceptualize energy policy more generally, and how did solar as a future option fit into that broader frame? What sorts of ideas did these specific and more general frames express, and how did actors try to change those ideas and frames? All of these questions require detailed empirical accounts for answers. In doing this long-term case study I developed a detailed understanding of the ways in which ideas and their associated problem frames got institutionalized as well as the formidable barriers to institutionalizing new ideas; it is more difficult to change institutionalized ideas than analysts often assume. The difficulty in altering institutionalized ideas points us toward the crucial parts of the policy process that must change if we are to have policies that retain flexibility, learn from experience, and incorporate diverse communities and ideas. Nowhere are these considerations more important than in policies concerning emergent technology, where the immense factual and conceptual uncertainties reinforce the importance of actors' values.

Numerous scholars have noted the importance of normative ideas in energy policy debates and attempted to document their influence.[17] A few scholars have studied in more detail the roles that particular values have played in energy debates and the values that advocates claimed were associated with certain energy technologies.[18] Partisans in these debates linked technological choices to social outcomes, even if only implicitly and even if the technological system they advocated would not, in fact, bring about the kind of society that they desired.[19] Moreover, the ways in which actors talked about the policies and energy systems that they desired tell us much about the normative ideas that underlie their proposals.[20]

INSTITUTIONS AND PROBLEM FRAMES

Problem frames, and the ideas that constitute them, operate within institutions. As Schön and Rein put it, "Frames are not free-floating but are grounded in the institutions that sponsor them."[21] Other scholars agree. Judith Goldstein and Robert O. Keohane argue that ideas become powerful when they become institutionalized, and that such deeply embedded ideas can explain the phenomenon of policy inertia, of institutions sticking to a policy long after one might have expected it to change.[22]

To understand the ways that ideas, problems, frames, and so on influence public policy, we must investigate the ways in which ideas get institutionalized. Particular ideas come to dominate the official definition of a problem and the conceptualization of its possible solutions. These ideas also shape the institution's rules, organizational norms, and operating procedures.

Substantial, enduring changes in policy require changes in the institutionalized ideas that influence policy, which can mean either changing ideas within an institution or changing which institution controls some policy. Frank Baumgartner and Bryan D. Jones emphasize the latter to change institutionalized ideas and policies:

This [policy] process is the interaction of beliefs and values concerning a particular policy, which we term the policy image, with the existing set of political institutions – the venues of policy action. In a pluralist political system, subsystems can be created that are highly favorable to a given industry. But at the same time, there remain other institutional venues that can serve as avenues for appeal for the disaffected.[23]

In short, if some policy advocates consistently fail to get the policy they want from some government institution, they can try taking their arguments to a different institution, perhaps a different congressional committee or executive branch agency. Jurisdiction over policy areas sometimes changes, and if that new institution becomes dominant, then the policy can change rapidly. The difficulty with this solution is that the new institution may not end up having decisive influence over the policy of concern, which in fact is what happened in the case of solar energy policy.

Alternatively, advocates can stick with the dominant institution and try to change the ideas that guide it. New ideas can change the meaning or understanding associated with some policy solution, in this case a technology, so that it looks like a more plausible solution to an old problem. Similarly, changes in ideas can change the way the problem is framed, so that the relevant government officials consider as a plausible solution technologies that they previously rejected or did not even take seriously.

Maarten Hajer's work on discourse coalitions alerts us to an important pitfall in the analysis of institutionalized ideas used to explain policy change, or the lack of it. He describes discourses as "an ensemble of ideas, concepts, and categories through which meaning is given to phenomena. Discourses frame certain problems, that is to say, they distinguish some aspects of a situation rather than others." The relationship of Hajer's discourses to the ideas and frames discussed above is obvious. He reminds us that we cannot conclude that ideas are influencing policy just because some institution has started using a particular discourse in its statements, but that we must look at the institution's practices and decisions before we conclude that the par-ticular discourse has become institutionalized and dominant in some part of policy making. Important actors may start speaking the stories of a new discourse, what he calls discourse structuration, but we must also analyze what the institutions *do* to see which discourses are in fact institutionalized.[24]

For the case of solar energy, and other future-oriented energy policies, we need to analyze which government officials were in a position to influence this kind of change and the institutional structures in which they operated, including the means by which nongovernmental actors had access to them. We will also need to analyze the ways that institutionalized ideas shaped the official definitions of problems and how some actors tried to change those definitions. The ideas held at the top levels of policy making, especially in the executive branch, are more important than are usually given credit in the policy literature. In the solar case, what appeared to be a substantial and enduring change during the 1970s, particularly at the agency level, was in fact ephemeral because, in part, of the stability of the way the issue was defined at the presidential level, despite vigorous efforts to change that definition. Making a large change in this type of institutionalized problem frame entails dramatic changes in a massive part of the nation's technological infrastructure, with all the accompanying political, economic, and social changes. Such policy changes must have high-level support, since they will conflict with many other ideas, goals, and interests held by previously persuasive stakeholders and hence encounter stiff resistance from those who prize the status quo.[25] Thus the key for this study will be how new values were, or were not, institutionalized in the Executive Office of the President (EOP). I will also analyze congressional actions to some extent, but on solar energy policy these were mostly reactive to executive branch actions, even in the late 1970s. The EOP was the key barrier to substantial energy policy change.

I do not mean by these comments to dismiss Congress as an important influence on policy. Assorted energy advocates used congressional committees very successfully as a means of promoting their technologies and keeping pressure on the executive branch. This pressure was felt most intensely in the appropriations process. My analysis will carefully depict the interaction of the Congress with energy advocates and the executive branch. That said, this analysis still focuses primarily on the executive branch because it retained the ability to set the dominant frame for the issue. Throughout the history of energy policy, the president and his advisors remained the crucial actors for undertaking new policy initiatives linked to new ideas about policy.

WEAKNESSES OF CONVENTIONAL ANALYSES

Despite their surface appeal, conventional analyses based on interest groups, simple notions of ideology, or rational economic calculations all fail to explain adequately the detailed chain of events in solar energy policy. A simple pluralistic look at the interest groups that supported solar energy could lead one to believe that it would have been generously supported and a high priority for policy makers, contrary to the actual history of solar policy. In addition to solar advocacy groups themselves, solar has gotten the enthusiastic backing of well-known environmental groups since the 1970s. Particularly vexing for interest group theory is that solar advocates' political resources stayed roughly constant during the time that solar policy was changing radically. To respond that the groups gained and then lost their influence in that short period of time (roughly 1974 to 1980) merely restates the question to be answered.[26] Solar has also enjoyed the strong support of the general public. Indeed, for decades public opinion polls have shown solar energy and energy efficiency to be the public's top choice for the energy technologies in which the government should invest for the future.[27] These polls, which political leaders allegedly watch so closely, clearly do not translate into public policy in any simple way.

A simple ideological explanation also fails to explain these outcomes. It is not enough to say, for instance, that President Reagan was opposed to solar on ideological grounds. Support for solar energy was declining sharply in top policy circles while President Carter was still in office. Moreover, the simple ideological explanation begs the more important question: Why were the values associated with solar technologies so anathema to conservatives? In earlier decades solar technologies had been championed by conservative advocates, and understanding how solar came to have particular values imputed to it requires a much longer and deeper historical perspective.

Rational economic calculation also fails to explain the government's actions. Policy makers faced great uncertainty when trying to decide about future energy options. We must base our explanations of their actions in terms of what knowledge was available to them at the time that they made their decisions.[28] In the early decades after World War II, solar's economic and technical feasibility appeared no more uncertain than other energy options into which the government was willing to invest massive resources, most especially nuclear power. Moreover, the government changed its policies in ways that were not justified by short-term fluctuations in fuel – especially oil – prices, as will be detailed in later chapters. For example, from 1980 to 1982, government solar research and development (R&D) funding fell drastically while the price of oil rose or declined only slightly.[29] My criticisms of simple ideological, interest-based, and rational economic calculation frameworks for understanding solar energy policy suggest that a full analysis needs a different approach, though, to be sure, those traditional variables will crop up repeatedly in my account.

The analysis here, by emphasizing the interaction of ideas with interests and institutions, will give us a better understanding of the reasons for the volatile fate of solar policy and how it fits into energy policy more generally. This analysis will also suggest how those who favor solar energy can better go about seeking policy support for it.

IMPORTANCE OF THE CASE

The broad importance of energy to all aspects of life in industrial societies needs little discussion. Energy is part of every major technological activity, from agriculture and manufacturing to transportation and telecommunications. The roots of energy policy stem from the U.S. government's deep involvements in energy technologies, resources, and markets, an involvement that goes back over a century and shows no indication of disappearing.[30]

The government has been and continues to be involved in the research and planning for future energy resources. The Cold War powerfully influenced federal government R&D priorities, and energy, especially nuclear energy, technologies figured prominently in those programs.[31] The Cold War influence went beyond picking R&D priorities. As Stuart W. Leslie has argued, the military security orientation of such programs led technology and science policy in particular directions, emphasizing state-of-the-art high performance often at the expense of technologies that could have important applications in the civilian economy.[32]

Such planning for the future seemed an immediate and pressing matter during most of the 1970s. It seems less so today, although there is no reason that it should. Planning for the future should not wait until a crisis strikes. Recent price increases remind us that the current low prices and ample supply of oil will not last indefinitely. A recent survey of studies of recoverable crude oil argues that world oil production is likely to peak somewhere between the years 2007 and 2014, and this conclusion does not assume any political events that will interrupt production.[33] Energy could be a front-page issue again before long.

Solar energy – or renewable energy, as such sources are usually called now – has the potential to be a major part of the world's energy sources as fossil fuels decline in production. As we will see, advocates have long depicted renewables as the resource that will enable the continuation of industrial civilization after the era of fossil fuels, and a recent spate of books and studies have updated and promoted that conclusion. Private analysts, solar and environmental advocates, government agencies such as the former Congressional Office of Technology Assessment, and some industry groups argue vigorously that renewable energy will be the cornerstone of future energy systems.[34] Thus, understanding the history and dynamics of solar energy policy is important for understanding the possible changes in a technological system of great importance, now and in the future.

Energy policy mostly focuses on existing sources of energy, their accompanying technological ensembles, and the conflicts of their associated regional economic and political interests. For example, the coal industry for years opposed increasing the quotas of imported residual fuel oil, typically used for home heating, into the United States, fearing that such imports would cut into their market share.[35] In this type of conflict, well-established economic interests argue over policies that would affect their shares of wealth and income. The technologies and market structures involved are mature, the various interests have close, long-term relations to government agencies, and everyone acts as if they have a clear idea of which policies will advance their economic interests and which ones will not.

In contrast, policy debates over solar energy are arguments over the shape of a large future technological system. Such policies necessarily confront immense uncertainties about interests and outcomes. This class of policies affects, in addition to energy, many of the most consequential technological systems of our time, including environmentally clean manufacturing, rapid changes in agriculture wrought by advances in biotechnology, and the linkages and developments in telecommunications and information technologies. Policies that governments adopt now will influence billions of dollars of investment in complex technological systems that will become constitutive parts of our society for years to come. The approach I take to this case thereby provides insights for analyzing some of these other issues.

CRITIQUE OF THE POLICY-MAKING PROCESS

Those who wish to challenge prevailing public policy must be able to challenge the sets of ideas that underlie the status quo. A democratic technology policy cannot content itself with giving citizens a set of cookie-cutter choices but must instead empower them to contest the underlying judgements and ideas that constitute those choices.[36] Woodhouse and Collingridge stress that intelligent democratic processes must take into account the views of diverse partisans, lest unwise policies go unchallenged. Clearly, partisans who cannot challenge institutionalized ideas have very little scope for challenging policies in general. Hajer argues persuasively that substantial changes in policy require the dominance of new discourse coalitions, which entails institutionalizing new ideas.[37]

Langdon Winner addresses the problem that philosophical and other theoretical analyses seem to have little effect on the technologies that our societies produce, even when some actors in the system recognize that ethical and other normative issues will be greatly affected by the new technologies. Winner concludes that "the trouble is not that we lack good arguments and theories, but rather that modern politics simply does not provide appropriate roles and institutions in which the goal of defining the common good in technology policy is a legitimate project."[38] This study takes Winner's critique seriously and asks why various technology policy processes, including those that provide channels through which advocates can participate, do not provide the deliberative institutions and roles that Winner calls for. In constructing technologies we do construct our future, and so our policies for the future, if they are to be democratic, require that citizens be able to challenge the institutionalized ideas that underlie the status quo.

PART I

BEFORE THE ENERGY CRISIS

1

Framing the Energy Problem Before
the Energy Crisis

Particular ideas, interests, and institutions shape the energy problem frame. In doing so they also influence the way in which decision makers and the public see solar energy and its potential to solve energy problems. This chapter analyzes some of the core values that make up the remarkably durable official problem frame that dominated energy policy. That frame did change slowly over time, but at no time did it present a conception of the energy problem that made solar energy look like a solution.

The very notion that there should be an energy policy implies defensible reasons for the state to intervene in the energy sector. Just this notion was controversial. Out of the New Deal and World War II came a mix of ideologies: Some lionized government planning, others advocated government intervention for security reasons, and conservatives sought a return to less-fettered markets.[1] Postwar volatility in markets for all fossil fuels made policy debates hard to resolve since policy makers had a difficult time deciding if they should be responding to gluts or shortages.[2] Controversies such as those over the ownership of off-shore oil leases and the expansion of publicly owned electric utilities kept value-laden, ideological issues on the front burner throughout the Truman, Eisenhower, Kennedy, and Johnson administrations, each having a different emphasis on the proper role of the state in energy policy, and each making at least some reference to the importance of private markets in the energy sector.[3] But all four administrations also recognized that government de facto played a substantial role in energy and would continue to do so.

Much of what follows focuses heavily on the presidents and their advisors, because new policy initiatives that require substantial funding and that could have dramatic consequences usually require presidential blessing if not instigation. Many initiatives for solar energy came from further down the hierarchy, from cabinet members or elsewhere in their

19

agencies. But these initiatives did not outlive their patrons, because top policy makers had not been persuaded to change the way they looked at the problem or the normative values that they associated with it. All four administrations saw the need to begin to develop new sources of energy for a postpetroleum energy system. But the existing problem frame raised large barriers for solar advocates, and they never institutionalized a new, more congenial energy problem frame.

THE NATURE OF THE ENERGY PROBLEM – CONVENTIONAL ANALYSES

Conventional analyses of energy policy have shown that policy makers focussed on four basic features of the energy problem: the availability of fuels, their prices, the redistributive effects of energy policies, and, by the mid- to late 1960s, environmental protection. Availability and price changed sharply after the Truman administration, and that change greatly influenced the framing of the energy problem. Immediately after World War II, Truman administration officials were very concerned about an oil shortage. Ralph K. Davies, testifying before the Senate Foreign Relations Committee in 1947, argued for approval of the Anglo-American Petroleum Agreement. Without it, he claimed that the government would need to resume rationing, a very unpopular measure. "We do not *face* an oil shortage. We are *in the midst of one* – now."[4] Nor was oil the only energy commodity in short supply; as Truman put it, "Everyone knows that our Nation's [electric] power supply is tight – that our margin of reserve is inadequate. In almost every part of the country increased production is being impeded and delayed by limited power capacity."[5]

Once the United States entered the Korean War, energy and other resource shortages were prominent topics in cabinet meetings.[6] Even before the war started, officials noticed troubling signs of an insecure energy supply. While domestic production of oil continued to grow, in 1948 the United States began to import more oil than it exported, making it a net importer for the first time.[7] Energy firms increased their production of all fossil fuels, but volatile markets made local shortages possible.[8] Both elites and the general public perceived energy shortages. For example, in 1948 the Sun Oil Company published a large advertisement in The *New York Times* entitled "Fuel Users Have a Right to Know: What's the Score on the Oil Supply?" The ad discussed recent increases in demand that had put pressure on supply, despite the industry's best efforts. "Sun Oil Company is working twenty-four hours a day, at breakneck speed, producing the greatest volume of oil products in its history." The ad goes on to ask consumers to conserve oil by keeping thermostats lower, installing storm windows, and so on.[9]

By 1952 these concerns about shortages disappeared from discussions of energy policy. The prospect of energy shortages that had so worried officials in the Truman administration did not trouble the Eisenhower, Kennedy, or Johnson administrations. Supply changed from short to abundant, and prices stabilized and then declined for almost two decades. President Johnson's Task Force on Natural Resources in 1964 framed the problem ahead as one of exploiting resources more effectively, not running out of them.[10]

Whenever these three administrations set about trying to assess the overall energy situation, their advisors and analysts gave them pictures of abundance in the short and medium terms and technological fixes in the long term. For instance, the Task Force report to President Eisenhower's Cabinet Committee on Energy Supplies and Resources Policy asserted that "There is no over-all shortage of energy fuels for future growth, nor are there shortages for any particular types." They added that supplies appeared adequate even in the event of full mobilization for war.[11] During the Kennedy administration, an energy study conducted by the Senate came to the same conclusion: "The Nation's resource base, in terms of each fuel, is adequate to meet projected requirements for the period covered by this study – i.e. to 1980." A 1963 study by the Federal Council for Science and Technology, a part of the executive branch, came to the same conclusions. Oil industry testimony before Congress likewise repeatedly reinforced the idea of abundance.[12] The Interdepartmental Energy Study Group, a large project started under President Kennedy and finished under President Johnson, estimated that supplies would be plentiful, with little increase in prices, through the end of the century. President Johnson's science advisor, Donald Hornig, reiterated that conclusion in a speech to the National Petroleum Council a year later.[13] These and other assumptions of abundance manifested a dramatic shift from the concerns of President Truman's 1952 President's Materials Policy Commission report, which is discussed below, and they dominated policy making as well as public discourse until events of the 1970s made such assumptions obsolete. As a key part of the core empirical ideas that made up the energy policy frame, they tended to filter out evidence and analyses that might suggest shortages in the near future.

Energy prices were a problem for Truman administration officials, although not for later administrations. Policy makers considered low energy prices essential for economic growth. But in the context of energy shortages in the Truman years, low prices caused a problem: They encouraged increased consumption, which in turn made shortages worse.[14] Thus the Truman administration embraced two possibly contradictory goals – national security, which required abundant supplies of energy for military and civilian use, versus low prices for economic growth. Things changed considerably in the Eisenhower, Kennedy, and Johnson administrations. Perhaps just as important as actual price patterns, most energy policy makers took price stability as a given and enduring feature of the energy system.[15] Although prices moved in complex ways, in the aggregate the real price (that is, with inflation factored out) of energy went down steadily between 1952 and 1968. This energy price is a weighted average of the prices of crude oil, natural gas, and coal.[16] Coal was the most expensive fuel, but its price declined in real terms. Oil prices were in the middle and held essentially flat, and natural gas prices, the lowest of the fuels, increased in real terms until the mid-1960s, when they began to drop. In absolute terms, coal's relative costliness gave price as well as convenience incentives for shifting to other fuels during this period. In addition, electricity prices also fell from 1950 to 1968, with consumers paying one-third less per kilowatt hour, after adjusting for inflation, by the end of the period, due both to the declines in fuel prices and gains in technological efficiency.[17]

The growing sense of an abundant and secure energy supply during this period made the questions of long-term energy alternatives seem less urgent, and so one might expect that policy for alternatives such as solar energy would grow less important as time went on. This contention, however, does not explain all of the events of these years. It is true that officials in the Truman administration made the most extensive and expensive proposals for the support of solar technologies, but those proposals never became policy and never changed the basic way that energy policy was framed among the president's advisors. And it was precisely during the times of cheap energy that the government, with strong agreement between the president and Congress, did in fact launch a very expensive and far-reaching policy designed to provide an energy supply decades into the future – the nuclear power program. Thus the conditions of abundance did not determine a policy outcome of inaction concerning future energy supplies. The important question then becomes which future energy sources got the most attention when there was no crisis to spur attention for all of them?

Another key feature of the energy problem was that energy policies were redistributive. Controversies over specific fuels, usually involving oil trade questions and decisions about favoring oil or coal, required presidential attention in all of these administrations. These were not problems of energy supply or technologies. Instead, these controversies focused on decisions that had very large financial consequences for interested parties, who contested them fiercely.[18] In particular, with declining prices and declining market share, the coal industry presented persistent problems for all postwar administrations. The industry lobbied actively over the issues that affected it, albeit not always successfully, seeking market protections such as restrictions on fuel oil imports. The manner and extent to which each administration decided to help the industry varied, with the Eisenhower administration the least interventionist.[19] This redistributive feature of energy policy meant that any policy change for a given fuel might be resisted by interests associated with other fuels. For policies aimed at the future, this problem might seem insignificant; but if such policies began showing results, they would develop enemies. Which enemies they developed would depend on the types of results they showed and the broader policy environment that shaped people's notions of their interests.

Finally, during the Kennedy and Johnson administrations, environmental problems became a part of officials' thinking about energy policy, and that part grew stronger by the end of the Johnson years. The environmental movement grew in the 1950s, had become a significant political force during the 1960s, and at least some officials in government understood that decisions about energy had profound environmental consequences.[20] An Energy Task Force in the Johnson administration listed a set of problems related to energy issues, and "pollution" was among them.[21] In addressing energy industry associations, President Johnson's science advisor, Donald Hornig, talked at length about the need for future energy developments to be sensitive to their effects on the environment, arguing that the industry must dedicate its efforts to finding ways to produce reliable energy without undue pollution. Hornig's audiences were not the most sympathetic to environmental concerns, so he must have placed growing importance on them to have stressed them as much as he did.[22] This new emphasis on environmental protection could have made solar energy look better to government officials, but only in the 1970s would the official problem frame make that connection. Environmental ideas were just beginning to make their way into the energy policy frame.

IDEAS, NARRATIVES, AND THE NORMATIVE FRAMING OF TECHNOLOGY

The conventional understanding of energy policy discussed above rested on a set of institutionalized ideas. Four different concepts framed energy policy in the United States after World War II – two normative goals and two causal or empirical beliefs about the physical and social nature of the energy problem and its relationship to technology and science. Although the policy frame varied over time in its emphasis on each normative value, and in the precise meanings and interpretations that it gave to them, those values were constantly invoked as the desirable goals of policy by each administration. Similarly, causal beliefs about the sources of the problems and what new technologies could do about them remained remarkably constant during this period, and this problem frame created serious barriers to the support for solar energy technologies. Two particularly revealing settings for debate and analysis during the Truman administration were the President's Materials Policy Commission and the UN Resources Conference. Both processes had the attention of the president and other high administration officials, both of them are rich as sources, and, in part, both of them set the terms of the energy problem frame to which later administrations adhered, emphasizing economic prosperity and national security.

On January 22, 1951, President Truman established the President's Materials Policy Commission (PMPC), sometimes called the Paley Commission, and charged it with analyzing the nation's materials problems over the long term.[23] Written with evocative language and colorful metaphors, the report analyzed policies that the government might adopt to cope with potential shortages or price increases. The major policy objectives were to prevent rapid rises in resource prices that would stifle economic growth and to prepare for the resource needs of the United States and its allies in the event that the Cold War turned hot. The central focus of the PMPC was economics, specifically the potential for rising real costs of materials: "The essence of all aspects of the Materials Problem is costs."[24] Resource shortages constituted a new problem for the United States, and the commission perceived the stakes as fairly apocalyptic:

The United States, once criticized as the creator of a crassly materialistic order of things, is today throwing its might into the task of keeping alive the spirit of Man and helping beat back from the frontiers of the free world everywhere the threats of force and of a new Dark Age which rise from the Communist nations. In defeating this barbarian violence, moral values will count most, but they must be supported by an ample materials base.

To explain the grounding assumptions that the commission adopted, the report listed a set of values that read like a liturgical profession of national faith:

First, we share the belief of the American people in the principle of Growth. Granting that we cannot find any absolute reason for this belief we admit that to our Western minds it seems preferable to any opposite, which to us implies stagnation and decay.

Second, we believe in private enterprise as the most efficacious way of performing industrial tasks in the United States. . . . We believe in a minimum of interference with these patterns of private enterprise. But . . . this minimum must not be set at zero . . . the coexistence of great private and public strength is not only desirable but essential to our preservation.

Third, we believe that the destinies of the United States and the rest of the free non-Communist world are inextricably bound together. . . . *The overall objective of a national materials policy of the United States should be to insure an adequate and dependable flow of materials at the lowest cost consistent with National security and with the welfare of friendly nations.*[25]

Clearly, the PMPC was not shy about staking out normative terrain.

The Economic Growth Value

The PMPC made economic growth one of the central goals that the government should seek. As a means to that goal, the report came down in favor of the private sector as the main provider of materials, including energy, but guided and influenced by government policy. Policy played many roles, since the government owned and bought many resources and regulated materials industries, especially monopolies. The government also funded R&D on resources, though on a modest scale. Moreover, some R&D was aimed at enhancing consumption rather than conserving resources.

The authors of the PMPC report clearly wanted the government to retain the powers to exercise whatever influence was necessary to avert serious shortages or price increases, but they also argued for a large role for the private sector.[26] To these ends the commission recommended three principles to guide government actions, the first two stressing the economic interpretation of resource problems. First, government policy should make it possible to obtain materials at the least cost possible, including importing them when foreign suppliers had genuinely lower costs. Second, policy should encourage consumers to conserve resources in the sense of using them efficiently. The PMPC report explicitly rejected the notion of conservation as hoarding resources or doing without; resource consumption that built economic growth and future prosperity was desirable. But such consumption did not justify profligate use.[27] The third principle was national security. These principles express the values on which the PMPC based its study. Seeking least cost and defining conservation as efficient consumption clearly put the emphasis on growth and economic efficiency. Other goals, such as distributional equity or the use of resources as means to any other social or political ends, vanish under a problem definition such as this. Likewise, only a narrow conception of technology could conform to such a problem definition, namely, technologies as the engines of economic growth.

The executive director of the study, Phil Coombs, used economists' definition of materials as economic resources, which is that they are scarce in the sense that they are increasingly expensive to produce, not in the sense that they are running out. "The materials problem of the United States is not, as some people would have it, that we will all wake up some morning in the future and find that we have suddenly exhausted our last barrel of oil or our last ton of iron ore, or our last pound of copper." Rather, the increasing cost of such resources would harm economic growth.[28] By casting the issue in these terms, Coombs eliminated two different approaches to the resource policy problem. First, since the problem appeared to be one of gradually increasing prices, it did not require a crash program to avert the disaster of a sudden depletion of resources and everyone's freezing in the dark. Second, since increasing prices endangered the economy, the existence of large quantities of low-grade ores and other resources did not diminish the problem. By excluding both of these extremes, Coombs cleared the way for the commission's analysis in the middle and provided a rationale for government intervention in these markets.

Later administrations also saw the need for a mix of private markets and public policies. While the Kennedy and Johnson administrations were more interventionist than Eisenhower's, all of them shared a large commitment to the use of the free market to achieve energy goals. Yet all of them recognized that public policy did and should play a role in providing energy to society. The Task Force Report to Eisenhower's Energy Cabinet Committee affirmed this belief in the market while still leaving room for state intervention:

It seems fair to say that, up until now, broad public policy in fuels has been to rely generally on competition and private enterprise to determine development and use of fuels. This is not to say that in particular instances public policy has not exerted considerable influence.

Similar sentiments found expression in the Kennedy and Johnson years.[29] In fact, the government's deep involvement as owner, consumer, and regulator of energy resources meant that energy markets could not resemble classical free markets. Still, the role of the private sector remained substantial even in the deepest crisis.

The National Security Value

Analyzing the role of ideas in policy requires understanding the ambiguity of shared concepts.[30] Although policy makers frequently invoked national security as a principle guiding energy policy, that principle could have several meanings. The Truman administration worried that the United States would not have a sufficient fuel supply for its military in the event of war. Although this concern faded with the growing abundance of energy resources in later years, it never entirely went away, and all administrations considered adequate stocks of energy necessary for the military. To address energy-related national security issues, President Truman, following a congressional mandate, created a National Security Resources Board (NSRB) in 1947.[31] The NSRB took its job very seriously. Less than a year after it was created, it recommended to President Truman that he seek legislation to expand and consolidate the government's power to allocate and control resources and that those powers be vested in the NSRB.[32] The report conveyed a sense of urgency, almost crisis, in describing the need for these expanded powers, depicting the economy as lacking spare capacity to produce these items, and arguing that the need for additional supplies in the event of war threatened great economic repercussions unless all demands for resources were coordinated by an expanded NSRB.[33] Roughly a year later, the NSRB concluded in another report that the country could not meet the resource requirements for the War Plan put forward by the Joint Chiefs of Staff.[34] Truman and other administration officials spoke publicly about the great importance of energy to defense and national security, one even claiming that it was a secure supply of high-octane gasoline that won World War II.[35]

Public officials also perceived that energy, and resources more generally, had another, more subtle relationship to national security. In addition to recognizing the need for resources to fight a war, a number of world leaders saw the shortages of such resources as the *causes* of international conflict and war. President Truman, in proposing a conference on conservation and resources to the Economic and Social Council of the UN, linked resources with world peace:[36]

The real or exaggerated fear of resource shortages and declining standards of living has in the past involved nations in warfare. Every Member of the United Nations is deeply interested in preventing a recurrence of that fear and of those consequences. Conservation can become a major basis of peace. Modern science has itself become a major international resource which facilitates the use of other resources.

He proposed that the conference be technical, divorced from ideology and politics. Three years later, delegates from dozens of countries, 22 nongovernmental organizations (NGOs), and 152 learned societies attended the United Nations Conference on the Conservation and Utilization of Resources.[37] Several administration officials, including the secretary of the interior, Julius Krug, participated in the conference. Reflecting most of the plenary speakers at the conference, the UN Secretary-General's report on it linked resources and peace:

Today the United Nations is embarking on a new phase of its programme to build the foundations for permanent peace. It is calling on science to mobilize technical knowledge in support of one of the high purposes of the Charter – to raise the standards of living. For behind most wars stand the spectres of hunger and want – effective warmongers of the past. Solutions to these problems, though not so spectacular as those in the political field, are of vital importance to world peace.[38]

In later administrations, only this first notion of national security – that the United States needed adequate energy resources to have a fully prepared military – exerted any substantial influence on the energy problem frame. As a report to Eisenhower's Cabinet Committee on Energy and Resources put it, "War and defense preparations have taught that . . . particular energy products, such as gasoline and bunker fuel, are as vital as munitions of war."[39] Policy makers did not regard growing imports as a problem. For example, Eisenhower administration policy makers were aware that the United States was, since 1948, a net importer of oil, with growing amounts imported into Europe as well as the United States from the Middle East. Yet the national security implications of these imports, while not ignored, took second place to the economic implications for domestic oil and coal industries since increasing imports of cheaper Middle Eastern oil affected employment and profitability in the domestic industries.[40] The alternative conception of energy and security – that abundant resources could prevent wars – remained largely outside official policy discourse, with the noteworthy exception of discussions about nuclear energy, which will be analyzed in the next chapter.

Victims Without Villains

Crucial to any problem frame is the causal story that gives it coherence. It is not enough to think that some things are normatively desirable. One must also have ideas about how the undesirable state of affairs came about, and so how it may be remedied. Policy makers' notions of causation influence which solutions they deem plausible.

After World War II a single causal story dominated virtually all policy discourse about energy and resources. That story is best demonstrated by some of the early policy narratives in the Truman administration, particularly from the UN Conference in 1949 and the PMPC in 1952. Detlev Bronk, president of the National Research Council, gave one of the opening plenary addresses at the UN Conference:

It would be folly not to recognize that the pressures of growing populations and the transformation of the materials of nature into scientifically created products to satisfy the increased wants of man for war and peace are rapidly depleting the world's resources. But we would lack reasonable faith in the powers of science if we did not believe that scientific research and the wise use of scientific knowledge can discover and create new resources for the needs of man and better conserve them for his future use.[41]

The PMPC provided a similar narrative in the opening of its first volume:

The nature of the problem can perhaps be successfully oversimplified by saying that the consumption of almost all materials is expanding at compound rates and is thus pressing harder and harder against resources which, whatever else they may be doing, are not similarly expanding.

The introduction goes on to talk about "the convergence of powerful historical forces," which includes growing demand for materials in the industrialized world and growing populations and material ambitions in the less-developed countries.[42]

These causal narratives defined the issues in two ways. First, speakers at the UN Conference sought a cause for threats to world peace and prosperity, and all found that threat in causal stories that centered on inadequate resources. This expressed a remarkable consensus. The speakers and attendees at the conference had all lived through World War I, the Bolshevik Revolution, global depression, the rise of Fascism, World War II, and the start of the Cold War under the Damoclean sword of nuclear weapons. Nonetheless, to these speakers, improvements in resources had the potential to cut across all of the ideological and political divides that rent the world and could make for the conditions of world peace.

Second, causal narratives in both the UN Conference and the PMPC removed blame for world problems from any identifiable actors and from the classical political vices of greed, imperialism, aggression, and so on.[43] Resource demand threatened to exceed supply due to large-scale social forces, the macroimplications of billions of microdecisions, and the vagaries of nature itself. For instance, growing populations result from reproductive rates, the results of countless individual decisions. Similarly, those populations use nonrenewable resources at increasing rates due to all of the small decisions that those many economic actors make.[44] The lack of an identifiable agency to blame puts this causal story in the category of inadvertent cause, where intentional actions have unintended consequences.[45] This sort of story removes blame – in this case rooting world problems in forces without villains – but still threatens large numbers of victims. Assigning blame is always strategic in making someone responsible for fixing the problem, and so a causal story that blames no one absolves everyone from that responsibility. Articulated this way, the growing pressure on resources is no one's fault, but is instead more like a force of nature. Therefore no one can be expected to stop the process; policy must simply adapt to it.

This story of unintended consequences consistently characterized the official perspective on energy policy from the end of World War II through the Johnson administration. The story's proponents continued to use the idea that problems of resources were the inevitable growth of demands on them by the growing world population, suggesting that policies for the future would have to provide for this growth in demand, since no one person or even group was responsible for it.[46] While analysts might be able to predict these bad outcomes, such predictions were likely to have no effect on people's behavior, since those struggling to improve their lot in life around the world are not likely to accept a construction of the situation that makes them responsible for global resource problems. Framing the problem this way was politically productive, since, by avoiding blame, this problem frame did not threaten most actors. It also suggests that the only solution, the only way to avoid serious shortages in the future, was to find ways of supplying ever more resources, at least until the world population leveled off. That need raised the issue of the role of science and technology in providing such resources.

New Technology as a Solution

Throughout this postwar period, policy makers saw scientific and technological progress as the keys to solving their problems.[47] New technologies not only provided greater abundance, but a politically and socially more desirable life, as the UN Secretary General indicated: "Scientific progress and economic development are not ends in themselves; they are means to a better and richer life for mankind, in which human rights and fundamental freedoms can more readily be observed and respected everywhere."[48] Other speakers at the UN conference echoed this theme. Leaders thought that technology could accomplish these goals both because of its ability to produce material goods and because it seemed removed from politics. Since resource problems were apolitical, and indeed without agency, then their solutions must transcend politics as well, they reasoned, and hence officials' repeated emphasis on science and technology as transnational, above the petty frays of political conflict. The image of technology approached that of a cornucopia, an instrument that could allow all the world's people, regardless of number, to live in prosperity. Officials depicted technology as universally empowering to the extent that it freed humanity from want and enabled the wider exercise of freedom.

Officials presented many ideas that certainly entailed potential changes and dangers, but those drawbacks were overshadowed by the promise of abundance. For instance, the secretary-general's report about the UN conference explored the tremendous potential of producing food from certain types of yeast, which would make much conventional farming obsolete.[49] He threw this out as an obviously beneficial development, despite the sweeping social changes that would accompany such a technological change in the production and consumption of food.

The policy discourse of the PMPC also emphasized this empowering and dispassionate quality of technology, namely, that it enabled an analysis of problems untainted by partisan or other political biases. In his discussion of the overall report with his staff, Executive Director Coombs made it clear that the analysis of materials problems required intelligent observation and analysis, not interpretation. He described the different parts of the final report as pictures taken from an airplane. "This [the attached guidelines] represents a picture from an altitude of 50,000 feet, which is about the proper altitude for the Introduction to the final report." In contrast, other parts of the report presented views from 10,000 to 40,000 feet.[50] Coombs posits these metaphorical aerial photographs as the very models of objectivity, which are more accurate than mere ground-based surveying and devoid of the distortions of personal bias and interpretation. Posing a policy problem a certain way constructs what is important and what is not. By seeing the commission's report as rigorously technical and unbiased, Coombs and others writing the PMPC emphasized those aspects of the problem that they saw as technical and ignored those thought of as more emotional or ideological, such as distributive questions or the just ownership of resources. Framing the problem in this way excludes certain kinds of arguments by ignoring these political and social questions, one of the functions of problem frames.

The image of technology in the PMPC report is, to say the least, a glorious one. For instance, "Technology, that complex accumulation of knowledge, techniques, processes, and skills whereby we maintain a working control over our physical world, has had so enormous a growth during the twentieth century as to dwarf all the previous accomplishments of its history." Elsewhere in the report, technology moved beyond the means of control to become the very agent of control: "Wherever it appears that known resources, exploited by prevailing methods will not meet demands established by prevailing use, there technology must take command and redress the balance." Here the PMPC report anthropomorphized technology. Imbued with its own agency, technology appeared as better than an unproblematic tool; it was a powerful ally. As the means for meeting the challenges of material shortages, the PMPC presented technology as the source of economic growth and national security, and hence associated those important values with it.[51] A report on energy R&D in the Kennedy administration contained similar notions of technology: "We can be reasonably confident that future supplies of resources for the United States will be adequate over the next several decades, *provided* we maintain a vigorous program of research and development in the physical and biological sciences."[52]

These images of technology as a source of ever-increasing abundance dominated official discussion about technology throughout the postwar period and posed serious obstacles for solar advocates. This shared meaning of technology had a similar effect on the evolution of energy technology systems to that posited by Trevor Pinch and Wiebe Bijker, even though the meaning operated at a different level of abstraction. For Pinch and Bijker, relevant social groups had a shared meaning about a particular artifact that relates to the artifact's specific design.[53] In my case a group of important policy makers had a shared meaning about a vaguely defined class of technologies, some that already existed and others yet to be developed. That meaning is that resource technologies are things that provided sufficient abundance, under conditions of exponentially growing demand, to achieve political and social, as well as economic, goals.

This meaning created a category that enabled policy makers to include or exclude future technologies in programs of government support. Technology policy makers are not systems builders in Thomas P. Hughes's classic sense. They are not, with a few exceptions, the people who, at the most immediate level, champion particular systems and overcome the economic, social, political, and engineering problems needed to build the system.[54] They are instead, as policy makers, the actors, operating with political authority, who set the ground rules under which systems builders must operate and who sometimes supply crucial resources that systems builders exploit. Therefore, shared meaning among policy makers structures the environment and the possibilities that systems builders face.[55]

INSTITUTIONALIZED VALUES BUILD THE ENERGY PROBLEM FRAME

The energy policy discussions from the Truman through the Johnson administrations all reflected the core values of either economic growth or efficiency and national security, with constant ambiguity about the extent of the state's role in the economy.[56] The possible shortages of resources or rising prices had nothing to do with identifiable villains, but instead resulted from global-scale, macroforces, the results of billions of uncontrollable small decisions. Technology appeared as the savior, the means by which societies could meet ever-increasing demands for resources, including energy. These values and related technical ideas dominated policy discourses about energy in key political institutions, particularly in the Executive Office of the President and among other senior executive branch officials, both in internal communications and in public pronouncements. They also were reflected in the policies that those institutions favored, including the lack of much action related to solar energy. In short, this problem frame, and the normative and technical ideas that constituted it, were institutionalized; they shaped the ways that key institutions of governance perceived and developed energy policy.

The Johnson administration began to develop a different economic approach to energy policy, abandoning more popular notions of prosperity or economic growth in favor of more technical notions of economic efficiency. That administration also began to consider the ways that environmental protection should influence energy policy. But neither of these changes made enough of a difference in the energy problem frame to affect solar energy.

2

Creating Policy for the Future

One can categorize technology policies based on the problems they are trying to solve and the length of time necessary for the technologies' development. Many technology policies try to solve current problems with already or soon-to-be available technologies, such as cleaning up certain kinds of pollution. These problems are well defined and the parameters of the relevant technology are also well known. A second type of policy still focuses on current problems but needs technologies that will require years or decades for their development. In this case, most authoritative actors have a mutually shared understanding of the problem, making it well defined, although that understanding might change over time. The uncertainty lies in the technology itself, since it may take any of several different forms in its development. An example would be biomedical R&D, such as that focused on cancer. Cancer comprises a current problem, with a widely shared set of ideas about it and well-established sets of institutions and interests involved in its diagnosis, treatment, R&D, and so on. However, the technologies that one needs to cure or prevent cancer are highly uncertain, with scientists pursuing many different possible avenues of research. Cancer is actually an umbrella term for a wide diversity of related diseases, which will no doubt require a diversity of treatments, making the technological future even more uncertain.

The third and most future-oriented type of technology policy seeks to solve an anticipated future problem, and do so with technologies that still require considerable development. These polices suffer from rampant empirical uncertainty about future technologies and their associated institutions and interests. It is often difficult for protagonists to know how different policies will affect their interests, or even what those interests are. Such policies will, more than usual, exhibit their advocates' normative social and political commitments and will of necessity construct the future technologies and their place in the world, since that place is in fact quite uncertain. These technology policies are policies for the future, and energy policies aimed at replacing oil fit squarely in this category.

Despite the support for solar energy expressed by some presidential advisors during the postwar period before the energy crisis, no one in these administrations perceived any potential for it to contribute to solving short-term problems, and it had no institutional support for long term-development, as did nuclear energy.[1] Decision makers' conception of the long-term problem made it difficult for them to take solar energy seriously. In general, solar energy remained relatively low on the policy agenda, and the limited constituency that tried to raise it did not involve actors with clear, large financial stakes, since its commercialization was so far in the future. Solar energy did not benefit from clearly defined interests or well-established institutional champions and solar advocates lacked a propitious definition of the energy problem that could help them mobilize such interests or institutional support. Thus when energy problems occurred, few saw solar as part of the solution.

From the end of World War II through the Johnson administration, officials considered three broad categories of technologies when they thought about policies for a future postpetroleum world: synthetic fuels, nuclear energy, and solar energy. What follows is an analysis of how government officials framed the problem they were trying to solve and how the different technologies fit into those frames. The combination of key ideas about the energy problem and potential energy technology solutions, along with the institutional structures for making energy policy, made it very difficult for solar energy to get a serious, sustained hearing in top policy circles. This chapter probes those linkages between problem frames and institutions in developing policies for the future.

SYNFUELS

Synthetic fuels (synfuels) are gaseous or liquid fuels produced from oil shale, tar sands, or coal. Various European countries had developed technologies for producing these fuels, some of them dating back to the nineteenth century, and the U.S. government sponsored a substantial synthetic fuels program during and after World War II.[2] Fuel shortages after the war made the problem of developing synfuels seem even more urgent to government officials.[3]

Richard Vietor makes it clear that national security was one of the driving motivations for the program. Officials understood the need for abundant fuel during World War II and some felt that relying on imported oil was risky, since imports could be cut off. During the winter of 1947–1948, the United States experienced a heating oil shortage, and the secretary of defense joined the secretary of the interior in calling for a dramatic expansion of the synfuels programs.[4] President Truman's President's Materials Policy Commission (PMPC) continued the national security argument for synfuels, since the United States had become a net importer of oil. The United States possessed vast quantities of oil shale and coal, and the technology prototypes already worked, so the key problem was lowering the costs. The PMPC's estimates of production and pricing made this argument seem plausible, because they claimed that by 1975 the United States could be producing 2.9 million barrels per day of synfuels and that gasoline from oil shale would cost less than 10 cents per gallon.[5]

Interior Secretary Julius Krug argued for a very aggressive program. He sought a national investment of $9 billion in synthetic fuel facilities that would produce two million barrels of synfuels a day. While he hoped that industry would make most of this investment, he thought that the government also should do so if necessary.[6] In May of 1948, he opened a government facility near Pittsburgh designed to extract oil from coal, one of three such units that the interior department planned.[7] In May of 1949, just a few months before the UN Conference, Krug made a speech urging the private oil industry to take over investment in synthetic fuels, and he requested that Congress authorize government loans for that purpose. However, many industry representatives were reluctant to involve their firms, believing that the high costs of synfuels made them a bad investment.[8]

However, 1948 was also the year that fuel stocks began to grow, partly due to growing imports from the Middle East, which undercut the government's rationale that synfuels were important, at least in the near and medium term. In that year the oil industry began to oppose the program in a major way and succeeded in slowing it down. From 1948 to 1953, the oil industry and the government debated strenuously the costs of synfuels, with industry estimates coming out much higher than those of the government. Despite the support of the president and the Departments of Defense and the Interior, the synfuels program stalled in Congress and died entirely once President Eisenhower took office.[9] The national security argument could not trump oil industry opposition reinforced by powerful arguments that synfuels were too expensive to invest in when conventional fuels were abundant.

Although the Eisenhower administration killed the synfuels program, the president did include synfuels in his 1954 charge to his Cabinet Committee on Energy Supplies and Resources Policy.[10] The committee's appointed task force did the study under very tight deadlines, with considerable help from industry, and said almost nothing about synfuels.[11]

A Federal Council for Science and Technology study of natural resource R&D during the Kennedy administration listed oil shale as part of the country's estimated reserves of fossil fuels, but said almost nothing else about it. The council said nothing about synthetic fuels from coal. The administration had enlarged two programs in the Interior Department dramatically in percentage terms: Oil shale R&D had risen from $778,000 in fiscal year (FY) 1962 to $1.4 million in FY 1964, and oil from coal had risen from $713,000 to $2.1 million in the same period. However, these sums are tiny when compared to government programs in the 1940s, and they pale in comparison to the $9 billion proposal that Krug formulated in the late 1940s.[12]

These different policies were grounded in different policy narratives. Krug repeatedly argued that U.S. petroleum stocks were dangerously low – only ten years' worth of proved reserves and maybe another thirty years' worth assuming new discoveries – and that America was taking a big risk by depending on oil imports from the Middle East. He posited that growth in energy consumption was inevitable, although he also argued for conservation measures. His solution to this alarming scenario was rapid and large investments in synfuels, building on and greatly increasing existing government programs.[13]

Krug's policy narrative locates the source of the problem in something impossible to control – the myriad actions of millions of energy consumers that result in rapidly increasing demand.[14] The growth of both the population and the economy makes such increased demand inexorable. Since there is no one to blame and no one whose behavior one can reasonably expect to change, the only solution is constant and rapid increases in energy supply. Increasing oil supplies mean increasing imports, which causes its own set of security problems. If one assumes that synthetic fluid fuels made from coal and oil shale are the only alternative means for producing large quantities of fluid fuels, then a synfuels program is the only place a policy maker can turn.

The oil industry disputed vigorously Krug's claims about the costs of synfuels, which they claimed were much higher than government estimates, and they also argued that domestic supplies of oil were more robust and that imports were less risky than Krug thought, concluding that a massive program in synfuels was premature. But note that Krug's argument did not, at one level, depend on the quantitative details of fuel costs. If the price of synthetic gasoline was $0.20 per gallon or even $0.40 per gallon, instead of Krug's $0.12 to 0.14 per gallon, Krug's narrative still retained its prescriptive force. If oil reserves would last twenty or forty years instead of ten, that merely put off the day of reckoning for a few years. Krug's policy narrative reveals the structure of his argument – that inexorable forces of increasing demand will soon enough cause severe shortages of fuels, retarding economic growth and endangering national security, and it does not much matter if it happens in 1960 or 1970 or 1980. If policy makers accepted Krug's narrative, uncertainties in synfuel prices paled in comparison with the consequences of severe shortages or the risks of imports, and in any event the price of petroleum products was likely to go up when their supply became short.

Krug adhered to numbers that made his case look as urgent as possible, but in the end the structure of his policy narrative made it irrefutable unless one expected to find very large new sources of fuels. None of this is to say that Krug was correct in his assessments of oil resources or synfuel prices, but rather that he and others in the Truman administration constructed the energy problem so as to make large investments in synfuels look reasonable and that such a construction of the problem had been at least weakly institutionalized in parts of the executive branch, as evidenced by its broad support for aggressive programs. The values of national security, economic growth, and the notion that the government must take a strong role in guiding these developments were all part of the problem frame, and the president, the secretaries of the interior (Krug and his successor), and the secretary of defense accepted that frame. Only determined opposition in Congress, led by a powerful oil lobby, kept the program from growing beyond the three synfuel pilot plants that the government constructed and ran.

The problem frame changed only when all of the people in key positions in the administration changed, that is, when President Eisenhower took over in 1953. Well before that, the government was collecting data that suggested that oil resources were not as small as Krug had suggested, and the public began to experience a long period of energy glut, instead of the shortages of 1945–1949. But those changes were not enough to change the frames of the people in key positions in the administration, so they continued to construct the world (represent it, as Stone would say) in such a way that they saw no reason to change their policies. Only the change in administration brought the change in the problem frame and the normative and technical ideas that went with it, suggesting that the frame had been institutionalized only weakly.

NUCLEAR ENERGY

Nuclear energy underwent a fate opposite to synfuels. Throughout the Truman administration officials expressed skepticism about the near- and medium-term potential for civilian nuclear energy. In one of his speeches about the looming oil crisis, Julius Krug mentioned nuclear power, claiming that it could not substitute for oil anytime soon. The projected shortages were going to be in fluid fuels, like gasoline and heating oil. Since nuclear power produced electricity and since it would take a long time to electrify all of the functions that then used fluid fuels, even a rapidly growing nuclear power program did not obviate the need for synfuels.[15] President Truman made strongly supportive statements about nuclear power in public, but internal discussions made it clear that the economic use of such technology remained, in the administration's view, probably several decades off. In addition, of the various civilian uses of nuclear technology, officials did not rank electricity production the most important.[16]

Near the end of Truman's term, the President's Materials Policy Commission (PMPC) voiced similar arguments about nuclear power and added some others. The PMPC did not question that reactors for energy could be built, but their costs and the need for nuclear materials in the weapons programs made their feasibility as civilian energy sources uncertain, at least for the near-term. While anticipating its great long-term potential, especially with the use of breeder reactors, they found it hard to predict when these developments would occur, except not any time soon. They expected that nuclear energy would not displace fossil fuels in any major way in the next twenty-five years.[17] They reiterated the basic problem of energy resources as one of increasing supply without increasing price. In its discussion of the potential for electricity from nuclear fission, which the commission classified as an unconventional source of electricity, the report stated: "At this time, it does not appear that nuclear fission can be regarded as a contribution in any substantial degree to electric generation during the next 10 or 15 years, and the probability is that the atomic energy industry will remain a heavy net consumer of electricity [due to military demands]."[18]

Even the Atomic Energy Commission (AEC) shared these doubts about civilian nuclear power in the near-term. In a classified report to the president dated at the same time as the PMPC report, the General Advisory Committee to the AEC stressed military developments as its top priority and regarded civilian power as a competitor with military programs for scarce materials and personnel:

The great scale of atomic energy production, present and planned, means that if the atomic materials were not required for military purposes they would be available on a scale large enough to be an important fuel for civil power. Where, when and under what circumstances power so generated could compete economically with power from other sources is not now known. The work of the Commission in developing atomic reactors has not been primarily directed toward answering this question.[19]

Clearly the AEC's emphasis on military applications overrode civilian applications.[20] Top government officials voiced these arguments, including, in the case of the General Advisory Committee of the AEC, private scientists who were advisors to the government.

This official position does not mean that everyone in the government shared these views or that the government had no civilian energy program. For example, on December 20, 1951, an AEC experimental breeder reactor in Idaho produced the first nuclear-generated electricity.[21] Moreover, many scientists in the national laboratories and elsewhere were quite enthusiastic about the potential for civilian nuclear energy and thought that it could be a significant part of the energy mix far sooner than did top officials and that it deserved much more government support than it got. One example, with some irony, was Farrington Daniels, a leading figure in solar energy. Daniels, a physical chemist, had worked for the government during the war and had ended up as director of Argonne National Laboratory. He was a principal designer of a prototype civilian nuclear energy reactor, the Daniels pile, and had left the lab and government service in frustration over the unwillingness of the government to support this kind of R&D adequately.[22] Clearly, despite such enthusiasm on the part of important nuclear energy advocates, the highest level policy makers before 1953 were very unsure about the magnitude and timing of nuclear energy and regarded it as a technology of the future, two or more decades away.

In the Eisenhower administration, civilian nuclear energy began to get more positive attention; in particular, it got a major boost from one of Eisenhower's most famous speeches, "Atoms for Peace," presented to the United Nations General Assembly on December 8, 1953. Remarkably, the promotion of civilian uses of nuclear technology was not the original intention or principal focus of the speech.

Officials wanted the speech, originally called "Candor", to lay before the public, forthrightly and in detail, the national security situation that the United States faced in its dealings with the Soviet Union. The president and his top advisors felt that the public did not understand the severity of the threat posed by nuclear weapons, especially the new hydrogen bombs, and by the designs of the Soviet Union. The speech aimed to mobilize the American people, to provide a stimulus similar to that of war, but in order to avoid a nuclear war. The populous needed to work harder, save more, and so on, to keep the nation economically strong, and it had to be prepared to adopt explicit civil defense procedures. One top aide described the speech as part of a process of "fiber-toughening for the long pull."[23]

Excerpts from sample drafts of the speech show consistently that civilian applications of nuclear energy were a sidelight, not the main focus of the talk, and in fact the references to it diminished and became increasingly vague as the speech was revised. Most of the talk was about the problems of "Atoms for War." In the June 17 draft, two pages of a fifteen-page speech were devoted to civilian applications, much of it about the medical use of radioactive isotopes. On nuclear energy per se this version of the speech began: "Finally, we have pushed back the frontiers of science and engineering in the field of power production to the point where we believe we are no more than a decade away from economic electrical power produced by the burning of uranium and possibly thorium."[24] The September 2 draft had even less about civilian uses, just eleven lines making up three short paragraphs. The image of nuclear energy was glorious, but vague: "Atomic energy in our lifetime will lighten the burden of man's toil, raise his standard of living, ease his ills, and add vigorous years to his life." In this draft C. D. Jackson, a senior aide, also introduced in one sentence the notion of some international control over civilian nuclear technology: "Under a system of effective international control, the whole world would share in these advantages."[25] That notion of international control of nuclear materials for global benefit became a core part of the speech.

In later drafts and the speech that President Eisenhower actually presented to the UN on December 8 he expressed, remarkably, near-term optimism. "The United States knows that the peaceful power from atomic energy is no dream of the future. That capability, already proved, is here – now – today."[26] In earlier drafts it first was a decade away, then sometime in our lifetimes, and now suddenly ready immediately.

Despite the importance of the "Atoms for Peace" speech, it actually took quite a while for the government to start a substantial civilian nuclear power program, and even longer for industry to get interested. In October 1953, two months before the "Atoms for Peace" speech, the AEC announced a pilot nuclear energy plant that it would build at Shippingport, PA. But that plant was controversial even among nuclear advocates, some of whom argued that it rushed into production a crude technology. They prefered a much-expanded research effort to develop more advanced reactors before moving to the pilot plant stage.[27] Four years after the speech, some former members of the AEC, along with a number of prominent nuclear scientists, criticized the government for going too slowly in developing civilian nuclear power plants and urged a more coherent, aggressive government program.[28]

During the Kennedy administration, nuclear energy policy had three principal actors: the White House (the Executive Office of the President and the president himself), the AEC, and the Joint Committee on Atomic Energy in the Congress. President Kennedy and his aides were publicly very supportive of nuclear energy, but they were not taken with the idea that the government should put dramatically increased funds into the technology and even considered decreasing the funding. The AEC and the Joint Committee were, on the contrary, very gung-ho, thought that the Eisenhower administration had left too much to the private sector, and wanted a dramatically increased government program.[29]

On March 17, 1962, President Kennedy formally requested that the chair of the AEC initiate a study of the role of nuclear energy in the context of other energy resources, specifically other ways of generating electricity. The AEC drafted a report and, remarkably, discussed it with the Joint Committee before presenting it to the administration, indicating that, while they nominally reported to the president, they considered the Joint Committee to be at least an equally important patron and ally. The AEC ignored Kennedy's request to analyze nuclear energy in the context of all energy resources and produced a report calling for a much-accelerated reactor building program. In their draft report they assumed that electricity demand would grow so dramatically that even the Joint Committee criticized the numbers. The AEC's final report called for building "seven or eight power-producing prototype reactors, approximately half of which would be advanced converters and the rest breeders," all at the expense of the AEC. It also argued for subsidies to get industry to build ten to twelve "full-scale power plants."[30]

The White House was unhappy with this conclusion and the way the AEC ignored its instructions, and on February 15, 1963, the president directed Dr. Jerome Wiesner, the director of the Office of Science and Technology in the White House, to chair an interdepartmental energy study to do what the AEC had not done, namely, to view nuclear energy in the context of other energy sources.[31] The Joint Committee saw this new study as a way of delaying an aggressive nuclear program and expressed its displeasure five days later by calling in Wiesner to testify at hearings and grilling him with some hostility about the administration's intentions for the support of nuclear energy. Wiesner held his ground, and while he was very supportive of nuclear energy in general terms, he was openly skeptical about the need for an immediate crash program.[32] In internal discussions in the White House, Wiesner was even more critical, arguing that the AEC report had failed to make a case for an aggressive government nuclear energy program.[33] The interdepartmental study was not completed until well into the Johnson administration.

During the Johnson administration the electric utility Jersey Central Power and Light ordered a turnkey nuclear energy plant (one that is ready to use once the owner walks in and starts it up, rather like turning the key to start an automobile) from Westinghouse.[34] The AEC, the TVA, and the director of the Office of Science and Technology, now Dr. Donald Hornig, all touted this purchase, and the one shortly after it by Niagara-Mohawk, as an indication that nuclear power had become competitive almost a decade earlier than the AEC had originally predicted and that this would pave the way for the rapid expansion of the industry. The estimated costs for electricity from these plants were projections that had no basis in experience, but that did not dampen officials' enthusiasm.[35]

Nuclear advocates used a policy narrative of loss of control and redemption.[36] Inexorably increasing demand for energy would endanger industrial society, causing us to lose control of the things that we needed to continue to prosper. Our present course of action – a growing consumption of nonrenewable energy sources such as oil and gas – was leading to a crisis of supply that would stifle economic growth and weaken national security. Nuclear power, particularly breeder reactors, could restore control by providing an energy supply that could expand almost indefinitely and enable us to reestablish control over our fate.[37] Interestingly, the AEC and the Joint Committee attributed economic growth to massive government intervention, arguing that the private sector could not be expected to take the risky investments that were essential to continued growth. From the Truman administration on, the AEC and the Joint Committee also stressed the importance of national security as another crucial condition that threatened to go out of control.[38]

The normative idea of progress also aided the acceptance and dominance of nuclear power in policy circles. By the middle of the nineteenth century, the concept of progress in the United States had shifted from a notion of people's spiritual, moral, and social improvement to that of technological advance. New technologies became the very embodiment of progress. When important decision makers came to associate a particular technology with progress, that technology became more desirable than its alternatives.[39] The notion of the frontier comprises another crucial part of the idea of progress. A technology is part of progress if it is on the technological frontier and can help take the society to and beyond whatever frontier it then confronts.[40]

Popular writings of the 1950s clearly associated nuclear power with notions of progress. In a rather breathless book intended for general audiences, David O. Woodbury, a popular science writer, depicted developments in nuclear technologies as the very essence of the frontier, with new fields of science and technology springing from nuclear developments. If we could develop the peaceful atom, "we shall leap sharply upward into a world of greater comfort and happiness, better health and security."[41] Gordon Dean, chair of the Atomic Energy Commission from 1950 to 1953, published a book describing for the public the then-current state of the U.S. atomic energy program and what sorts of problems lay ahead. Although more serious in tone and substance than

Woodbury's book, Dean also clearly accepted the notion that nuclear technology was a major part of progress, economic and otherwise. He also used the notion of the frontier, the idea that nuclear technology was taking us to the next uncharted territory, and left no doubt about what to do:

> Mankind has recently entered a room, the door to which is labeled the atomic age. We are in that room, and we have found that it is so large and so dimly lighted that we cannot yet begin to perceive all that is in it. But we have crossed the threshold, and we cannot turn back. All we can do is go forward as boldly, and yet as wisely, as we can.

One does not turn back from the frontier and promise of progress.[42]

Depictions of nuclear technologies as part of progress were not left to the random publications of individual authors. The government and industry made substantial efforts to advertise for atomic energy, depicting it as friendly and a part of social progress. The public relations and advertising campaigns were massive and continued for years.[43]

These narratives and their associated problem frames constructed the energy problem and nuclear power technology in such a way that they fit together almost uniquely. Since the general problem is growing energy demand, about which policy can do nothing, the solution is a technology that can produce ever-increasing blocks of bulk energy. Because existing fission technology could not, in fact, do that at the time, nuclear advocates depicted the current generation of reactors as a necessary step toward the ultimate solution, breeder reactors, the only technology that could fulfill such demand.[44] Even the skeptics in the Kennedy administration, like OST Director Wiesner, accepted the general problem frame; they just did not think that it merited the large and sudden increase in public funding, since the crisis was not going to be acute any time soon and other technologies, including renewables and the improved use of fossil fuels, might play a role in stretching out the supplies of oil and gas. But they did not, from the evidence of their internal and external statements, question the basic logic of the issue.[45]

Thus most senior policy makers of this period shared this meaning of nuclear power technology as a progressive, frontier, cornucopia of energy, one that provided symbolic gratification as well as practical solutions to energy problems. Note that the meaning of the technology is not enmeshed in its detailed designs, but rather in its general outline and structure.[46] This shared meaning led to a consensus for substantial policy support for these technologies, with the only dispute among government officials being over how much and how fast.

The AEC, the Joint Committee, and, to a lesser extent, the Executive Office of the President had institutionalized these problem frames and policy narratives. They showed up repeatedly in the ways that officials discussed the problems, the institutions responded to questions and challenges from the outside, and even in the ways the institutions were organized and charged to operate. The Joint Committee was the only standing, permanent committee in Congress that had members from both the House and the Senate, suggesting that its subject was more important than interhouse rivalries. The AEC could simply defy the president when he ordered them to study nuclear power needs in the context of other energy sources, and it could get away with it because of the structural protection that it got from the Joint Committee. These policy frames and commitments remained constant for decades and transcended the individuals who happened to occupy the leadership positions in these institutions. So durable were these institutionalized frameworks that when opponents of these institutions sought to make changes in nuclear power policy, they found it easier to abolish the institutions than try to reform them.[47]

SOLAR ENERGY

Although it had nowhere near the prominence or funding of nuclear power or even synfuels, solar energy did crop up when White House staff, and sometimes agency officials, discussed future energy policy, both internally and externally. Different administrations expressed varying degrees of enthusiasm for it, but they all conceptualized it in basically the same way. All of these instances show the interplay of a complex mixture of ideas, government officials, outside actors, and the contingent events outside of energy policy in shaping problem frames and policy development. Ideas were not the only factors influencing these events, but they played a greater role than other analyses might suggest. The interaction of ideas with more conventional policy variables provides a better explanation of events than the conventional variables alone.

In Truman's administration solar issues appeared on the policy agenda twice in major ways – just after the United Nations Conference on Resources in 1949, and in the deliberations of the President's Materials Policy Commission of 1951–1952. Julius Krug, then Secretary of the Interior and the official representative of the United States to the 1949 UN conference, gave a plenary speech in which he suggested ten specific areas of resource development that he thought would best contribute to higher standards of living. The first three, in order, were nuclear energy, solar energy, and synthetic fuels, especially from oil shale.[48] Krug embraced solar's potential during the conference. As interior secretary, he already had jurisdiction over several energy sources, and he made it clear at this conference that he wanted to add solar energy to his department's programs. He suggested that a solar program in the hundreds of millions of dollars might be appropriate for this effort.[49] The program never developed into anything, in part due to the mobilization for the Korean War, which put a heavy emphasis on short-term fuel needs, and also due to Krug's resignation as interior secretary only a couple months after this conference.[50]

Exactly why Krug was so enthusiastic about solar remains unclear.[51] He had long experience with energy issues, working with the Wisconsin Public Utilities Commission in the 1930s on electrical rates and, later, as chief power planning engineer for the Tennessee Valley Authority (TVA). When the war started, he joined the War Production Board (WPB) as head of its power division and, after a brief stint in the Navy, became chairman of the WPB during the last year of the war. In 1946, Krug was named Secretary of the Interior, replacing Harold Ickes, and the press depicted him as nonpolitical and a very able administrator.[52] During his tenure as interior secretary, Krug issued repeated warnings about impending shortages of oil and natural gas.[53] As part of the solution to this problem, he advocated an aggressive program to develop synthetic fuels from oil shale, coal, and tar sands. But his emphasis on solar was new and suggests that he had recently decided that solar offered another partial solution. Thus a reconceptualization of solar technology and its broader energy context did penetrate to a cabinet-level official during the Truman administration. Yet, the failure to adopt policies that promoted solar energy in any substantial way or with any permanence foretold a pattern that would be repeated for decades. Krug never institutionalized his advocacy of solar energy and the problem frame that went with it, so his policy initiatives did not survive his departure from office.

The staff of the PMPC also discussed solar, and their report concluded that solar energy, like nuclear energy, offered alternatives for the future, not the present. The PMPC assumed that energy demand would double by 1975 and that hydro, oil, and gas would be insufficient to meet that demand without raising costs substantially. While they projected that conventional sources would suffice until 1975, in the long-run the nation would need new sources of energy. It was in this long-run that solar energy could begin to play a role. In one of the few places in the report that mentioned solar, the report stated, "Long before then, the Nation should begin its transition toward currently unconventional sources, notably solar and atomic energy."[54] Significantly, solar energy appears nowhere in the PMPC's volume on energy and infrequently in the bulk of the report, while a chapter, "The Possibilities of Solar Energy," appeared as the last avenue explored in Volume IV, "The Promise of Technology."[55]

This chapter was the only extended discussion of solar energy in the PMPC report. Largely a summary of the various technologies then in existence and the research that was being done on them, the structure of the chapter followed that of other contemporary writings on solar, albeit expressing more enthusiasm than some. It began by noting the immense amount of solar energy that strikes the earth and argued that the task for R&D was to increase the efficiency of solar technology in converting that energy to useful forms. The chapter reviewed specific solar technologies, including domestic space and hot-water heating, wind, photovoltaics, and ocean thermal energy. It made the claim that solar space heating could be put into 13 million homes, including some apartments, between 1950 and 1975, accounting for ten per cent of the nation's total energy. The chapter called this scenario the "maximum plausible market" by the year 1975 and did not propose any means by which this market potential could be realized.[56] The chapter concluded with the argument that solar is the only option in the long-term to replace fossil fuels and that the transition to it should begin long before shortages inevitably drove up the price of conventional fuels. It assumed that populations around the world would continue to grow, that their growing standard of living would make ever-greater demands for energy, and that nuclear power would never be more than about one-fifth of that energy load, thus leaving solar as the only option left. The chapter then called for large increases in funding for solar research.

Significantly, the PMPC judged both solar and nuclear energy as viable alternative power sources for the future, contrasting them to conventional fuels rather than to each other. There was great uncertainty in the costs and feasibility of both of them. There were, of course, also great differences, not least of which was the massive military, and later civilian, expenditures on nuclear developments compared to the tiny funds spent on solar. Nonetheless, at that time the PMPC had no compelling reason to conclude that solar was any less practical for civilian use in the long-term than nuclear, and some of the language in the report reflected this equality. Both had great potential, and both needed a great deal of work before they could realize that potential.

Top officials in the Eisenhower administration gave solar energy little credence. The Cabinet Committee Task Force report lumped solar in with nuclear and shale oil as future resources. "The prospect of using newer sources of energy, such as nuclear power, oil products from shale or coal, and solar energy, appear farther in the distance than would be of any significant concern in this study."[57] The privately sponsored World Symposium on Applied Solar Energy prompted the main discussions about solar energy among administration officials. The government officials most interested in promoting solar were one step lower in the hierarchy than was the case in the Truman administration. Orme Lewis, Assistant Secretary of the Interior, and Howard Pyle, Deputy Assistant to the President, were trying to get the president involved in the upcoming solar symposium and in the subject more generally. They sought the attention of White House staff by discussing what the president should do with regard to the symposium and by circulating a speech by Dr. M. E. Spaght, a vice president of the Shell Oil Company. In summarizing Spaght's speech, they emphasized his use of the ideas of income energy, principally solar, and capital energy, which comprised fossil fuels and uranium.

The speech argued that we could live on income energy indefinitely, but that the current costs were too high and that we had better soon find ways to bring those costs down, since we would exhaust our capital energy in about a century.[58] These ideas presented a very different frame for the energy problem than the one that dominated the administration, and Pyle and Lewis tried to circulate them among the top White House staff. The aides appealed to the desirability of having the president be part of a growing phenomenon:

It occurs to me [Pyle] that this general subject and the vast possibilities in the field parallel in some respects the atoms for peace idea. This solar energy thing has unlimited possibilities and might conceivably be another way in which the President could reflect the great vision he has in planning for the future. . . . It's going places inevitably, and there's no reason why the boss shouldn't be identified with it.[59]

However, it was not so easy to get the top White House staff interested in solar energy. In response to Lewis's request that the president send a welcoming message to the symposium, Bryce Harlow, a senior aide to the president, expressed skepticism:

Orme agreed that before the President would pay the slightest attention to all of this solar energy business, he would have to be interested by someone with a scientific background who could show factually exactly where the science is now and what its future holds in store.[60]

Lewis and Pyle did get the president to send a friendly but noncommittal letter of greeting to the symposium delegates, but little else.[61]

The Kennedy administration said little about solar energy, with the most discussion coming in the May 1963 report on natural resources R&D. This report discussed some "important gaps and imbalances" in the current division of energy R&D funds, and mentioned renewable resources first:

As shown in the inventory tabulations of work in progress in 1963, only about 0.3 percent of the $1.5 billion spent on energy resources research and development is directed toward renewable resources and no research and development at all is underway on tidal power, wind power, and naturally occurring temperature gradients in tropical and arctic waters.[62]

The report made technological and institutional recommendations, but only in general terms:

> The Subcommittee believes that research on solar energy ought to be increased beyond the agency proposals [for the coming fiscal year]. . . . At the present time, the most promising ways of utilizing solar energy beyond photosynthesis are as a supplemental source of energy for space heating, drying, and desalination of sea water. No Federal agency has primary responsibility now for research directed at development of solar energy and as a result no coordinated program of solar energy research is in existence.

The report goes on to endorse an Interior Department proposal that it house such a research program. It also proposes that the government fund R&D on wind and tidal power because they may be locally important, even if they do not have the potential for national impact on energy supplies.[63] Thus the report begins to discuss the institutional problem of supporting solar energy research, the lack of an institution that would develop and champion such work.

IDEAS THAT THWARTED SOLAR ENERGY
R&D INITIATIVES

A consistent set of causal stories and values is woven through these proposals and discussions of energy policy and solar energy. To elucidate those stories and values, consider at length a specific example, the PMPC in the Truman administration, which provides us with a window on the thinking of those who were trying to change the way that top policy makers conceptualized natural resources policy, including energy policy. As a study that had the president's and other officials' attention, the PMPC report was in a position to influence the ideas associated with those policies. Although it came too late in Truman's term to affect policy, it did set out a new way of thinking about these issues. Applying Stone's method of narrative analysis to both the report as a whole and to the chapter on solar energy can help us to see what kinds of stories, symbols, and metaphors were used in portraying both resource issues and solar energy in particular.

The basic story of resources in the PMPC follows a classic theme of a loss of control, which dominated the thinking of the staff throughout the report. They saw World War II as a turning point that marked the end of the United States' self-sufficiency in resources. Since that time, demand for resources, and energy in particular, had increased steadily and promised to keep increasing. Economic growth, coupled with growth in population, would continue to increase demands on materials, potentially leading to rapidly rising prices and shortages, stifling prosperity, and threatening security. These large-scale trends appeared to have a certain inexorable quality to them, and only continuous efforts to stay just ahead of disaster offered any solution:

One thing seems certain about the materials problem: it will persist. Its forms will alter; its severities may be controlled, and partial solutions will brightly present themselves – but the forces that brought the problem into being will increase rather than diminish. The central fact seems unalterable: as industrial civilizations grow in complexity they compound demands made upon materials ... the reason the Malthusian doom is so overdue is that Malthusian calculations have never given sufficient weight to the extraordinary ingenuity of mankind in extricating himself from situations before they become wholly and finally intolerable ... the materials problem may never be solved, but it can be compensated. We will accomplish this, however, only if we recognize that as physical resources decline, the resources of ingenuity must rise up to serve mankind in their stead.[64]

Thus the PMPC presented a narrative of a situation heading steadily toward disaster. Only planning and ingenuity could rescue the nation. But even that rescue could not be permanent; it required continuously finding new ways of supplying materials and energy.

The solar chapter in the PMPC report exhibits the same narrative structure as the broader report, only this time with a happier ending. Globally increasing population and per-capita energy demands make inevitable dramatic real increases in the costs of energy unless alternative sources are ready to take up some of the load in twenty-five or thirty years. Because the report projected that nuclear energy would only bear a fraction of the load, solar would have to take the place of conventional fuels. Since the United States had spent almost nothing to develop economical solar energy, it appeared to be time for a massive commitment to it to avoid this collision of increasing demand with dwindling supplies.[65] The ending to this narrative was happier because the potential supply of solar energy is very large and will continue at the same rate indefinitely. This type of narrative seeks to persuade by arguing that the normal course of events is leading to a very bad outcome and that only the change recommended by the author can prevent tragedy. Actors who seek to promote substantial policy change tell such a narrative because they need to provide a compelling reason for change since, on the surface, all seems right with the world. Similar stories characterize the policy statements of the later administrations, though they are not worked out as elaborately. Those who favored solar energy saw it as the solution, or part of the solution, to an ever-increasing demand for energy, one that threatened loss of control over social processes.

Although solar advocates used these stories about solar energy, they could not persuade top officials that solar energy was in fact a good fit with the energy problem in its dominant problem frame. With a few exceptions, officials were quite resistant to changing their definitions and frames of the energy problem. Again, the most developed example comes from the PMPC. Early on in its work, the PMPC perceived energy as key to the nation's ability to meet the challenges of adequate materials, and advances in technology as key to an adequate energy supply. Since conversion from raw resources to usable materials took energy, and since future resources would come from lower grade deposits, the demands on energy needed to supply resources were sure to increase, and rapidly. The PMPC expressed little concern with energy as a consumer product. In fact, when they described energy as part of the set of materials under concern, the word "material" was put in quotes. As with all materials, the objective was to expand supply without a substantial rise in costs.[66] Even more fundamentally, the PMPC accorded solar little attention because it regarded solar, like atomic energy, as promising long-term replacements for fossil fuels but of no supply significance for the next twenty-five years, a conclusion that was fully consistent with contemporary technical writing.[67]

Both the entire report and the solar chapter of the PMPC used a mechanistic metaphor, depicting the trends in resource use as rolling along autonomously. While such trends resulted from human actions, they seemed independent of human control or choices, the unintended macrooutcomes of millions of microdecisions. Since the causes of these trends appear deeply structural, rooted in normal and unalterable human activity, there was no point in trying to change them; one simply sought to keep ahead of them. Concerned people explored numerous strategies for keeping ahead, such as substituting more abundant resources for scarce ones and using scarce ones more efficiently, but they never considered altering the underlying structural causes.

Solar's Lack of Institutional Structure

The institutional structure associated with energy policy did little to promote solar energy. As the May 1963 report in the Kennedy administration pointed out, solar did not have a centralized institutional champion in the government, unlike nuclear power. Instead, agencies pursued it only for their own narrow mission purposes, such as NASA working on photovoltaic cells for its satellites. There was no institution in government charged with thinking about a comprehensive program for developing solar technologies and, just as important, no institution to fight for that program. Sometimes highly placed individuals developed an interest in solar energy for various idiosyncratic and contingent reasons, such as Interior Secretary Krug in the Truman administration, or Lewis and Pyle in Eisenhower's. Nonetheless, those interests were not put into place as institutional structures that would stay in government and continue to support solar programs after those particular officials who advocated solar energy left office.

Research and procurement programs for solar technologies reflected this lack of institutionalized support. Government interest in solar technologies during most of the 1950s and 1960s showed up mainly in the military services and the space program, both of which had small research programs that were mostly concerned with photovoltaics (PVs), devices that convert light directly into electricity. Because of their light weight and lack of moving parts, NASA used PVs to power satellites, and they powered the Vanguard, one of the first American successes in space. The government bought PVs in substantial quantities in the late 1950s and 1960s.[68] Science advisors in the Kennedy administration saw solar as promising, and went further to argue that government-funded R&D favored nuclear too heavily and should be reoriented toward other energy sources, solar among them.[69] This notion of trade-offs between two sources never made it into the public discussions, largely because powerful forces in Congress, such as the Joint Committee on Atomic Energy, were quite hostile to cutting nuclear funding for the benefit of other energy sources. And indeed, the budgets of those years continued the trends of large funding for nuclear and little for others, particularly solar.[70]

Even so, during the Kennedy years solar R&D funding increased steadily, though remaining substantially less than nuclear or conventional fuels. Total energy R&D reached about $717 million in FY 1962, $909 million in FY 1963, and an internal study expected it to reach about $1 billion in FY 1964, with most of the money coming from the Department of Defense, the AEC, and NASA, with the rest from the Departments of the Interior and Commerce and the NSF.[71] The solar energy component (classified as "direct solar energy") of this R&D program grew from about $1.7 million in FY 1962 to about $5.4 million in FY 1964. The indirect solar energy R&D, mainly hydro, wind, and biomass technologies, grew to about $2.4 million by FY 1964.[72] Biomass includes plant matter that can be converted into fuels such as alcohol.

These data demonstrate several things. The budget for solar energy R&D was much larger than is often thought, and it increased rapidly in this period, from $2.1 million to $6.6 million over a three-year period. Most of that budget fell into the Defense Department and NASA, and so it probably developed power systems for satellites.[73] The small NSF budget for solar was growing rapidly in the biomass area. In contrast, the AEC spent no money at all in the solar areas, while its funding of nuclear R&D topped $400 million by FY 1964.[74]

These data demonstrate most tellingly that each agency focused on a small number of solar energy applications relevant to its particular mission. No government institution existed to try to develop a balanced plan of R&D for solar, conceived of broadly, or to act as a champion for solar in competition with all of the other claimants for federal research funds. The FCST report tried to provide the beginnings of that centralized analysis, but it had little effect on policy, despite its presidential mandate. Thus the institutional structure for energy policy left solar energy with only a small fraction of the total energy R&D funding, and only then when it suited the particular needs of certain agencies. While most people recognized that solar had great potential, it still seemed an energy source of the future, ironically a more distant future for the Eisenhower, Kennedy, and Johnson administrations than for Truman's. Solar never got serious consideration as a source that might be a major part of the future U.S. energy system and so it lacked the support that such a role might have entailed. In a technology policy for the future, with all its attendant uncertainties about interests and technology, a technology needs institutions that embody favorable ideas to get serious attention from decision makers. Solar had none of that, and so it never got that attention.

3

Advocates Construct Solar Technology

From the end of World War II through the 1960s solar enthusiasts sought to shape public understanding of solar technology and to influence government policy toward it. During this period solar advocacy began to mature, with the establishment of research programs, professional and advocacy associations, technical journals, popular writings, and conferences. Within this growing group of advocates, consisting mostly of scientists and engineers, a core of experts emerged on whom the government could and did call for advice about solar issues. However, debates within this core about the potential for solar energy made it difficult for advocates to depict it as a technology that government policy makers should take seriously, especially given the framing of the broader energy debate.

SOLAR TECHNOLOGY: STATE OF THE ART AFTER THE WAR

Even before World War II some solar technologies enjoyed experimental or even commercial use.[1] For example, by October 1939, Palmer Putnam, a consulting engineer and a central figure in solar energy circles, persuaded a Vermont electric utility and a turbine manufacturer to test his design for a large wind turbine that would feed electricity directly into the utility's grid. By October 19, 1941, they had finished a large, 1.25-megawatt wind turbine with 175-foot-diameter blades, sited on the top of Grandpa's Knob, a treeless mountain near Rutland, Vermont, and began generating electricity. The machine ran well for two years, until a bearing wore out that took two years to replace due to war-time shortages of such parts. It began operation again in 1945 and ran for several months before a blade broke off, after which the machine was permanently retired.[2] Modest-sized firms in the private sector funded the entire project. Putnam involved many eminent people from the mainstream of the engineering world in this renewable energy project, including Vannevar Bush, the former dean of engineering at the Massachusetts Institute of Technology (MIT) and the head of the federal government's entire R&D effort during the war, along with several other professors from MIT and Harvard, including the chair of MIT's civil engineering department. Surprisingly, the costs of the wind power were not drastically higher than power from conventional sources. In 1945, Putnam and his colleagues estimated that they could put up more wind turbines for the utility of the same design at a cost of about $190 per kilowatt of installed capacity. The utility needed a cost of about $125 per kilowatt for the wind machines to be competitive. Putnam estimated that it would cost several hundred thousand dollars to build and test new designs that might bring the costs down sufficiently, but the manufacturer felt that it could not risk more money on such an uncertain enterprise, and the project was abandoned.[3]

Prior to the war, commercial firms also sold solar hot-water heaters, which became commonplace in Florida, California, and other parts of the South.[4] From 1936 through 1941, the solar hot-water market boomed in Miami, with the total number of installations in southern Florida estimated at 25,000 to 60,000. By 1941 solar hot water installations in new Florida homes outnumbered electric by two to one.[5] Solar systems also supplied hot water to subsidized low-income housing projects in California, Florida, and Georgia. The largest such installation, apparently put in during the war, operated at a complex in Georgia, where flat plate collectors connected to 153 storage tanks served 480 dwellings. This system provided 72 gallons of hot water per dwelling per day, which government officials considered adequate by public housing standards of the era.[6] Due to materials shortages, manufacturing of the systems ceased during the war, and the industry never entirely recovered thereafter due to declining prices for fossil fuels, maintenance problems with systems already installed, and increasing per capita use of hot water.[7]

Before and after the war, solar home heating also gained a modest popularity. In 1945, *McCall's Magazine* published a collection of articles about passive solar homes that had appeared earlier in the magazine. The houses, all modest in size and mid-priced or lower, were not called "solar homes," but many had large south-facing windows, and their descriptions expressed an intent to use the sun's heat to provide for some heating needs.[8] In the building boom after the war, some developers marketed houses explicitly as solar heated. But the popularity of such homes declined in the late 1940s, due both to declining fuel prices and to the poor performance of some of the homes.[9]

Researchers investigated a number of other solar technologies just before and after the war, such as flat plate and concentrating collectors for the generation of heat and photovoltaic cells that converted sunlight directly into electricity. But all of these technologies were in the research stage, and none were yet commercial. In the case of photo- voltaics, one researcher called for substantial basic research that was "completely divorced from any present considerations of a practical nature."[10]

With a few exceptions, scientists and engineers made only modest progress in developing solar technologies between the end of World War II and the late 1960s. In a comprehensive review of solar technolo- gies published in 1964, Farrington Daniels presented a list similar to those published fifteen or twenty years earlier, including solar domestic heating and hot water, solar cooling, solar furnaces, solar heat engines, and photovoltaic (PV) cells, along with a few more obscure technologies. Photovoltaics had enjoyed the most dramatic improve- ments since the war, with their efficiencies growing from about one per cent in 1953 to about fourteen per cent in 1964.[11] Nonetheless, high prices still characterized all solar technologies. A 1963 book reported PVs producing electricity at about $100 per kilowatt-hour. An Italian firm made solar pumps for about $1,000 per horsepower and solar stills desalinated seawater at a cost of about $700 per acre- foot, compared to $2 to $40 per acre-foot for conventional water supplies. Despite these prices, Merritt Kastens argued that some solar technologies were only about a factor of two from being com- mercially competitive.[12]

TECHNOLOGISTS' CONSTRUCTION
OF SOLAR ENERGY

Scientists and engineers working on solar technologies dominated public discourse about them in the 1940s, 1950s, and 1960s. In techni- cal and popular arenas, they presented not just research results but a whole conception of and framing for solar energy and where it fit in society. They agreed on many points, and all used the same data. They all acknowledged that immense quantities of solar energy reached the earth, that existing technologies used that energy with very low efficiency, that the energy was intermittent, and that energy from such sources was expensive compared to fossil fuels. Despite these common points of departure, they did not all draw the same conclusions about solar energy. They did not all share the same understanding of the meaning of the technology.[13] They disagreed among themselves about the potential for solar technology as a substitute for fossil fuels. That disagreement stemmed primarily from two things: the nature of the energy problem that solar was supposed to solve and the extent to which they thought that deliberate, targeted research and development programs could accelerate or change the path along which a technology develops. One can, roughly, place the experts in two clusters based on these disagreements.[14]

The Guarded Cluster

Hoyt Hottel, a professor of chemical engineering at MIT and head of one of the best-known solar research programs, exemplified the cautious, guarded cluster of solar experts. In an address to the Smithsonian Institution in 1941, Hottel referred to solar enthusiasts as "cranks" who brought more "rosy optimism" than knowledge to their work and argued for the "informed pessimism" of a good engineer. He pointed out that the conversion efficiencies of solar energy technologies were very low, rendering irrelevant the large quantities of solar energy that strike the earth. He was also dubious that these efficiencies could be increased dramatically, leaving little room for policy impacts on solar's future.[15] By espousing lower expectations for solar technologies, Hottel both provided reassurances that he was a careful, sober technologist, that is, one who was credible, and suggested that the exploitation of solar had to wait for the results of extensive research.[16] Other solar researchers, such as F. W. Hutchinson of Purdue University, shared Hottel's skeptical view of solar energy.[17]

Even more enthusiastic solar researchers and advocates such as Farrington Daniels could also be very guarded about the short-term prospects for solar energy. He warned at an opening plenary address at a 1955 symposium, the "Sun For Man's Use," that solar technologies could not yet enter the mainstream and that excessively optimistic proclamations coming out of the conference would only hurt solar later when they failed to materialize.[18]

Throughout the 1950s, many solar researchers kept this guarded view of solar's commercial value. But they still promoted it on the grounds that fossil fuels were limited and that solar and nuclear were the only long-term substitutes. It was still unclear what role solar would play due to "the low intensity at which the energy is received, its intermittent nature and the consequent difficulty of energy storage, and the low efficiency of present energy converters."[19] This guarded, cautionary approach informed government understanding and policy, discouraging high levels of intervention on behalf of R&D. In Gusfield's terms, the guarded technical community owned this issue, that is, its definition and understanding of the issue made up the official definition.[20] Of course, numerous factors in addition to expert opinion influenced government officials' views of solar energy. Nonetheless, cautious elites in the technical community contributed to those official views.

Ambitious, Imaginative Advocates

Another cluster of solar advocates expressed more ambitious and hopeful scenarios for solar's future. Perhaps the most important of these was Farrington Daniels, who, though cautious about the short-term, believed that focused R&D could greatly improve the prospects for solar technology. Daniels was a major figure in American science, elected to the National Academy of Sciences in 1947 and president of the American Chemical Society in the 1950s. A physical chemist, Daniels had worked on the Manhattan Project during the war at the Chicago Metallurgical (later Argonne National) Laboratory and after the war produced the first design for a civilian power reactor, the Daniels Pile. The Atomic Energy Commission refused to support the project, largely because it did not want any diversions from its military program. He left Argonne in 1947 and returned to the University of Wisconsin at Madison, where he took up the study of the application of solar energy.[21]

In a 1948 talk Daniels framed the energy problem and solar energy within it:

When we have used up our coal and oil, exploited our available land with intensive farming, and trebled our population, can we then call on the sun to give us still more means to satisfy our ever increasing demands for food, fuel, and power? *The answer is yes.* But there is a long challenging road of research and development which must be followed first – and we must not get the idea that we are about to step into a new era of physical and economic abundance.[22]

This article contrasts strikingly with the cautious advocates. Daniels had very few technical disagreements with them, acknowledging the economic shortcomings of many solar technologies. Yet he was very positive that the possibilities of solar could be realized with sufficient investment in research, reflecting his belief that a strong R&D policy could affect this technology's development. This core belief framed the technology very differently. His fluid notion of technology meant that applications of resources and talent could dramatically alter technological outcomes, which implies that technologies are changeable through policy decisions. This view is hardly surprising for a physical chemist who came of age during the flowering of quantum mechanics and worked on the Manhattan Project. The skeptics did not share that view of technology's plasticity.

Daniels's is a classic narrative of decline, one of the fundamental types of stories told in policy narratives. Such stories seek to persuade us to a course of action, not simply by a recitation of facts and analyses, but by depicting the situation so as to make any other course of action look irresponsible because it would leave us to a terrible fate.[23] Thus Daniels reconstructed the energy problem as one in which large-scale forces resulting from human behavior steadily moved us toward trouble, only to be arrested by increased intensity in scientific and technological research on solar energy. His positive outlook for solar energy grew out of this larger energy context, which gave more urgency to developing new energy sources and technologies.

Other solar experts, such as Maria Telkes, Eugene Ayers, Palmer Putnam, and M. E. Spaght, joined in this more ambitious advocacy for solar energy, and all of them identified the lack of R&D funding as the factor that prevented solar energy from making the progress that it could.[24] In 1952, Ayres used, and apparently introduced, a financial metaphor for energy, categorizing energy sources into two groups – capital and income. "More and more we will be required to live on our energy income and be less dependent on our energy principal within the next few decades."[25] This metaphor suggested a strong argument for investing in solar energy as a source of energy income and appears to have been persuasive to the officials in the Eisenhower administration who promoted solar within the administration, since they referred to a speech by Spaght that used it.

Such metaphors can serve to reconceptualize an issue in our mind. They powerfully invite us to see a phenomenon as one thing rather than another and shape the way we understand that phenomenon.[26] If we see energy sources as all of a piece, as interchangeable fuels and technology that heat our homes, light our lamps, and so on, then we conceptualize them as standard private economic goods, no different than toasters or baseballs. Our only concern with them is price and, perhaps, reliability and service. However, categorizing energy sources as either capital or income sources compels us to think about them differently. The capital versus income distinction implies that energy is not merely a private economic good, but rather that energy sources are of two qualitatively different types. Since spending one's capital is considered a profligate, unsustainable thing to do, this distinction carries the suggestion that we should use as much income energy and as little capital energy as possible.

Finally, environmental values gradually began to come into the ambitious advocates' frames for solar energy. Farrington Daniels invoked the idea of stewardship, the need to leave future generations sufficient resources, as the reason to expand the use of solar energy as quickly as possible. Eugene Ayres likewise talked about how the status quo would leave the world grossly depleted in important resources. Bringing the problem back to the present, Maria Telkes listed the lack of pollution as one of the virtues of solar energy. The idea of stewardship seemed most important to these advocates, with pollution a secondary concern.[27]

Interestingly, throughout the 1940s, 1950s, and 1960s, environmental advocates, with rare exceptions, paid no attention to solar energy. In histories of the environmental movement and in the writings of its advocates, solar energy does not even show up, much less occupy an important place.[28] The solar energy and environmental movements apparently had no overlap. Leaders in the solar energy field did not figure in the environmental movement prior to the energy crisis. With one notable exception, environmental advocates did not discuss solar energy as part of their program of reform.

Murray Bookchin provided that exception. In his book *Crisis in the Cities*, published in 1965 under the pen name Lewis Herber, he cataloged the many environmental health problems that grew out of ever-growing cities and urban sprawl. In the book's last chapter, "In the Long Run," he addressed energy and the city. The "urban blight" and suburban sprawl and their attendant diseases, which fossil fuels for cars made possible, and the finite supplies of fossil fuels themselves, made their use, to Bookchin, simply unsustainable in the long-run. He ruled out nuclear power as a large-scale replacement for fossil fuels because of environmental difficulties of nuclear waste disposal. He concluded that only an energy system based on a wide variety of renewable sources would ultimately work, and so he championed solar heating, photovoltaics, wind, tidal power, and other renewable energy sources.[29]

EARLY ORGANIZED SOLAR ADVOCACY

Solar advocates began serious organized activism during President Eisenhower's administration. Through the 1950s and 1960s they held conferences and meetings and built new institutions. Although their institutions declined in the 1960s, they remained active and reemerged vigorously in the 1970s. Rather than attempt a comprehensive chronicle of their activities, what follows demonstrates the ways in which solar advocates tried to build institutions and to influence public opinion during the 1950s and 1960s, and the values that they sought to associate with solar technologies.

Conferences and symposia on solar and other energy resources flourished in the early 1950s as experts debated where current developments in solar science and technology pointed. For example, a 1953 symposium at the University of Wisconsin tried to define the state of the art in using solar energy. The symposium's organizers attempted "to bring together all the scientists who had worked on the utilization of solar energy."[30] Farrington Daniels claimed that they only missed a few such experts, so the forty-one invitees suggests the field's size at that time. The symposium included many of the more publicly active figures in the field, including Daniels, Hoyt Hottel, George Löf, Palmer Putnam, and Maria Telkes.[31] Despite their disagreements about solar, most of them spoke to its overall potential and emphasized its difficulties and problems. Solar had great potential and deserved much more research support, all agreed, but its moment had not yet arrived. In an interesting construction of solar's future uses, Daniels made an analogy between the diffuse versus concentrated physical nature of energy sources and the population densities that they could best serve:

In the long-range development of new energy resources to supplement our fossil fuels, it is likely that atomic energy, with its concentrated energy, its complicated safety devices, and its requirement of a minimum "critical size," will be used in large expensive central stations near urban centers. Solar energy, on the other hand, with its universal availability and simplicity and its need to cover large areas, will find its place first in isolated and rural areas.[32]

Conferees perceived solar and nuclear energy as policy complements, not antagonists. The published proceedings assessed space and hot-water heating as closest to commercialization, and photochemistry and photovoltaics as holding promise for the longer term.[33]

A much larger and wider ranging Mid-Century Conference held the same year aimed at a comprehensive look at all of the nation's resources, including energy. A group of prominent individuals had founded Resources for the Future (RFF) before the 1952 election, and with a Ford Foundation grant they planned the conference. This high-visibility event had attending or on its advisory boards university presidents, corporate CEOs, journalists, and labor officials, as well as scientists and engineers who worked on various resource issues.[34]

The RFF leaders conceived this conference in the mold of the 1908 Roosevelt–Pinchot conference that had earlier promoted the ideas of conservation and resource development. Concerns that growing populations, economies, and military needs put ever-greater pressure on natural resources motivated the RFF organizers, who felt the need for wise policies to prevent problems decades down the road.[35] This was an explicit attempt to influence policy for the future. The section of the conference that addressed energy reflected these themes. Speakers saw the reserves of coal, oil, and natural gas as substantial but feared that the growing demands for them could create trouble later. Panelists discussed nuclear and solar as unconventional energy sources. Farrington Daniels co-chaired the energy section with George Gadsby, president of Utah Power and Light. The first three speakers during the solar discussion were Hoyt Hottel, Maria Telkes, and George Löf, followed by people from research institutes, oil companies, utilities, municipal governments, and the National Science Foundation.[36] The discussion had the usual profusion of reports of developments in various solar technologies, from photovoltaics to heat storage, and the standard assessments of them all as promising though not currently economical. Several speakers also pointed out that, compared to nuclear, solar energy had received virtually no research dollars from the government, although they disagreed about how much money it should receive.

On March 17, 1954, a group of financiers, scientists, businessmen, and educators founded the Association for Applied Solar Energy (AFASE) in Phoenix, Arizona. The group embraced a free-market ideology, believing that a promising future for solar energy required stimulating industry involvement. Henry Sargent, a utility executive and the first president of the AFASE, emphasized the importance of business:

[The AFASE] would serve as a means of presenting to industry and business accurate information on the present state of the art [of solar technology]. Its purpose in doing so would be to enlist the support of private capital in the development and application of those phases of solar energy utilization which give promise of economic feasibility.

As one of their first actions, they began to organize a large World Symposium on Solar Energy for the following year.[37] Lewis W. Douglas, who had also chaired the RFF conference two years before, chaired the symposium. The Advisory Committee also contained some familiar names: C. G. Abbot, Vannevar Bush, Godfrey L. Cabot, Hoyt Hottel, George Löf, and Maria Telkes. Farrington Daniels gave a keynote address at the opening plenary session. Most of this group became active in the AFASE as a small but well-established circle of leading solar technical experts.[38]

In his opening remarks, Lewis Douglas, a banker and insurance executive as well as a former member of Congress, claimed that science and technology in general, and solar in particular, offered an answer to Malthus, and together they would enable humanity to defy the claim that scarcity was inevitable. "The economic, social, and the political implications of this proposition," Douglas said, "penetrate deeply into the organic structure of human society itself."[39] Sargent, AFASE President, stressed the necessity of involving the private sector because "the ultimate success or failure of an endeavor of this kind lies largely with the business man."[40]

After the 1955 symposium, the solar community remained active but experienced steadily declining fortunes. The substantial popular media coverage of the 1955 symposium quickly tapered off, with neither dramatic technologies nor policy changes to keep up interest.[41] The AFASE launched two separate journals, *The Sun at Work*, a popular magazine for AFASE members, and *Solar Energy*, a technical journal. But neither these nor other conferences and popular publications sufficed to maintain sufficient public interest.[42]

In the 1960s several organizations sponsored numerous meetings and conferences that made solar energy look like a very active and rapidly developing field during this decade.[43] Nonetheless, the principal advocacy organization, the AFASE, experienced considerable difficulty. By the end of 1962, membership had dropped thirty per cent. In 1963, AFASE leaders reorganized it into the Solar Energy Society (SES), more of a professional scientific society. Farrington Daniels, active since the founding of the AFASE, became the SES's first president and its first elected officer, which Harvey Strum describes as a shift in control away from many of the people who had founded its predecessor. However, the financial problems persisted, and in 1967 the SES suspended publication of *The Sun at Work*.[44] The Arizona businessmen who had contributed in the early days of the AFASE reduced their support because American industry had not gotten very involved in solar energy. In turn, industrial membership declined because industry leaders saw no apparent payoff in the short- or even medium-term. In addition, declining electricity prices during this period further undercut the solar heating industry.[45] The cost of solar technologies had to come down for them to appeal to business people.

This brief review of solar advocacy demonstrates three things. First, in the period before the energy crisis, experts in solar energy did constitute a policy community in John Kingdon's sense.[46] A group of experts drawn from industry, academia, and the lower levels of government debated among themselves policy proposals for better government support of solar energy. This small group all knew each other, were aware of each other's work, and shared a common foundation of consensually agreed on technical knowledge.

Second, members of this community disagreed substantially with each other over both the future potential for solar energy and the extent to which government policy could affect that future. The more negative views of this community dominated the thinking of the most senior government officials.

Third, the disagreements within the community demonstrate clearly the complex nature of technical policy knowledge. The members argued over what sounded like technical subjects: the future possibilities for solar energy technologies and the extent to which they could replace fossil fuels. However, the analysis of their positions shows that these technical-sounding disagreements were grounded in political and social disagreements over the ability of government to shape future technologies and the nature of the energy problem that solar energy needed to solve. All advocates engaged in boundary work to make their differing positions appear to be grounded in technical considerations, once again making political and social disputes implicit, hidden behind the technical arguments.[47]

4

Solar Energy's Incompatibility with Official Problem Frames

In light of the conferences, technical and popular publications, the creation of new institutions outside of government, and the intermittent interest of senior government officials, why was there so little official action on solar energy before the 1970s? The customary explanations of short-term policies or markets do not hold up to closer scrutiny. Clearly, due to the relatively high cost of solar energy from the 1940s through the 1960s and the declining prices of fossil fuels during the same period, the research, development, and diffusion of solar technologies would have required the support of some institution willing and able to take a very long-term view of the future needs for energy resources. While one often hears the glib complaint that governments never take long-term perspectives on policy issues, in fact such institutions and leadership were very much in existence in the decades after World War II. These long-term investments showed up in Republican and Democratic administrations alike, such as Eisenhower's initiative on the Interstate Highway System, Kennedy's support of a greatly expanded space program, and Johnson's Great Society programs.[1] Although always constrained by budgets, all of these administrations invested in future-oriented projects, ones that required a certain amount of vision and commitment to the nation's development. Solar technologies could have been, but were not, included among them.

Another standard reason given to explain the failure of solar energy to develop in these years focuses on the lack of any pressing short-term need for it. Although conditions changed at the end of the Johnson administration, abundance and decreasing prices in most parts of the energy market characterized the postwar period to 1968. This situation, framed by conventional thinking of the day, left solar without a problem to solve and made solar technologies too expensive in comparison to conventional technologies. The economics of solar certainly made it very difficult to develop a consumer market composed mainly of individuals putting solar devices on their homes, or of industrial markets in transportation or manufacturing.[2]

But this explanation fails to account for two historical realities. First, at least since the 1880s, U.S. energy markets have been in part political markets. Besides the traditional set of atomized small buyers and sellers who constitute the microeconomists' conception of a market, the production and supply systems that deliver energy to consumers have included governments at the national and state levels, large utility monopolies, large supply companies, and a variety of financial institutions. All of these institutions and their interests influence the prices that consumers see and the energy choices from which they may pick. Second, and perhaps more importantly, energy technologies could also be developed quite independent of consumer demand. Public policy makers in fact made immense investments in energy technologies in the United States and elsewhere and developed them extensively, all without any real short-term economic incentives. In the most striking case, nuclear technology's advocates succeeded in politically constructing it as the technology of the future.[3]

As discussed in Chapter 1, in the 1940s energy specialists had generally equated nuclear and solar energy as long-term alternatives to fossil fuels, regarding each as expensive but promising future energy technologies and calling for research and development in them. It was in the Eisenhower administration that nuclear energy jumped into the foreground of energy policy, leaving solar behind. Advocates of nuclear energy managed to lay claim to the proximate future and billions of R&D dollars, while policy makers continued to relegate solar energy to the distant future, if they considered it at all. The rise of nuclear power is a complex story that involves scientists in and out of government promoting it, along with a special congressional committee, some officials of the fledgling Atomic Energy Commission (AEC), and a host of popular writers.[4] Even though some top officials remained skeptical of the need for a large government nuclear energy program, it continued growing in size. The "Atoms for Peace" speech did not turn around nuclear policy in one stroke, but it did articulate publicly a policy frame in which nuclear power could play a significant role. In this speech civilian nuclear power became not merely the positive side to a troubling technology but rather part of an international process of spreading prosperity in a way that would lessen the chances of another world war.[5] Eisenhower's speech gave the idea of civilian uses of nuclear energy an enormous boost, and coverage of peaceful nuclear technology expanded into the popular media dramatically with almost entirely positive assessments.[6]

The rapid development and expansion of policies for nuclear technology, with its many technical and economic uncertainties, had nothing to do with solving short-term problems of energy supply. Indeed, solar energy had the support of some of the same people who supported nuclear energy development. For instance, Representative Craig Hosmer (R-California), who had introduced the earliest bills to support solar developments in the 1957–1960 period, strongly supported Project Plowshare in the 1960s, a proposal to use nuclear explosives to dig canals, harbors, and the like.[7] Yet solar research never received anything approaching the resources given to nuclear. Why was nuclear so successful and solar not? The failure of solar energy to attract more substantial policy support must lie beyond any scientific or objective assessment of its potential. Instead, the contrasting histories of nuclear and solar energy in the 1950s and 1960s demonstrate the symbolic and valuative components of policy making, as well as their interaction with public and private institutions that led in the nuclear case to massive investment in a technology. Despite a small constituency, interested bureaucrats, and a few sympathetic representatives and senators, the advocates of solar energy never made the pluralist penetration of policy making. As the Truman through the Johnson administrations tried to solve energy problems, three particular features of the energy problem definition contributed to the inability of solar advocates to make much headway in getting government support for solar energy. These were the emphasis on economic growth and free-market mechanisms, energy's low priority for high-level policy makers, and the belief in the need for exponentially increasing supplies of bulk energy. In addition, solar energy suffered from the fragmentation of energy policy, which, coupled with the reigning problem definition, made it difficult for solar energy advocates to find an institutional champion within government.[8]

In this chapter I will draw together the materials developed earlier and show how political pressures can affect policy only if they are congruent with the problem definitions and values that structure the way institutions and decision makers conceptualize the issue.

SOLAR'S STRUGGLES WITH INSTITUTIONAL PROBLEM FRAMES

Solar advocates tried a number of times to press their case to government officials and often found a sympathetic ear somewhere in the White House. But they could not change the dominant problem frame at the top level. For example, solar advocates tried to influence President Eisenhower, but with little impact. The first symposium sponsored by Association for Applied Solar Energy (AFASE) offered a way for solar advocates in and out of government to try to get the attention of top-level policy makers. People from the Stanford Research Institute (SRI), one of the co-sponsors of the conference, met with various government officials who might have an interest in solar energy.[9] As detailed in the previous chapter, Orme Lewis, an assistant secretary of the interior, and Howard Pyle, deputy assistant to the president, both worked with the symposium organizers and circulated the pro-solar speech by M. E. Spaght, pushing for the president's involvement in the symposium.[10] Despite Lewis's and Pyle's enthusiasm, and Spaght's business credentials, the president's top aides remained skeptical. Although Lewis and Pyle did get Eisenhower's welcoming message for the symposium,[11] this level of visibility did not translate into greater administration support for solar energy. In addition, symposium sponsors did little to lobby the administration, consistent with the free-market ideology that they espoused at the conference.[12]

The Resources for the Future (RFF) conference was also quite visible to policy makers in the White House, and, in fact, its organizers initially had a close relationship with President Eisenhower and his aides. However, after receiving considerable criticisms from conservative members of the business community, the administration kept cordial but distant relations with the RFF and the conference.[13] More importantly, the problem frames articulated at the conference – the urgent need to avoid future resource shortages and the wide scope for government action toward that goal – never penetrated administration thinking.[14] A conference in which solar received a sympathetic hearing did not influence official problem frames.

Solar advocates' repeated efforts to get the attention of policy makers failed, despite the visibility and entrée that some of these advocates had. The reasons for this failure grow out of the structure of decision making for energy policy and the empirical and normative ideas that were institutionalized as officially accepted problem frames in these institutions. Since solar had little in the way of short-term consequences, it could not address the shortage or price stability concerns just after the war or compete with cheap fossil fuels in later years. As a longer term resource of potential importance, it seemed to have a claim on funds for R&D, much like nuclear energy, and its advocates spoke in such terms. However, the fragmented decision-making structure suggests why getting such funds was an uphill battle, since no agency became a bureaucratically entrenched champion for solar energy. This conclusion, of course, raises the question of why there was not such a home, since it was possible to create one, as Julius Krug had in fact intended to do in the Interior Department. Krug's resignation, over a different issue, before he could create a home for solar energy speaks partly to the contingent nature of policy outcomes. But that explanation leaves unanswered the question of why no one else in Interior or elsewhere took up the cause of solar energy. The answer lies in the way technical and normative ideas associated with any technology can become institutionalized. Of course, interests also shape policy.[15] That said, solar advocates never succeeded in institutionalizing ideas, especially normative values, favoring the promotion of solar energy, and that lack of supporting institutionalized values influenced both the interpretation of empirical ideas and the arena in which the assorted interests sought their preferred policy.

As Lindblom and Woodhouse have argued, elites choose policies from a restricted set of choices based on uncertain and incomplete information and while under partisan pressures.[16] Under such circumstances, what are the "obvious" two or three policies from which they choose? As argued by Schön and Rein, that set of choices is heavily influenced by decision maker's problem frames – the way they see the world and various possible policies fitting into that world. Solar advocates presented their technology in a way that did not fit with official established problem frames.

Solar advocates varied in their detailed assessments of various solar technologies, but they presented a technological narrative that was remarkably consistent in its overall structure and content. Surveying the various advocates discussed in Chapter 3, we see a story with three basic parts. First, all of the advocates started by showing that the potential resource of solar energy is immense, that the quantity of energy reaching the earth's surface dwarfs humanity's consumption. Second, they depicted the fundamental problem of using solar energy as either the very low efficiencies with which such energy was currently used or the problems of storing such intermittent energy, or both. Third, they all concluded that the only way society could prevent severe energy shortages and make effective use of solar energy was to fund R&D that would enable scientists to struggle against these limits and raise the efficiencies of converting and storing solar energy, lowering the costs so that solar could provide large and increasing quantities of energy to satisfy humanity's insatiable demands. In this narrative, the scientists and engineers were working to solve their problem before declining stocks of fossil fuels caused great suffering and social disruption.

Could this narrative persuade a government agency or presidential aides? At one level, the narrative has to be empirically compelling, or at least plausible. Did anyone have reason to believe that solar's great potential could, in fact, be tapped? On this score, solar was clearly at a disadvantage compared to nuclear power after World War II. Nuclear scientists and engineers, working in a crash R&D program during the war, had produced a series of breakthroughs in creating nuclear technologies and the technology itself was novel, exotic, and not that well understood. Nuclear weapons had revealed dramatically that nuclear technologies could produce immense quantities of energy. Such a technology seemed ripe for more breakthroughs that could resolve its cost and engineering uncertainties. In contrast, solar technologies were, for the most part, quite familiar and so seemed less amenable to big breakthroughs. How much more efficiency could one expect to squeeze out of wind turbine blades or the copper pipe, painted metal, and glass that made up solar collectors? Fifty years later, we know that the answer is "quite a bit," particularly for photovoltaics, wind power, and passive solar design.[17] However, decision makers forty years ago could only use the knowledge available to them at the time, coupled with whatever conceptual frameworks they used to think about the future. And that framework, from the 1940s through the 1970s, put a heavy emphasis on breakthroughs – the creation of novel technologies that they perceived as qualitatively different from previous technologies.[18] It is hardly surprising that solar advocates like Daniels said that the greatest potential for radical improvements lay in the most exotic solar technologies, such as photovoltaics.

An agency also might adopt a technology if it comported well with that agency's beliefs, values, and problem frames. At this level, the Department of the Interior was not an institution likely to champion solar energy. This department was concerned with the exploitation and management of existing resources, including fossil fuels, not with long-range alternatives to them.[19] Fossil fuels themselves were not under some "energy office" but instead delegated to separate bureaus and offices, which were quite independent fiefdoms. Even the partial exception to this rule, synthetic fuels from coal and oil shale, fit the larger pattern. Run by the Bureau of Mines, part of Interior, the synfuels program was to some extent an attempt to find alternative uses for an already existing resource, in the case of coal, or to produce a traditional product from a novel resource, in the case of oil shale. In both cases policy makers believed that the technologies were very close to being economically competitive and so did not think that they needed the extensive development that everyone thought that solar technologies required.[20]

One agency was very compatible with the solar narrative in that it believed in the need for long-term alternatives to fossil fuels and the immediate necessity for large R&D investments to develop them. Unfortunately for solar energy, that agency was the Atomic Energy Commission (AEC), and it was committed to a different technology. In short, solar energy, as it was then conceptualized, did not fit with the institutionalized problem frames of any government agency, and so had no champion within government. Alternative ideas that might have favored solar, particularly values like ecological stewardship, found no place in official problem frames.

NUCLEAR POWER'S FIT WITH INSTITUTIONAL
PROBLEM FRAMES

By contrast, institutionalized problem frames worked quite differently for nuclear power. Most obviously, nuclear power had an institutionalized home in the AEC, which was charged with promoting it. Also important was the way in which nuclear power advocates could articulate a problem that their technology seemed likely to solve, and do so in a way that was congruent with the values that framed the larger issue of energy.

People often point to the obvious linkages between military and civilian nuclear technologies as a reason for the government to support civilian nuclear power. The nuclear weapons program developed a considerable background knowledge on technologies relevant to civilian uses and created its own line of power reactors for naval vessels.[21] Nonetheless, as I demonstrated in earlier chapters, some parts of the military nuclear establishment were ambivalent about sharing the technology, materiel, and personnel with the civilian sector. In addition, this linkage with nuclear weapons often impeded broader public acceptability of civilian nuclear power.[22] Thus, one must look to other political activities, particularly a broad debate over energy, to fully account for the growth of the civilian nuclear power program.

President Eisenhower's "Atoms for Peace" speech, driven by his desire to mobilize the country for the Cold War, gave considerable impetus to nuclear power. Among other things, the speech got his ideas into a wider public literature. For example, in addition to the daily press, a book published in 1955 by popular science writer David O. Woodbury used the same title, *Atoms for Peace*, and asserted everything that Operations Candor and Edify (the media campaign that followed the speech) pronounced. Woodbury gave breathless accounts of new developments in nuclear technology and stern lectures about the need for all Americans to accept the responsibilities that came with the Atomic Age. Most importantly, he tried to dispel people's fears of nuclear technology, recounting how he once woke up in the middle of the night to see the sky lit as brightly as day. At first Woodbury and his wife stood together trembling, thinking that the end of the world had come. Suddenly he realized the source of the mystery and declared, " 'It's that atom bomb [test] over in Nevada!' . . . We laughed and went back to bed."[23]

An institutional public relations campaign in the 1950s and 1960s joined private writings like those of Woodbury. As Michael Smith details, a consortium of the AEC, reactor vendors, and electric utilities launched a massive effort to convince the American public that nuclear power was their friend and would transform their lives dramatically. Starting in the 1950s the consortium produced millions of copies of booklets promoting nuclear power and in the 1960s produced films seen by over 100 million people in theaters and on television. They also created traveling exhibits and demonstrations that went to schools all around the country.[24] These messages conveyed a sense of nuclear's immense, almost magical, power, but also that that power had been tamed and controlled. They evoked a world that was effortless, clean, and prosperous thanks to the wonders of nuclear-generated electricity.

"Atoms for Peace" and the following public relations campaign afforded nuclear technologies wider public and policy attention and, coupled with institutional support from the AEC and the Congressional Joint Committee on Atomic Energy, increased government resources for civilian nuclear developments. The speech and its fallout also took place in the context of a rapidly worsening Cold War. Even before the speech, some senior government officials and advisors had worried about competition with the Soviets over building civilian power reactors. They pushed for an aggressive reactor development program as a matter of international prestige. They argued that nuclear power was a high-status, cutting edge technology and that U.S. technological leadership required that it have the most advanced nuclear power system. While not everyone in the administration accepted that argument, it clearly motivated many senior officials.[25]

The Eisenhower administration had cut the budgets of the AEC and other agencies during its first year in office, and the AEC eagerly sought to get resources back for its various programs. With this new legitimacy, ironically from the same administration that first cut the AEC budget, it succeeded. Not only did the federal government fund research on nuclear electricity, but also on nuclear ships, airplanes, and rockets. As a measure of funding enthusiasm, nuclear airplane and rocket research received over a billion dollars in the 1950s alone, but neither ever tested a prototype.[26] In addition to increased funding for nuclear technology, later in the 1950s legislative and executive changes made it easier for private firms to get into the business of producing reactors. Of course, "Atoms for Peace" did not create these changes out of whole cloth. An assortment of powerful actors had been pushing for many of these policies for quite some time before the speech, but policy changed quickly when such interests received the assistance of legitimating discourse and high-level support.[27]

These problem frames and accompanying policies became deeply institutionalized, allowing the AEC and its congressional supporters to pressure President Kennedy in 1962 to increase substantially the support for the AEC and its reactor building program. As I discussed in Chapter 2, in response to these pressures, President Kennedy ordered the AEC to undertake a study of the general state of energy resources and where nuclear power fit into the whole picture, in effect asking the AEC to justify its requests based on broad national needs. The AEC delivered its report in November 1962, and, not surprisingly, it saw a rapid expansion of nuclear power as the only solution to meeting energy demands that it expected to increase very rapidly. The AEC tied nuclear power to the two major values that had driven energy policy since the Truman administration: prosperity and national security. The report claimed that nuclear power would contribute to economic growth by producing cheap electricity everywhere. Furthermore, nuclear power could enhance national security by housing the reactors in very strong buildings, or underground, making them relatively invulnerable to attack.[28]

Kennedy's aides were less than happy with the AEC report, seeing it as promotional instead of analytical. Yet because of the AEC's strong support in Congress, administration spokesmen could not openly criticize the report. For instance, in February 1963, testifying before the Joint Committee on Atomic Energy, the president's science advisor, Jerome Wiesner, trod lightly on the report:

I feel it is a very useful report, representing much effort and thought on the part of the Commission and the other groups whose studies it reflects. The report proposes a pattern for nuclear power development, several aspects of which I feel are generally appropriate.

Faint praise indeed. Wiesner also testified that the report failed to do what the president had requested, namely, putting the nuclear program into the context of resource policy more generally.[29] Wiesner wrote a much more candid internal memo to McGeorge Bundy about the failings of the AEC report:

In answer to your question concerning the Administration's position on atomic power, I believe we could be considerably less ambitious on this field. Even the AEC study completed last fall . . . fails to make an urgent case for nuclear energy development, though I am sure they would interpret the document differently.

The report is in two parts, an analysis which indicates that there is no energy crisis, and a part devoted to a description of an ambitious development program. A number of groups in the Government . . . did not believe that the AEC study provided adequate justification for an aggressive program and recommended that the President not endorse it.

One of the most serious deficiencies in the AEC study is that it failed to examine adequately non-nuclear energy resources research, and a new study has been initiated to remedy this deficiency.[30]

Despite these concerns, the strength of the AEC's institutionalized problem frame and congressional support prevailed, and Wiesner's call for redistributing expenditures went largely unheeded for another decade.[31]

Frank R. Baumgartner and Bryan D. Jones, in their analysis of the nuclear case, argue that critics of civilian nuclear energy were, by the late 1960s, able to shift the venue of decision making to different congressional committees, which led to the decline in government support for these technologies. This new venue embraced different problem frames.[32] But the controversy over nuclear energy in the Kennedy administration, only a few years prior to the events that Baumgartner and Jones analyze, suggests how difficult it is to disrupt some policy monopolies. President Kennedy's science advisor had become deeply skeptical of both nuclear energy policy and the line agency responsible for it, but the constituencies for that agency in the scientific community, industry, and Congress were still firmly in place. Jerome Wiesner's criticisms of nuclear energy policy were technical in nature and consistent with the dominant values that framed energy policy. He claimed that current and projected energy supplies and prices were adequate for anticipated demands, and so prosperity and national security did not require an aggressive nuclear program. In making these criticisms Wiesner did not take account of the symbolic importance that advocates attached to nuclear technology. Moreover, different groups provided very different interpretations of what was required for national security. As Michael Smith has pointed out, one of the themes that the AEC and its allies used in promoting nuclear power was a connection to national security: If the Soviets develop it first, that will harm U.S. interests by giving the Soviets more prestige with less-developed countries.[33] Such a notion of national security may be more vague than estimates of barrels of oil, but it had a powerful influence on problem frames nonetheless. Policy-making fragmentation thus facilitated the development of insulated policy systems in this case. No one – including the Office of Science and Technology – was institutionally located to challenge these narrow perspectives in a way that led to a change in policy. That would only come later with the rise of new social movements.

SOLAR ADVOCATES ADOPT ESTABLISHED PROBLEM FRAMES

Throughout this period, solar advocates argued for greater government support of solar energy, largely in vain. Time and again, their claims failed to persuade key policy elites, even when they got a hearing. The most important presidential and congressional actors held to a framing of the energy problem that made it impossible for solar advocates to present a compelling case that their technology fulfilled either the normative or pragmatic requirements of energy policy, partly due to the way those requirements were deeply intertwined. Most solar advocates during this period tried to reaffirm conventional problem frames and values, usually by making no explicit mention of normative issues in their writings, or if they did, they simply repeated the requisite emphasis on prosperity, which required reasonably priced energy for endless economic growth, and national security, which required both secure energy supplies and cutting-edge technologies. Solar advocacy around the time of the PMPC in the early 1950s and Farrington Daniels's mid-1960s book on solar energy both illustrate these practices.

The PMPC saw solar energy through the eyes of most of the leading solar advocates of the day, including Daniels, Hottel, Putnam, and Telkes.[34] These scientists and engineers characterized solar energy and its limitations in ways that did not suggest associating any new values with solar energy. To the contrary, they proposed that solar technologies could, over the long term and with sufficient research support, replace a significant part of the conventional energy system, operating within conventional social and political institutions and furthering conventional political and social goals. They believed that future generations would simply unplug fossil fuels and plug in solar energy. In that sense, their technology seemed quite compatible with conventional ideas and problem frames. The only hitch seemed to be the pragmatic question of whether they could make a convincing case that solar technologies could deliver ever-increasing blocks of bulk energy in the not-distant future, and at prices that would not stifle economic growth.

Put in these terms, however, the pragmatic problem reveals its normative entanglements. The requirement, after all, that energy prices not increase much while supply does is a normative one in that it assumes that ever-increasing consumption of resources is a desirable future trajectory. The narrative about solar in the PMPC, and among most technical advocates, tried to address this problem, though without universal agreement. It told the story of an immense resource with very low efficiency of use. The problem was how to increase such efficiency so that prices would come down, a task about which researchers like Hoyt Hottel expressed skepticism, and one that even Farrington Daniels acknowledged would not be easy. Could technologies based on pipes, mirrors, and photosynthesis compete or even compare with nuclear power as the breakthrough technology of the future?

Daniels's Use of Conventional Problem Frames

Probably the best-known work of solar advocacy in the 1960s was Farrington Daniels's *Direct Use of the Sun's Energy*. Comparing his book to the two major government energy policy reports of the time demonstrates how congruent Daniels's advocacy was with the official definition of the energy problem and solar's place in it. His fundamental problem frame stemmed from the exponentially growing demand for energy. He argued that increasing global populations and increasing incomes would require ever-greater consumption of natural resources, including energy. This growing demand would, in the not-distant future, lead to a shortage of fossil fuels, since their supply was clearly finite, and this shortage would mean that societies would need alternative fuels to maintain a good standard of living.[35]

Daniels argued that solar energy could be that alternative source, but the book is cautious, indeed, ambivalent, about when that might be or the extent to which solar energy could support a high-consumption lifestyle. The book is organized by different technologies, and in every case it stresses the caveat that solar cannot compete with cheap fossil fuels. He also states at one point that solar energy is too diffuse to have much impact on urban or cloudy areas. Despite these qualifications, his book does advocate greater research on the use of solar energy. He points out that it could have immediate cost advantages in sunny remote areas, where fossil fuels were already expensive. While solar was too expensive then in most applications, recent advances in research and the potential for mass production suggested that the costs could come down. Short-term research should be targeted at applications in less-developed countries and long-term research at applications in industrialized countries. Solar had the further advantage that "There is no gamble in solar energy use; it is sure to work." The only question was whether the costs could be brought down or if the costs of alternatives would go up sufficiently. He noted that solar R&D had been almost totally neglected by both the government and the private sector, especially when compared to the then-booming programs in nuclear power and space exploration. This neglect of R&D, a common theme in solar advocacy, carried with it the suggestion, sometimes implied, that more generous R&D funding would have substantial results for making solar more competitive.[36]

Daniels drew an analogy between population density and energy density. Since solar was an energy source of low density and nuclear was one of high density, he argued that they would serve populations of corresponding densities, rural and urban. This analogy provided a clever way to try to carve out a market and political niche for solar energy. His arguments could catch the interest of rural constituencies, providing a new possibility for institutionalized champions for solar. But in an increasingly urban society there were limitations to this strategy as well. Second, Daniels and others constructed solar technology as one that could benefit primarily the poor in less-developed countries, which at that time were mostly rural. A technology projected to be compatible with the practices and resources of the Third World was likewise very different from one being touted as the replacement for fossil fuels in the United States or Europe. Daniels' construction of the energy problem and solar energy limited its appeal.

The Federal Council on Science and Technology (FCST) report on energy R&D came out one year before Daniels' book and had a similar description of the general problem. How could the United States provide increasing quantities of energy at low costs well into the future? The data that compared R&D on various energy sources made clear that solar received vastly less government funding than conventional or nuclear power technologies. In FY1963, for example, solar got $3.8 million in R&D funds versus $16.9 million for fossil fuels and $534.1 million for nuclear power.[37]

The Interdepartmental Energy Study (IES) released during the Johnson administration, just two years after Daniels' book, contained a different approach to analyzing energy R&D needs. Like Daniels' book and the FCST study, the IES concerned itself with R&D, which was its mandate, and it also suggested that the key government activity for solving future problems should be developing new energy-producing technologies, not subsidizing some industry or otherwise intervening in the market directly. The difference with the earlier studies was in the way the IES framed the energy problem. While acknowledging the importance of energy and national security, the IES stated up front that it would focus on energy's economic aspects. While all of the earlier studies had also considered economic issues of energy, the IES took a much more technically rigorous approach to the subject. The IES argued that the proper goal for energy R&D policy was the optimal allocation of resources, a basic premise of microeconomics, and it explicitly rejected goals such as economic growth or other popular economic notions. Following from this goal, it advocated the use of a cost–benefit analysis as the best way of analyzing policies. The IES group acknowledged the extraordinary technical difficulties of actually carrying out such calculations and so argued that their approach would give at best "a heuristic description of the overall problem."[38]

The IES authors' problem frame also contained other assumptions. First, from historical data they concluded that high incomes required high energy consumption and, therefore, policy should seek to sustain such consumption. They argued that industry R&D paid too little attention to long-term energy needs, suggesting a need for government involvement. In addition, they noted that technical and economic uncertainties severely limited the ability of policy makers to target R&D in any precise way. It was hard to know just which technologies would emerge from particular R&D programs and whether those technologies would be competitive, given the uncertainties about the future social and market conditions into which they would emerge. Their conception of R&D was quite sophisticated for the time. They explicitly rejected the linear model of R&D, noting that sometimes technological developments preceded scientific understanding. They also acknowledged the social and economic influences on R&D:

Not everything that is scientifically possible and technologically feasible will be produced. The cathode-ray tube, for example, has been known since at least 1870. It was ignored then because society at the time needed large-scale industrialization and concentrated therefore on motors, generators, and lights. Had society been ready for precise measurements, been preoccupied with high-speed warfare, or had leisure, the cathode-ray-tube technology of oscilloscopes, radar, or television would have arisen many decades earlier. Comparable examples in every field prove how often technology is the handmaiden of socioeconomic justification and desire.

These social influences and economic and technical uncertainties implied that R&D policy could not be precisely targeted. "The most that can be done is to analyze R&D in terms of the past and present, to determine what factors are involved and how they interact, to search for the obvious gaps and imbalances, and then to combine all these findings into a comprehensive yet flexible plan for energy R&D."[39]

This IES perspective on technology parallels nicely the constructivist school of technology studies. It recognizes explicitly that there is no abstract optimal way to design or develop a technology, but rather that the social and economic goals of the actors involved heavily influence the outcome. The brief example of the cathode ray tube suggests the notion of interpretive flexibility: It can become an oscilloscope or a television depending on what people want to do with it.[40]

What is missing from the IES notion of technological development is the concept of social conflict: that different actors may attach different meanings to a technology and seek to solve different problems with it. Thus government policies aimed at developing new energy technologies need not, in this perspective, resolve political or social conflicts over which technologies to promote or how to shape their design. The IES commitment to the optimal allocation of resources assumes that there is an abstract optimum for such allocation that is removed from explicit social conflicts. Their constructivist notions of technology do not extend to constructivist technology policy. The irony, of course, is that if the government had adopted the IES recommendations, it would have changed substantially its allocation of R&D resources. It was precisely the actors who had achieved political stabilization and closure on this technology policy – the AEC and its congressional allies – who beat back calls for such changes, at least for a few more years.

The IES said very little about solar energy, relegating it to a few pages in a chapter on "Other Energy Sources," and said nothing about it in a chapter on the "Environmental Aspects of Energy Development." In a large foldout table the report gave a brief summary of the state of technological development and the capital and operating costs associated with all energy sources, including solar. It depicted most solar technologies as only long-term options due to their being technologically immature or too expensive, or both. For example, the table listed photovoltaics, which it called technically well developed, as having capital costs of $200–400 per watt, vastly higher than fossil fuel plants, and included the comment that these costs would probably not go down significantly.[41] These economic perspectives on solar technologies, coupled with the fundamental problem frame of the report, explain why solar was not taken seriously in IES. If you believe that the technological goal is ever-increasing amounts of bulk energy and that price is the only reasonable signal to use for setting policies, then solar's capital costs make it look quite unattractive.

These estimates of solar costs contrast with the report's estimates for nuclear power. The same table gave no current estimates for the capital costs of a nuclear power plant, from which one could conclude that there was little basis for making estimates of future costs. Nonetheless, the table did list a future capital cost of $0.165–0.175 per watt, several thousand times less than the current costs for photovoltaics. The higher end of this estimate is taken from the 1962 AEC report discussed earlier, the one that the president's science advisor had so criticized.[42] Thus in two cases of technologies with highly uncertain future costs, the report's authors gave a large benefit of the doubt to nuclear technology and virtually none to solar; this did not bode well for future policy for solar R&D.

Note the way technical and normative ideas subtly mix here to produce a technical-sounding conclusion: that solar is unlikely to be a significant energy source in the future compared to nuclear. The technical claims about future capital costs are, of necessity, highly speculative and could include factors such as public and private levels of investments in R&D, the benefits of scaling up production, and the cost of capital for the necessary production. The nuclear estimates, as mentioned above, came from an AEC study that other government officials had heavily criticized. The solar estimates came from unnamed "solicited review papers and panel discussions," so we have no way of knowing how the forecasts were made and if they were done in a manner consistent with the nuclear projects.[43] The report combined these technical speculations,

which rested on a flimsy bed of evidence, with the fundamentally political and social assumption that the point of energy technologies was to
produce exponentially increasing quantities of bulk energy at low costs.
The report then expressed this set of combined ideas as the allegedly
technical conclusion that solar was not going to be a large part of the
country's future energy system.

These official studies show why it was hard for government
policy makers to take arguments like Daniels' seriously, despite his
prestige and establishment credentials. His book and the official studies
had similar general problem frames, though the IES used a much
more technical interpretation of economics and what that meant for
policy. Moreover, Daniels did not claim that solar could be an important energy source in the United States now or in the near future. The
FCST report and the IES agreed, but the IES relegated practical solar
energy to a more distant future, with greater uncertainty of result,
than did Daniels. Given that view of solar energy, Daniels' claim
that solar deserved much more support was not so compelling, considering the contrasting official optimism about future nuclear power costs,
the uncertainty of the price of solar, and the emphasis in the IES on
microeconomic efficiency.

THE FORMIDABLE BARRIER OF
PROBLEM FRAMES

The officially accepted frame of the short-term energy policy problem
remained consistent from the Truman through the Johnson administrations. It emphasized the care and feeding of the various fossil fuel industries, carefully catered by their associated Interior Department agencies.
The long-term problem definition called for the replacement of fossil
fuels. By the middle of the Eisenhower administration the replacement
was nuclear energy, which alone among alternatives seemed to have the
capacity to provide large blocks of energy, and solar advocates could not
change that perceived need, and indeed accepted it themselves.

Changing the ways in which people think about policy problems is a
daunting task. Convincing a few people of the need for such change,
even if they are very important people, is not sufficient. One must
affect numerous actors' beliefs and values about the policy issue. Clearly
no one accepted the notion that solar energy was the immediate solution
to the most pressing problems that the nation faced with regard to
fuels, and the values that advocates tried to associate with it were either
not convincing or not of great concern. Advocates like Daniels and
Putnam presented solar as a long-term solution that would allow
the continuance of industrial civilization. Almost alone among advocates, Eugene Ayres associated it with a new and better form of society.

Neither of these ideas found broad interest, much less acceptance, among officials, and there is no evidence that the presidents of this period embraced them, thus depriving them of a powerful leadership voice that could have influenced issue definition by changing the terms of the macropolitical debate.[44] Furthermore, solar advocates did not speak with one voice about the values associated with solar energy, and they lacked a strong organizational voice to speak for them. As a result, advocates of solar energy left the energy policy subsystems undisturbed and found no home for themselves in government structures or in the mind of the president.

In contrast to the solar advocates, advocates of civilian nuclear energy promoted their technology in very different ways. Possibly emboldened by recent technological breakthroughs and the immense quantities of energy available from the fission of uranium, they promoted nuclear power with great enthusiasm, uninhibited by fears of overselling the technology and then disappointing the public. For instance, before a commercial nuclear power plant was ever in operation, Lewis Strauss of the AEC made the now-well-known prediction that electricity from such power plants would be "too cheap to meter." Nuclear proponents also quickly settled on specific nuclear technologies – the light water reactor in the short-term and the liquid metal fast breeder in the longer term.[45] The relevant social groups, as Pinch and Bijker would call them, reached closure and stabilized the artifact, at least in policy terms. These sorts of claims enabled nuclear advocates to present a narrative about the future of their technology that was congruent with existing official energy problem frames and fulfilled the symbolic need for U.S. leadership in a crucial technology.

The values explicitly associated with energy in this period remained remarkably constant in name, but they did change slightly in the way that policy makers conceptualized their meanings. Energy was a source of economic prosperity and national security, everyone agreed. By the end of the Johnson administration, however, the popular economic notions of growth or prosperity were being supplanted by more technical ideas of optimal resource allocation and the quantitative methodologies that went with them, in particular the cost–benefit analysis in the IES. Concerns about environmental problems found articulation only at the official level by the end of the Johnson administration. Moreover, while government officials in the Johnson administration linked environmental concerns to energy production, such concerns were not yet linked to solar in a compelling way.[46] The values that advocates tried to associate with solar also stayed consistent throughout the period. They saw solar as a future energy source, as renewable after fossil fuels ran out. As merely a replacement, most advocates did not associate solar energy with an explicit articulation of any alternative social or political arrangements that would accompany a solar future.

The concept of income energy versus capital energy introduced by Eugene Ayres and M. E. Spaght in the 1950s added the only wrinkle to traditional values in the advocates' arguments and had the potential to change solar advocates' articulation of the fundamental problem. Implicit in the claim that we should instead live on energy income, and therefore within our means, is the notion that we should be living differently than we do, that is, more frugally. It follows that living in a world that runs on solar energy means consuming less primary energy, in the sense of number of barrels of oil or kilowatt-hours of electricity, and hence building different technological ensembles that provide energy services. But during the 1950s and 1960s, no one drew out such conclusions. Officials did not find this narrative compelling.

PART II

DURING THE ENERGY CRISIS

5

Problem Frames During the Energy Crisis

In the 1970s a situation of energy abundance and falling prices turned into one of shortages and escalating prices, greatly raising energy policy's salience. This short-run crisis opened a political opportunity to take a longer term look at energy sources and government support for them, as the crisis strained public confidence in the existing system. In short, the energy crisis was an opportunity to revise the existing problem frame and institutionalize a new set of ideas to guide that frame. The crisis did give rise to new energy policy institutions, and those institutions to some extent centralized energy policy making and gave a new institutional home to advocates of solar energy. Nonetheless, the core ideas driving energy policy at the presidential level changed very little, and the possibilities contained in the new institutions were never realized. Before turning to the official energy problem frame, it is important to understand the new institutional structures that helped to formulate and implement energy policy.

My emphasis on debates within the White House does not imply that the White House alone set policy. Decades of studies have shown that there are many important actors in a political system as fragmented as that in the United States, such as executive branch agencies, Congress, interest groups, and the courts. That was as true in energy policy as in any other issue area. Nonetheless, one of the most important of those actors was the White House. Presidents Nixon, Ford, and Carter may not have gotten all that they wanted, but all of the other actors had to react to their initiatives, and the president and the White House staff could and did severely constrain what other actors, particularly executive branch agencies, did. Therefore, in thinking about the way values become institutionalized, seeing how they were debated within and pushed by the White House, is a good place to start.

CENTRALIZING ENERGY POLICY INSTITUTIONS

The organization of policy-making institutions is not simply a question of efficiency or effectiveness. Rather, such institutional structures affect policy outcomes and the ability of interested parties to influence those outcomes. Groups involved in energy policy clearly understood this implication of centralizing policy institutions, and those who benefited from the status quo resisted it. In addition, the fragmented nature of energy policy fit well with the pluralist political context in which it was embedded, providing further resistance to change.[1]

Nonetheless, major organizational change held a high priority in President Nixon's administration, and the growing energy crisis increased the issue's salience. The White House sought centralization to evaluate energy alternatives in an integrated way and to make trade-offs among them. The Nixon administration produced a bewildering array of informal groups and new offices in a very short period of time within the Executive Office of the President (EOP), some of which are discussed below.[2] President Nixon also sought a centralized cabinet agency, the Department of Natural Resources (DNR), later called the Department of Energy and Natural Resources (DENR). Presidents Ford and Carter also sought, and eventually got, this new agency.

Energy Policy Institutions Under Nixon

In April 1973, President Nixon established the National Energy Office within the EOP and appointed Charles DiBona, a systems analyst, to head it.[3] Although DiBona thought that he would be the key White House aide on energy, conflicts with powerful White House and agency officials undercut his role. The fights over turf got fierce and DiBona lost them.[4] Less than three months later the president created the Energy Policy Office and appointed former Colorado Governor John Love to head it. Officially, Love was the top White House aide for energy and reported directly to the president. In practice he fared little better than DiBona and resigned before the year was out.[5]

After the oil embargo of October 1973, reorganization proceeded apace. The president created the Federal Energy Office, which was later replaced by the legislatively mandated Federal Energy Administration. The FEO had a rather stormy beginning, but the second person to head it, John Sawhill, reorganized it and reduced much of the internal overlap, which began to create the centralized policy and regulatory agency that the president wanted.

White House staff organizations settled down considerably during the Ford and Carter years. While due partly to their different styles of managing the White House, certainly much of the settling came from closure on the Executive Branch reorganization for energy, the creation of the Energy Research and Development Administration (ERDA), and then the Department of Energy (DOE). These new institutions settled the matter of which line agencies were responsible for energy, so there simply was not as much to fight over concerning who would control energy policy. Within the Executive Office of the President, both Ford and Carter designated key aides who focused on energy, along with some staff from the OMB.

The institutional difficulties that President Nixon experienced in centralizing long-range planning for energy policy in the White House, where he could make unilateral decisions, demonstrate how hard it is to change policy institutions. In one sense, the changes may have seemed irrelevant to policy outcomes, since officials articulated values consistent with those since President Truman, emphasizing economic growth, national security, or both.[6] While they often compromised with powerful established energy interests, the administration clearly tried to pursue policies aimed at national security goals and at the deregulation of energy markets, despite its wage and price controls in other areas. Nonetheless, White House officials felt that the lack of centralization hampered the detailed articulation and implementation of these goals. Moreover, these new institutions within the EOP did not open the policy process to new constituencies, particularly not to groups that had new ideas to offer about energy policy. The specific political players came and went, but organizations such as environmental or solar energy groups had no place in the process. For example, a proposed President's Energy Advisory Council was supposed to be "an outside advisory council to enable major groups concerned with and knowledgeable about energy matters to contribute to energy policy." The initial list that the White House staff suggested to the president included people from industry, environmental groups, a few academics, and other political officials.[7] However, the council that eventually got appointed looked quite different, with ten people from industry, five from academia or other research institutions, and one from a national laboratory.[8] Moreover, decision making within the Nixon administration was so Byzantine that it was not clear what influence these advisors could have had.

The Nixon White House's centralization effort included proposals for a Department of Natural Resources (DNR), which later added "Energy" to the title (DENR). The idea of a new cabinet-level energy department developed early in the administration, and proposals appeared under several names. By late 1970, the DNR idea seemed to some aides like an inexpensive and politically safe energy policy initiative, unlike things such as price deregulation:[9]

There is one additional area, however, which involves no cost and only a limited political impact. I am referring to a reorganization of the government's energy activities. This is sorely needed. Specifically, it would involve a reorganization of parts of Interior and legislation to split out some of AEC's activities.... The selling point would be that for the first time, fossil and atomic fuels could be under one roof so that the proper tradeoffs can be made.[10]

They were seriously mistaken about it being easy and low-cost.[11]

White House staff knew that their DNR proposal would encounter resistance from Congressman Chet Holifield, Chair of the House Government Operations Committee and therefore able to hold up any of Nixon's reorganization plans that required congressional approval:

Holifield has one burning desire – to go down in history as the father of the breeder reactor ... [he] is so emotionally involved that he is nearly irrational on the subject.... [Supporting the breeder reactor] will assure that Holifield will report out a DNR bill and presumably the other reorganization bills. The DNR bill, however, as reported out, will *not* include the AEC activities presently written into our bill. Holifield will not give up control of either the enrichment plants or the reactor program to DNR.... Now our choice is whether to accept a DNR without the AEC programs or go to the mat with Holifield.[12]

Nixon's staff urged him to stick with the more comprehensive reorganization and to offer Holifield support for the breeder and some other nuclear programs only if he acted favorably on the DNR bill. "Holifield will probably explode and accuse us of blackmailing him, etc. – but after the fireworks are over, I am virtually certain he will cave [in to our demands]."[13]

The administration did give strong support to the breeder program, but Holifield, while expressing gratitude, continued to defend the AEC's turf.[14] In April 1973, the administration tried again, this time with support from Senator Henry Jackson, proposing a Department of Energy and Natural Resources (DENR). Again they failed, in part due to Nixon's increasing distraction over Watergate.[15] Finally, by late 1973, just prior to the embargo, the administration focused its efforts on ERDA, trying to make it more than a "warmed-over AEC," and gave up on grander reorganization schemes for the time being.[16]

These failures to centralize policy making reflected how much the Nixon administration had given in to a powerful policy iron triangle, consisting of industry, agencies, and members of Congress. The proposed ERDA would in fact be a "warmed-over" AEC, which would absorb the energy research divisions of other agencies, such as the Interior's Office of Coal Research. The Nuclear Energy Commission (later called the Nuclear Regulatory Commission) would absorb the regulatory functions of the AEC, and the commissioners would go with them, leaving the ERDA to be run by a single administrator. The new proposed DENR, in the meantime, would absorb all of the rest of Interior, as well as all non-research energy functions from around the government, such as policy studies, collecting data, selling electric power, and so on.[17] Chet Holifield had not been the one to cave in.

Many members of Congress supported an ERDA bill, particularly one that would set up a separate regulatory apparatus for nuclear power. They were unhappy with the AEC and its dual role as the regulator and promoter of nuclear power, which they saw as a conflict of interest. The time was ripe for this sort of reorganization.[18] Nonetheless, the ERDA bill remained months from passing despite the October 1973 oil embargo and the deepening energy crisis. The political crisis surrounding the collapse of the Nixon presidency absorbed the time of Congress and the administration, and it was not until Gerald Ford became president that Congress moved on its passage.

The case of energy policy centralization in the Nixon administration demonstrates how the executive branch of the government tried to make sweeping institutional changes but did so without seeking any substantial changes in the values associated with the energy policies and without a strong outside constituency pushing for the change. For instance, the Nixon administration was most certainly not antinuclear, but it had other reasons for wanting to make changes that would possibly imperil the policy treatment of nuclear energy. As a result, it encountered strong resistance from both congressional and industrial sources. At that time, nuclear power policy, and especially the Joint Committee on Atomic Energy, was under attack, and both would soon be forced to change. Nonetheless, they could still resist the Nixon administration's attempted centralization. Moreover, since the administration did not bring any new groups into the fray, it had no allies to counter opposition pressures; in Schattschneider's terms, Nixon did not enlarge the scope of conflict.[19] One potential set of allies in this cause, the environmental groups concurrently fighting nuclear power, were anathema to the Nixon administration. They represented a set of values to which Nixon and his supporters could only feel hostile. The Nixon administration's notions of environmental protection, while increasingly important, were narrowly construed to mean that one should burn cleaner fuel, if possible. Because groups representing nuclear power contended strongly that their technology was, in fact, clean and environmentally benign, this set of values left the Nixon White House with no argument to curtail this sector of energy production. Thus the administration failed in this period to get any of the reorganizing legislation that it wanted.

Ford and ERDA

After President Nixon left office, Congress passed some reorganization legislation, and President Ford signed the ERDA bill on October 11, 1974, and the Executive Order that activated ERDA and the Nuclear Regulatory Commission (NRC) on January 15, 1975.[20] ERDA brought together, for the first time in one agency, almost all of the federal government's energy R&D programs, though nonresearch aspects of energy policy were still split among Interior, the Federal Power Commission, and the Federal Energy Administration.[21] In terms of its formal institutional structure, ERDA seemed to create a new arena for energy policy that would give voice to advocates of energy sources other than nuclear or fossil fuels. It seemed to provide a way that the ERDA administrator, the agency's top official, could make the necessary trade-offs in terms of funding for different energy sources. Separate assistant administrators managed programs for fossil energy; solar, geothermal, and advanced energy systems; nuclear; environment and safety; national security; and conservation. For the first time, the federal government possessed significant centralization in energy policy.[22]

The administration understood the political importance of ERDA's structure. In one sense, ERDA was an Atomic Energy Commission that had absorbed energy R&D programs from other agencies, and constituencies for nonnuclear energy feared that their programs would be lost and diminished in an agency dominated by AEC personnel. Those fears were understandable. ERDA staff initially consisted of 5,988 full-time staff from the AEC, 1,106 from Interior, 17 from the EPA, and 13 from the National Science Foundation (NSF), of whom 8 had worked on solar energy programs and 5 on geothermal. Outnumbered at the start by roughly 1,000 to 1, solar constituencies had good reason to worry about being dominated. That said, ERDA did have separate, structurally equal solar and conservation programs, which grew quickly. The administration acknowledged and sought to alleviate numerous constituencies' concerns about nuclear domination of ERDA, pointing to its new structure.[23]

Carter and DOE

President Carter spoke out for the creation of a Department of Energy (DOE) before he was elected, during the 1976 campaign.[24] The authors of the National Energy Plan, produced in the first ninety days of his administration, continued the push for it, stating the same need for a rationalized, centralized institution:

Although organizational changes alone will not solve any energy problem, creation of the Department of Energy is a necessity if the elements of the Plan are to be carried out in a coherent and effective manner.... Only through creation of a Department that combines the skills and expertise now dispersed through numerous Federal agencies will the Government obtain the comprehensive overview of interrelated energy problems and the organizational coherence needed to implement the National Energy Plan.[25]

President Carter got his DOE legislation in August 1977. The DOE did consolidate energy policy, bringing in ERDA as well as several other energy agencies. The department did achieve a formal level of rationalization. That said, it also had numerous difficulties. It was born as a huge, complex bureaucracy, cobbled together from other agencies, not built from scratch. It exhibited many of the unfortunate characteristics of such organizations, often rigid and unresponsive. It became quite unpopular with numerous constituencies.[26] Solar advocates were among those who quickly grew to dislike the new department.

THE ENERGY CRISIS AND PROBLEM FRAME BEFORE THE EMBARGO

The United States experienced energy crises before the oil embargo of October 1973. Both the mass media and government officials referred to assorted shortages as an "energy crisis."[27] As is often the case in a crisis, energy policy changed substantially between 1969 and 1973 and, more slowly, so did solar energy policy. Nonetheless, the problem frame for energy policy proved quite durable, despite numerous pressures for change engendered by the crisis. Its core values – national security and economic rationality – framed a problem to which solar could contribute little. This period has a very complex history, and I will sample events from it to analyze the developments most relevant to solar. A more complete account can be found in the sources cited and in the more specialized literature on individual fuel sources.

The Growing Energy Crisis

By the late 1960s Americans began to experience tightening energy markets. The real price of electricity stopped declining, and by some measures began to increase. Petroleum markets similarly began to tighten, with prices staying flat or beginning to nudge upward. These problems contrasted sharply with the period from 1950 to 1970. For example, during that earlier time, the real, inflation-adjusted price of electricity fell from 3.8 cents per kilowatt-hour to 2.3 cents, and per capita consumption of it more than tripled.[28]

From its beginning, the Nixon administration also faced less subtle problems with energy. On hot summer days large numbers of air conditioners, combined with lighting and other electric loads in offices, produced demand that exceeded many urban utilities' capacities, causing power shortages – brownouts rather than total blackouts.[29] Even more troubling were fuel shortages. The winter of 1969–1970 was unusually severe, resulting in shortages of heating fuels as well as talk of more shortages to come.[30] The United States' increasing dependence on imported oil, particularly from the Middle East, concerned some policy makers. The Arab members of the Organization of Petroleum Exporting Countries (OAPEC, part of OPEC) had threatened to cut off oil supplies as early as February 1972.[31] Thus, in a few short years, consumers began to experience energy shortages – a notion that almost no one would have associated with energy only a few years earlier.

Media Presentations of the Energy Crisis

Several popular and technical writers interpreted these events as a crisis. They saw exponentially increasing consumption of fossil fuels as leading to severe shortages in the not-distant future, depriving future generations of the chance to live an affluent life and consigning the less-developed countries to permanent immiseration.[32] The mass media reported shortages, actual or impending, in electricity and fluid fuels. In August 1969, *Business Week* reported that electric utilities, frustrated by the delays in getting nuclear power plants online, were increasing their investments in coal-, oil-, and gas-fired power plants as a way of meeting the growing demand.[33] A November 1969 *Business Week* issue included a ten-page "Special Report" entitled "Why Utilities Can't Meet Demand," claiming in the article's first sentence that "Things have never been worse for the utilities than they are right now." Numerous cities had experienced power shortages in the two previous summers, and some planners feared that future summers could be even worse. The utilities had created part of the problem themselves, heavily advertising air conditioners and other electric appliances, only to be caught by surprise when consumers bought such products more quickly than they expected, increasing electricity demand more quickly than the utilities were prepared to handle. Utility executives also attributed their woes to labor shortages and costs, conservationists who challenged power plant construction, manufacturers who missed deadlines and produced faulty equipment, and overly stringent government regulations. In addition to these problems, the article devoted a full page to coal shortages. Utility stockpiles were dropping, other demands for coal were increasing, and utility and coal executives expected the tight coal market to continue.[34]

A little more than a year later, Consolidated Edison, the New York City utility, faced a "mini-crisis" due to a cold snap in the Northeast, forcing it to cut voltages to its customers and to plead with institutional customers to cut electricity usage.[35] As the summer of 1971 approached, the chair of the Federal Power Commission said electricity shortages "can be expected to continue over the next four or five years."[36]

Major media also expressed concerns over petroleum supplies. The oil companies were engaged, in the words of a *Newsweek* article, in a "frantic search" for sources of crude, including making high bids to explore for oil off of Alaska's North Slope. Firms and governments from other industrialized countries likewise were searching for new oil fields, including off-shore fields. All the while, relationships between American and European petroleum firms and OPEC, particularly those in North Africa and the Middle East, were becoming increasingly tense. OPEC countries threatened to cut off supplies to the United States, Europe, and Japan, arguing that they were not getting a fair share of the oil revenues. And all of this was happening more than two years before the oil embargo.[37]

The issue reached television on September 4, 1973, when NBC aired a three-hour long documentary entitled "NBC Reports: The Energy Crisis – An American White Paper." The show included interviews of seventy-eight different people espousing assorted interpretations of the problems and advocating various solutions related to energy, concluding with the overall message that the situation pointed to a seemingly inexorable crisis coming out of the increasing use of ever-more-scarce resources.[38]

In addition to the popular media, policy analysts were developing arguments about the nature of the crisis and publishing their views in widely read, though not quite "popular," journals. In framing the energy problem, some analysts portrayed energy as an economic good and others emphasized its physical nature and relationship to the ecosystem. In an example of the former, M. A. Adelman of MIT argued strenuously that the rising price of oil did not reflect any real scarcity, but instead resulted from a combination of the OPEC cartel's manipulating the market and its being aided in doing so by U.S. foreign policy. If the industrialized nations could break the cartel, oil would be cheap and in secure supply.[39]

Other perspectives were more critical of the economic approach. Environmental writers argued that the market prices of energy did not capture the externalities associated with its production and use, and some expressed skepticism that such externalities could ever be captured by pecuniary prices:

Because [environmental] damage is difficult, and perhaps impossible, to reckon in dollar terms, it is necessary to go beyond the market system in order to appraise the true costs of energy. As externalities cause the channels of money flow to diverge ever more widely from the channels of true costs and benefits, adequate appraisal of energy costs increasingly presupposes a shift away from strict reliance on traditional economic theory, with its confidence in pecuniary price as a measure of product costs. . . . These traditional misperceptions suggest the need for a new perspective, an "ecological perspective."[40]

Other analysts simply ignored the economic dimension to energy entirely. In a famous book on the environment, Paul and Anne Ehrlich wrote of energy as if it were simply a physical quantity being used up too fast:

Our supplies of fossil fuels – coal, petroleum, and natural gas – are finite and will probably be consumed within a few hundred years, possibly much sooner. . . . The most recent and thorough estimate, by geologist M. King Hubbert, gives us about a century before our petroleum reserves (including recent Alaskan discoveries) are depleted.[41]

This tension between these ways of seeing energy continued throughout the debates of the 1970s.

Official Problem Framing Under Nixon

To understand how solar energy fit into the larger energy policy context and why the normative and pragmatic ideas associated with solar energy technologies were a poor fit with those that framed energy policy more generally, we need to examine the ideas associated with energy more generally. Although the government devoted rapidly increasing resources to solar energy R&D, the relevant government agencies never institutionalized values that made solar appear a likely solution to their problem.[42]

Early in Richard Nixon's first term, government officials saw evidence of short supplies and increasing prices. Fossil fuel use had long since become integral to all parts of American society and culture. Industrial production, a high standard of living, and, above all else, the American obsession with automobiles, required a ready supply of energy for the good life.[43] In this context, and with this problem frame in mind, officials identified insufficient supply, not excessive demand, as the energy problem, occasionally pointing to a need to conserve as a short-term policy.

How, exactly, did policy makers articulate this problem? Early in 1971, White House aides presented the problem in a memo to President Nixon as one of inadequate supply: "We will have a serious shortage of fuels, and most particularly clean fuels, during the next five years."[44] Their greatest concerns emphasized winter shortages of natural gas and heating oil and summer shortages of electricity. This memo echoed the concerns of an oil industry report sent earlier to the White House staff, arguing that the shortages resulted from government policies that had put the industry in a squeeze between its costs and the prices that it could charge.[45] By early 1972, presidential aides called the imminent shortages "the energy crisis." They expected electricity shortages in the summer of 1972 and natural gas shortages the following winter, and they attributed the crisis to misguided government policies that restricted supply.[46] By early 1973, the notion of an energy crisis, interpreted as inadequate supplies, was in full swing in popular parlance as well as government circles.

White House staff noted repeatedly in memos and public statements that the United States, with only six percent of the world's population, consumed over a third of the world's annual energy production. Although they stated this fact without any apparent sense of moral opprobrium, by 1973 the administration concluded that the only answer in the short-run entailed encouraging Americans to reduce voluntarily their demand for energy by reducing driving, carpooling, keeping temperatures lower in the winter and higher in the summer, and so on.[47] By this time the oil industry, both in communications to the public and with the White House, tried to further this conception of the problem. In documents claiming to "set the record straight," they argued strenuously that they were victims of demand growth and policy constraints that made it impossible to keep up with demand.[48]

Administration spokesmen stressed the centrality of energy supply and its necessity for the good life, even when they tried to convince the public of the importance of conserving energy in the short-run. As John Love, then assistant to the president for energy and formally the top White House energy official, put it:

I do not believe that it is an overstatement to claim that the distance man travels from his cave – that is both his social and material progress – can be measured by his use of energy to improve his environment, to produce goods, to make things grow and to provide mobility. . . . To a large degree, the development of a Nation can be measured by its use of energy. Americans are the greatest energy users in the history of the world. With only six percent of the population, we use 35 per cent of the energy produced in the world. . . . What a tribute that is to our intelligence and innovativeness.

Love continued by saying that rapidly increasing demand caused some difficulties, and he called for conservation. But nothing in the letter, or Love's other public statements, suggests that he took Americans to task for their heavy use of energy. Quite to the contrary, he regarded such use as the pinnacle of not only material but *social* achievement.[49] Love's statements reflected, more baldly than most, the thinking of many in the administration. Note the values that he associated with technologies for producing and consuming energy. He emphasized the role of energy as a source of economic prosperity and legitimated it with the important value of economic growth, the same value that had consistently driven thinking about energy since the Truman administration. But Love took these notions further by equating a high-consumption society with a socially well-developed society. Love believed that energy technologies within a high-consumption system constituted the means to encourage social progress. Even more pointedly, consuming ever-increasing quantities of energy was the measure of a good society; consuming energy was the foundation of the good life. Technologies of ever-increasing complexity made possible the exploitation and consumption of energy resources. Thus the value of an energy technology increased with its ability to produce energy in ever-greater quantities. Perspectives such as Love's saw energy production technology as the thing that made modern society possible and dictated a constant upward spiral of production and consumption. By putting such technologies in place society could maintain its status quo. We can understand the shared meaning of these technologies to Love and his compatriots by understanding that they linked the technologies to this particular social and political outcome.[50]

This valorizing of energy consumption strongly framed the administration's views of the energy problem. If increasing consumption was an unalloyed social good, then energy policy should seek maximum production to overcome shortages. Administration officials saw conservation, especially as it refers to reduced activities, as an unfortunate and temporary expedient that was to be set aside when production rose to meet demand. Similarly, solar energy appeared as a weak solution in such a problem frame, unless advocates could make a persuasive case that it could produce large quantities of bulk energy. The administration's emphasis on production carried through right up until the embargo. Thus, at a cabinet-level meeting on energy chaired by Love just six days before the embargo, he emphasized the president's wish that disagreements among government agencies be resolved so as to maximize the production of energy.[51]

The administration's public positions framed energy in the same way. On June 4, 1971, more than two years before the embargo, President Nixon sent to Congress the first comprehensive energy message.[52] Responding to the brownouts and heating fuel shortages of the previous two years, the message made public the administration's concern about a growing energy crisis. The president used the message to outline his view of the energy problem and to present sweeping new policies and institutions that could solve the problem. This message suggested the ideas that underlay his administration's conception of energy policy.

The message described the proximate cause of the problem as twofold: rapidly growing demand and a greater need for clean fuels to reduce pollution. The message claimed that, in the previous four years, the growth in energy demand had accelerated, growing faster than the economy as a whole, due largely to low energy prices. During the same period, the public and the government had put greater emphasis on environmental protection, making even greater demands on clean fuels. The solution to this problem was a greatly expanded supply.[53] To that end, the president proposed a list of policies for both the short- and long-terms.

One could break Nixon's list of policies into three parts: R&D on new technologies for the longer term; a set of stop-gap measures for the short-term; and reorganization of energy agencies to better analyze, plan, and implement such policies. The R&D program's top priorities were pollution control technology (so that users could burn dirtier but more plentiful fuels), coal gasification, and, most importantly, the breeder reactor. "Our best hope today for meeting the Nation's growing demand for economical clean energy lies with the fast breeder reactor."[54] Indeed, the president made the breeder reactor demonstration program the first specific item that he mentioned in his energy message, and said that he wanted a successful demonstration plant completed by 1980. He also called for the creation of a Department of Natural Resources (DNR), which we discussed previously.[55] Some observers think that this combination of items in Nixon's policy speech reflected a truce with Senator Holifield, a strong supporter of the breeder who also opposed the DNR.[56] For all three programs the president requested from Congress additional funding for FY 1972, due to start in less than a month, over and above what they had already approved.

Note that all three of these technologies were intended to produce large quantities of bulk power. The solution to accelerating demand growth is accelerating supply growth. Most of the message emphasized expanding supply and said nothing about controlling demand. The noteworthy exception is a section, far down on the list of "other" policies, on "Using Energy More Wisely." Here the message makes a plug for greater energy efficiency, and suggests better housing insulation standards and energy efficiency information for large appliances. More importantly, this section argues for more economically efficient pricing of energy in which all costs of energy sources are incorporated into energy prices:

We believe that part of the answer lies in pricing energy on the basis of its full costs to society. One reason we use energy so lavishly today is that the price of energy does not include all of the social costs of producing it.[57]

Here is a classic argument for economic efficiency. By internalizing the social costs of energy consumption into its price, consumers will pay more directly for those social costs and, as economically rational agents, will seek to minimize their costs by taking actions to reduce their energy consumption until the marginal cost of more energy efficiency equals the marginal cost of buying more energy. In short, environmental protection provides the rationale for raising energy prices, which will then depress demand. Although raising prices was buried in the energy message, it occupied a very prominent place in the administration's internal discussions, as we will see in the next section.

Finally, the message argued for the consolidation of energy policy into a single agency, the Department of Natural Resources. The president emphasized that energy policy was scattered all over the government, making it impossible for the administration to approach the problem comprehensively and make necessary comparisons and trade-offs among different energy sources.[58] Government officials had voiced this desire to centralize energy policy since the Truman administration, and it finally began coming to fruition under Presidents Nixon, Ford, and Carter.

The themes of the 1971 energy message remained constant in the administration's public pronouncements. For example, about seven weeks before the oil embargo of October 1973, President Nixon held a publicized, hour-long meeting with his energy advisor, John Love, and other top administration officials, including Roy Ash, Director of the Office of Management and Budget (OMB), George Shultz, and Henry Kissinger. A draft of the statement released after the meeting made clear the seriousness of the situation. "*The energy challenge is not a cliche. It is a fact of overwhelming consequence to the future of our country. . . . [W]e cannot wait until we are on the edge of an energy crisis. We cannot wait until the last minute, because the last minute is now.*"[59] (Emphasis in original.) The policy response articulated in this statement contained, at the broadest level, the same four major components: the use of market forces to bolster supply; a recognition of the need to protect the environment or at least placate environmental constituencies while doing so; the use of research and development for long-term solutions; and the need to centralize energy decision making in one cabinet-level agency, instead of having it scattered all over the government. By that September the administration already had seven energy bills pending in Congress that embodied these policy responses, including one to create a new Department of Energy and Natural Resources, and the remaining six to make it easier to produce or import energy. All seven reaffirmed the conventional approach of trying to bolster supply.

Deregulating Energy

Deregulating energy was a central part of the administration's private discussions of energy policy. The Nixon administration believed that government policies were at least partly responsible for the fuel shortages and that deregulating oil and natural gas prices and controls would alleviate most of the shortages. John Whitaker put the matter succinctly in a 1971 memo to the president:

These actions [ones other than deregulation] skirt the hard policy decisions, require little or no new funding, all have little political appeal or impact and, not surprisingly, would have no real effect on the energy shortage. . . .

The fact of the matter is that there are meaningful possibilities to increase the supply of clean fuels. One is to deregulate, at least partially, the price of natural gas. The resultant increase in price would stimulate additional exploration and production. The other is to modify or terminate production controls and import quotas on oil. Both items, as you well know, are political hot potatoes.

Nixon did indeed know that these were "hot potatoes." At the end of the memo, Whitaker suggested two options, neither of which was to deregulate. Option one entailed not even discussing deregulation internally, much less in public. Option two assigned a small group of top-level officials to study the possibility of deregulation and then recommend to the president whether or not he ought to deregulate. Nixon agreed to option two, but wrote by hand on the memo, "But in *complete* confidence. *Don't* stir up the political issue. If it can't be done *without* fanfare (which is probably the case) – go to option 1."[60] Whatever Nixon's views on the virtues of the free market, in his first term he intended to tread very gently on the issue of deregulation.[61]

President Nixon did not mention natural gas price deregulation in his June 1971 energy message, but it remained a topic of discussion for White House staff concerned with energy policy, and he did mention it in his 1971 Annual Economic Report. Nixon and his staff continued to believe that allowing gas to rise to its market price would solve the supply problem. A memo to the president in July 1972 discussed the conclusions of five separate energy models – one corporate, one government, and three academic – which all said that the supply of gas was quite elastic with respect to price, and that the deregulation of new gas prices alone would solve the energy shortages. But the memo also noted the potential political backlash, advising Nixon that such an initiative should wait until after the election. Deregulation would enrage consumers and only please the oil industry, which was probably unnecessary, for "if the Democrats nominate McGovern, the oil industry and its sympathizers will have no political alternative to the President."[62]

Industry pressure for price deregulation continued after the 1972 election. Tom Paine, a vice president with General Electric and former Nixon administration official, wrote to the president and attached a brief paper on the energy problem that emphasized the need for freer markets in energy resources. The letter was widely circulated among the staff, including George Shultz, John Ehrlichman, and Henry Kissinger, along with a very complimentary cover memo written by Peter Flanigan.[63] Although Paine may have been preaching to the converted, it did not hurt his cause to keep up the pressure. Frank Ikard, President of the

American Petroleum Institute, in his letter of June 23, 1973, to Peter
Flanigan, a senior White House aide, defended the oil industry from
charges of creating a phony shortage and argued that prices were too
low and needed freeing.[64] The day after Christmas 1972, the White
House staff presented Nixon, now entering his second term, with a
memo detailing ten new energy proposals for the Congress that would
convene in a few weeks. "The principle underlying these proposals is
that government interference with the free market system should be as
limited as possible, and that this system is best capable of providing sufficient clean energy at an acceptable price." True to this credo, the first
of the proposals called for the deregulation of newly found natural gas.[65]
On April 18, 1973, President Nixon made good on his commitment to
deregulating prices, proposing partial deregulation in his energy message
to Congress.[66] The bill had a tough time in Congress, as the administration knew it would. By September 1973, the administration did not
think that the bill had a very good chance of passage in 1973 or 1974.
Nonetheless, at the September 8 energy meeting of the president and his
top advisors, complete deregulation remained one of the topics on the
agenda.[67]

The administration's emphasis on price deregulation suggested little
in the way of a short-term role for solar energy. Even significant increases
in conventional energy prices would not create a solar energy industry
overnight. Many of the technologies were immature and the industry was
still small and fragmented. A basic policy orientation that sought to
reduce government involvement in energy markets suggested that an
aggressive solar R&D program or other forms of subsidy were not likely
to be forthcoming.

Environmental Protection

Environmental protection developed into a very important issue during
the Nixon years, and the president signed the landmark National
Environmental Protection Act (NEPA) into law on January 1, 1970.
While NEPA grew out of a congressional initiative, and many observers
believed that Nixon's support of it was less than whole-hearted, it
institutionalized environmental protection as a concern that his administration could not ignore. Moreover, the act established within the
White House structure a staff agency called the Council on Environmental Quality (CEQ).[68] Although the ways in which environmental
concerns influenced energy policy reflected this new organizational structure, which now included the CEQ, policy outcomes were also constrained by the policy and ideological commitments of top officials.
In the following analysis, we will see that the values associated
with environmental protection did not penetrate as high in the structure

of decision making as standard pluralist accounts of environmental policy claim.

Pluralism sees environmental concerns as one among many, each with its own constituency pushing the government in its favored policy direction. According to this interpretation, environmentalists' successes derived from the resources that they brought to bear and the skill with which they used them, relative to competing groups. While this account has much to commend it, it misses some crucial parts of the way environmental values entered into policy making during the Nixon years.

Two phenomena are relevant here in forming a more complete account: the segregation of environmental concerns within the policy structure and the perfunctory internalization of environmental concern at higher levels of decision making. Consider the environment in energy policy. The agencies leading the charge for making environmental concerns central to policy making were, not surprisingly, the EPA and the CEQ. In late July 1972, an EPA official, Robert L. Sansom, sent a memo to White House aides John Whitaker and Richard Fairbanks in which he presented both EPA and CEQ views on energy and, particularly, energy conservation. This memo offered a starkly different conclusion from the supply orientation present in most White House discussions of energy. It asserted that a "significant reduction in energy use (up to about 20 per cent by the latter part of this century) can be effected without impairing our standard of living if a coordinated program is undertaken." Sansom then emphasized the environmental aspects of energy production and conservation and ranked energy production technologies according to their environmental effects. Sansom knew that his analysis was at variance with the way that the administration typically looked at energy, for in the introductory part of the memo he wrote, almost apologetically, "You will note our summary is from an environmental viewpoint."[69] Environmental concerns thus entered energy policy discussions from a relatively new agency and peripheral White House office, in contrast to the views of those agencies and persons at the center of energy policy making.

Environmental concerns did, to some extent, penetrate everyone's thinking about energy policy in the early 1970s, but in such a way as to not alter or even challenge the fundamental thinking about energy policy. Frequent references in White House memos and other writings to the necessity of providing "clean fuels" or "clean energy" show that environmental concerns had entered the official lexicon of presidential aides.[70] Yet clearly such concerns defined criteria that were desirable but not central. For instance, the same memos that noted the need to find clean fuels also outlined the ten new energy initiatives that the administration proposed in April of 1973. All of the initiatives were aimed at boosting supply, not finding ways to improve the efficiency of energy use, and many of the supply proposals clearly threatened environmental concerns, such as speeding the exploitation of off-shore oil and accelerating coal use.

I do not suggest that the EPA was irrelevant to public policy during the Nixon years. Clearly it had a powerful effect on policy in implementing the statutes in its domain, and these laws multiplied in the 1970s. Moreover, it is significant that the language of environmental concern entered the official lexicon of energy policy at all. To some modest extent, therefore, the value of environmental protection was becoming institutionalized. However, the large-scale changes in institutional venue and policy framing, posited by Baumgartner and Jones as the indication of an old policy monopoly's replacement by a new set of arrangements, had yet to take place in energy policy.[71] Environmentalism remained a new value for which advocates fought in a variety of policy arenas, but by 1973 they had only modestly succeeded in energy policy. Solar energy advocates increasingly tried to sell their technology to policy makers on the basis of its environmental benefits, but they were as yet knocking on the wrong door. Environmental values had not yet been institutionalized at the top level of energy policy making, and hence the environmental appeal of solar continued to be, to a large extent, irrelevant to White House officials concerned about energy problems. For the time being, the problem remained framed as one of increasing supply.

POSTEMBARGO

The oil embargo of October 1973 raised the intensity of activity in American energy policy.[72] Nightly newscasts, people's daily experiences of lines at gas stations, and rapidly increasing energy prices revealed a severe energy crisis. Public opinion polls measured a strong reaction to the crisis, coming as it did on the heels of several other major social upheavals.[73] Politicians at every level responded.[74] The Iranian Revolution of 1978–1979 reduced for a time that nation's oil exports and again led to sharp price increases, ensuring that energy remained a high-salience issue throughout the 1970s.[75] How did ideas influence institutions in energy policy, how were the issues framed, in what sense did partisans see energy technology as encouraging a particular kind of society, and how could solar energy fit into all of these questions? The official frame of energy policy changed less than one might expect, despite the issue's greatly increased intensity and salience. Nonetheless, the sense of crisis reemphasized issues of national security in energy debates.

Problem Framing and Policy Response: Nixon and Ford

In energy policy, as in so many other ways, the Nixon administration felt embattled by the end of 1973. Senator Henry (Scoop) Jackson, with whom the administration had begun a series of cordial, quiet meetings only a year before, now accused the president of a slow and inadequate response to the energy crisis. In turn, an internal memo to Nixon reflected the administration's changed perceptions of Jackson and addressed the need to counter Jackson's "demagoguery." The memo advised the president to "accentuate the positive" as a tactic instead of meeting Jackson's charges head on, by which Nixon wrote "good" in the margins. He wrote "OK" next to another paragraph which suggested that "This is not to say, however, our people cannot subtly attack demagogues. . . . (This type of information will be distributed orally rather than by memorandum.)"[76] The memo continued with a six-page list of accomplishments by the new Federal Energy Office, an office established within the White House to coordinate federal energy policy, in the month of September alone and fourteen "major" initiatives by the president, most either organizational or aimed at boosting domestic supplies, including the new five-year R&D program. In one initiative, for instance, four months before the embargo the administration had begun an energy conservation program for the government itself. The program was successful, and by early 1974 it had exceeded its original target by a large margin.[77] The Nixon administration also had twelve pieces of legislation pending before Congress, although most were not moving along well, and the White House was considering eleven more. The bills moving along best were those creating the Federal Energy Administration (FEA) and the Energy Research and Development Administration (ERDA).[78] On the other hand, President Nixon vetoed a bill that did pass in February, an Energy Emergency Act, because it contained a number of unacceptable measures, such as price rollback requirements.[79] In short, President Nixon and his advisors felt that Congress was hindering them in dealing with the energy crisis.

The Ford administration held similar sentiments. Early in Ford's tenure, one top aide circulated a memo to other White House staff listing sixteen pieces of energy legislation awaiting congressional action.[80] By 1976, President Ford had gotten eight of the bills he wanted passed, and Congress had added six of its own, but the administration still had fifteen energy proposals on which Congress had not acted.[81]

A set of consistent empirical and normative ideas dominated White House discussions concerning new energy policies and institutions, and those ideas did not bode well for policy toward solar energy. These ideas made up the official frame of the problem and suggested who owned this issue. Some of these ideas harkened back to every administration since Truman. The essence of the problem in this view was a growing shortage of inexpensive fossil fuels resulting from the more or less natural evolution of personal and industrial use of previously abundant energy. As demonstrated above, presidents and their spokespersons frequently cited the statistic, publicly and internally, that the United States, with only six percent of the world's population, used about thirty-five percent of its energy production. Moreover, they cited this fact, not as a criticism of American energy use, but rather as the natural consequence of millions of rational microdecisions that together had a macrooutcome that posed difficulties for energy supply. From the Truman administration on, this way of depicting the problem presented it as an unintended consequence and suggested that there was no specific villain and no one to blame. But Presidents Nixon and Ford did introduce an important difference in this conceptualization of the energy problem. They identified a villain, even if an unintentional one, namely, government interference in the market. The centrality of free market ideology was crucial to the way that these two presidents saw the issue, and so it is worth examining how their top aides argued on its behalf.

In the last year of his presidency, Richard Nixon became increasingly isolated in the White House, distracted by the unfolding Watergate scandal. Two aides, Roy Ash of the Office of Management and Budget and Herbert Stein, Chair of the Council of Economic Advisors, retained some modicum of access to him, at least in regard to energy policy. Ash had come to the Nixon administration from Litton Industries where, as a senior executive and eventually president, he had been one of the key people responsible for building Litton from a small electronics firm into a gigantic conglomerate. A self-made corporate success, it is not surprising that Ash held strong views about the importance of unfettered markets.[82] He was clearly a dominant player in White House policy making, and his preferred outcomes often won when White House staff disagreed with each other. He sent numerous memos, some on specific programs and some on the energy problem more generally, to the president and other aides, emphasizing the importance of free markets and the need for the private sector to be deregulated in order to solve the energy problem.[83] "We must *allow*," he wrote, "and hopefully *help* and *lead* the private sector . . . to adjust to new market conditions in the 1974–1980 period. *For it is the private sector which will solve the energy problems of this period.*" (Emphasis in original.) President Nixon agreed, writing "Makes great sense" on this memo.[84] Ash was also aware of the implications of massive decontrol and the political difficulties in carrying it out. Consequently, he recommended "that *particularly* we avoid meddling with the private sector in ways which interfere with its ability to produce. (Publicly, we probably must join in the clamor against the oil companies to some degree and take some specific steps so as to be perceived this way.)" (Emphasis in original.)[85] While some of the Nixon energy policy may have been based in cynicism, Ash had a very clear idea of the nature of the problem and of how he preferred policy to work.

Herbert Stein, Chair of the Council of Economic Advisors, named the administration's postembargo energy program "Project Independence" and strongly influenced White House policies.[86] Stein sent at least two of his speeches on energy to President Nixon, whose handwritten notes on them suggest that he read them through, marking one "Brilliant" and another "Very thoughtful."[87] In these speeches Stein asserted his view that deregulated markets, and the higher prices that such actions would entail, were far preferable to continued regulation and rationing schemes in dealing with shortages. If higher energy prices had undesirable distributive consequences, then those should be addressed directly by taxes, employment policies, or other means, not by interfering with the markets for one commodity.[88]

Project Independence

"Project Independence" was President Nixon's policy initiative to free the country from dependence on foreign oil and as such laid out the general problem frame for energy policy. He announced "Project Independence" in a televised address to the nation on November 7, 1973, less than one month after the start of the OPEC price increases and embargo. Despite the sensational proximate causes of the energy shortages – the Mid-East war and oil embargo – the president put the energy problems in a broader, longer term context:

> But our deeper energy problems come not from war, but from peace and abundance. We are running out of energy today because our economy has grown enormously and because in prosperity what were once considered luxuries are now considered necessities. . . . Now, our growing demands have bumped up against the limits of available supply, and until we provide new sources of energy for tomorrow, we must be prepared to tighten our belts today.[89]

As so many studies had before him, he depicted energy shortages arising out of the beneficial processes of economic growth; the tens of millions of microdecisions to install air conditioning, drive larger cars, and so on added up to an unintended consequence. Lacking villains, this story instead spread the responsibility among the public at large, whom he urged to "tighten our belts." The address included a long list of administrative actions and legislative requests intended to increase domestic supplies and reduce consumption, such as lowering speed limits, shifting to daylight savings time year-round, reducing airline flights, reducing government energy consumption, finishing the Alaska pipeline, and relaxing some environmental standards.[90]

Belt-tightening is not a very attractive long-term policy, and the president had a different plan for the 1980s. He made the goal of "Project Independence" that the United States be self-sufficient in energy by 1980, a little more than six years away. Drawing comparisons with the "Manhattan Project" and "Project Apollo", President Nixon called for self-sufficiency as the way to ensure American freedom of action abroad and prosperity at home. "Today the challenge is to regain the strength that we had earlier in this century, the strength of self-sufficiency."[91] As policy narratives so often do, this one harkened back to a better time when American strength was uncompromised by foreign dependence.

Conspicuously absent from the values framing this crisis was that of free markets. Indeed, one could read Nixon's statement of the problem to suggest that free markets got the country into this mess in the first place. In any event, price decontrols did not show up anywhere in this speech's list of policy options. However, the president was clearly considering such market-oriented actions. The next day, in a special message to Congress discussing his legislative wishes, he included price deregulation for new natural gas. The president simply included gas deregulation as one item in a long list, not giving this modest step any special prominence, and saying nothing about deregulating oil markets.[92] The fact that the president, now in his second term and ineligible to run again, said nothing about deregulation in his televised speech suggests that he still considered it a "hot potato."

The "Project Independence" study got organized starting in January 1974. Some presidential advisors, such as William Simon, favored a strongly market-oriented approach and saw no need, from an economic perspective, for imports to go to zero. Simon favored importing up to fifteen percent of oil and gas from diverse sources. This approach was not favored by all of those working on the study, and from March 1974, when the work got underway in earnest, to the November 1974 release of the study's report, there was constant fighting within the administration over the extent to which the report would mainly favor oil and gas deregulation, possibly coupled with new energy taxes. A staff that reached 500 people at its peak produced the final report, a huge, multi-volume work that was produced under a very constraining deadline.[93]

Project Independence described the source of the energy crisis in much the traditional way, as the unintended consequence of growing affluence and cheap energy, which was in turn partly responsible for such a rise in affluence. It noted that per capita U.S. energy consumption was eight times the world's average.[94] A separate volume, entitled *An Historical*

Perspective, elaborated on these trends, showing that total and per capita energy use had increased steadily since World War II in all regions of the world, but most steeply in Japan, Western Europe, and the United States. This historical volume also presented another cause of the problem, the loss of control over production and distribution by the large multinational oil companies, including the "Seven Sisters," to the countries that owned the oil.[95]

This report put a much heavier emphasis on economic efficiency than did President Nixon's announcement a year earlier. Several features of the report showed that the project had engendered strong debates over key ideas. First among these was energy independence itself:

To some, energy independence is a situation in which the United States receives no energy through imports, i.e. it produces all of its energy domestically. To others, independence is a situation in which the United States does import to meet some of its energy requirements, but only up to a point of "acceptable" political and economic vulnerability.

The report's authors stated that they did not intend to actually recommend policies, but instead to discuss trade-offs and present a framework for analysis.[96] Nonetheless, buried deep in the report is a chapter on the definitions and methodologies that drove the analysis, and here they made it clear that they were using the latter definition of independence, one based on some imports. They argued that the nation should seek the least total national costs, which is a sum of both the market costs of energy and the costs of vulnerability associated with imported energy. They emphasized that this point of least cost was not at zero imports, since the market costs of energy are very high under that scenario.[97] Here issues of national security are expressed as straightforward economic costs, such as the costs of establishing an emergency oil stockpile. Operating on these assumptions, and by analyzing policy options that assumed modest (in retrospect) oil prices, this definition of the problem left little for solar in the short-run, as will be discussed in later chapters.

The Federal Energy Administration put great effort into the *Project Independence Blueprint*. The *Blueprint* was leaked to the press in draft form and came under heavy criticism from various agencies, especially Interior Secretary Rogers Morton.[98] The *Blueprint* argued that nothing the government could do would have any effect on the nation's energy problems for the next three years, but that efforts to increase domestic supply and decrease demand could pay off by the 1980s. The report devoted 250 pages to conservation. While it did not consider demand reduction to be an adequate policy without policies to boost domestic supply, the draft report contained a number of government regulatory measures for curbing demand, concluding that voluntary conservation would be inadequate. Sawhill wanted policy to include a substantial twenty or thirty cents per gallon gasoline tax, but President Ford made his opposition to such a tax known before the draft was released. Indeed, advocating this tax may have contributed to Sawhill's being fired on October 29, 1974. Regarding solar energy, the report argued that a five-year, $1 billion program could have noticeable effects on energy consumption through space heating and electricity generation.[99]

President Ford and his principal energy advisors articulated a very similar conceptualization of the energy problem. From their perspective, the energy crisis had the same origins and the same solutions as discussed by Nixon's advisors, some of whom had carried over to the Ford administration.[100] Such views received support from legislators in energy-producing states.[101] The Ford administration wanted to make more progress on energy matters than had Nixon's, and the Energy Resources Council (ERC), headed by Rogers Morton and Frank Zarb, put together a briefing book for the president that set out the general goals of the administration and the types of programs that could meet them. Some of the goals of this energy policy contradicted each other, particularly the desires for free markets and for national security.[102]

The briefing book argued that several principles should drive energy policy, the first of which was to provide energy at the lowest possible cost "consistent with our need for secure energy supplies." This policy statement also asserted the need to "[p]rotect the environment in every way consistent with our national energy needs." The ERC explained the free market principle this way: "Look first to the private sector and our free market pricing system as the most efficient means of achieving the Nation's goals, but act through government where the private sector is not able to reach the national energy goals." They affirmed a commitment here to the free market, but not as an end in itself, and they offered no suggestion of how to resolve the conflicts of principle and practice that might arise.[103] The ERC put the national security implications of the energy crisis very starkly, emphasizing the relationship between the two:

What is essentially at stake is the economic balance of power achieved by the Western World over the last century and a half. . . . Prior to the late 1960s the United States was not only self-sufficient, but had sufficient surplus capacity that it set the price and direction of the world petroleum market. Energy consumption grew rapidly at 4–5 per cent per year. Since then, however, the U.S. situation has seriously deteriorated: . . . The restoration of American dominance in setting the goals and establishing the price of energy must be the ultimate objective of our national energy policy.[104]

Since the United States had become a net importer of energy in the Truman administration, the ERC's interpretation entailed rewriting a bit of history. But whatever its factual inaccuracies, the narrative structure of this analysis tells of a happy past, when the United States dominated world markets and so had all of the energy that it wanted at low prices. That situation had changed, and the goal was to restore the good old days, a bluntly described American hegemony over international energy markets.

Clearly, seeking this national security goal meant compromise with free market goals. Deregulation of domestic energy markets would certainly result in higher prices for all fuels, especially in light of OPEC actions. Higher prices should depress demand as well as stimulate domestic production and thereby make it easier to reduce dependency on energy imports. However, the ERC's notion of the free market did not extend to international trade, since the whole purpose of its policy was to reduce imports faster than market dynamics. Moreover, in a properly functioning market, no single buyer establishes the price of a good. Despite these complications, Ford and his advisors considered the deregulation of energy markets their primary policy instrument for achieving energy independence, both ideologically and in terms of the expected impact on reducing imports.[105] In numerous other memos and messages to outside constituencies, the administration continued to promote this set of sometimes conflicting principles of energy independence and low prices for secure supplies on the one hand, along with price deregulation of domestic supplies on the other, which everyone knew would result in higher prices. Occasionally they also mentioned a need to relax environmental regulations.[106]

Ford's White House staffers frequently came into conflict with agency personnel, particularly ERDA and the Council on Environmental Quality (CEQ), over the issue of government intervention in the private sector, even though the CEQ was also part of the White House. The White House staff, including those in the OMB, tried hard to keep the agencies more consistent with the basic principles of the president's plan, especially the emphasis on the free market and increasing domestic supply. The White House feared that the agencies, especially the ERDA, would appropriate too much power for themselves, with the help of Congress, and would thereby interfere with the market. So to ensure its authority over policy, for example, the White House chose to clear ERDA's annual plan for R&D, which it was required by statute to submit every year, resulting in constant battles over the wording and emphasis of the various drafts. Hugh Loweth of the OMB complained to ERDA that its R&D draft plan for 1976 failed "to emphasize the role and importance of the private sector."

He pointedly explained the ideological significance of word choices, for instance:

> I note that the legislation does not call for a "National Plan," but only a comprehensive plan. By calling the document a National Plan for Energy RD&D [Research, Development, and Demonstration] I believe we have overstated the Federal Government's role and capability in this area. As we have discussed, we are concerned that this title could be misinterpreted to mean that the Federal Government somehow intends to determine and direct the timing and nature of private sector actions and investments in energy RD&D and energy production capacity.[107]

Loweth lost the battle over the title of the document, but the White House got most of what it wanted in other respects.

The White House also disagreed sharply with the ERDA draft about its emphasis in the executive summary on conservation, which the draft interpreted as energy efficiency, as being the most important set of energy technologies to foster, more important than any supply technologies. Some called the dispute at the staff level "irreconcilable," especially when it centered around specific sentences, such as "Conservation (energy efficiency) technologies are identified as being of the highest national priority for national action." Presidential aides, particularly OMB staff, rejected singling out conservation over supply since both were important, asserting that such priorities countered previously stated policies, and, moreover, they would open the door to criticizing the president for not spending enough on conservation. Glenn Schleede, a staffer on the Domestic Council (part of the Executive Office of the President, i.e., the White House staff) who focused on energy issues, advised his superior on the Domestic Council that the issue could cause problems if the White House tried simply to override ERDA:

> On merit, I believe that there is no strong basis for ranking energy conservation technologies highest. . . . The whole issue has apparently raised an emotional state among the ERDA staff and thus presents a real problem for Dr. Seamans and Bob Fri [Administrator and Deputy Administrator of ERDA, respectively].

Schleede recommended that the differences be "papered over" instead of resolved. He offered specific wordings to the effect that conservation technologies now "ranked with several supply technologies as being of the highest priority for national attention." He also suggested putting in words that would emphasize the primacy of the private sector in actually deciding which technologies got deployed when.[108] Schleede got his compromise. The final published version of the ERDA plan used his exact words in the executive summary when discussing the new importance of conservation technology, except that the published document substituted the word "action" where he had suggested "attention."[109]

Such battles between ERDA and the White House occurred whenever there were statements to be made about energy because they entailed profound implications for the choices of which ideas would dominate policy. Thus, in discussing a message to be sent to an energy conference, Schleede described the significance of this contentious process:

I'm not surprised by the ERDA draft but I'll confess to some disappointment. It runs directly counter to the whole thrust of the President's policy on Federal vs. private sector roles. The emphasis should be on the private sector's primary responsibility for developing and bringing into use new energy technologies. The Federal Government's is the supporting and assisting and facilitating role.

ERDA persists, understandably I guess, it [sic] perceiving of itself as the center of everything . . . we've run into this same problem in ERDA reports . . . and in other things that ERDA writes for us.[110]

Despite these conflicts, the White House and the ERDA agreed on many points. ERDA's 1976 annual R&D plan listed the fundamental goals toward which energy policy should lead, and these conveyed a set of values or ideologies with which the White House could be very comfortable, such as preserving national security, maintaining a strong and growing economy, preserving the status quo in terms of lifestyles, and protecting the environment.[111] Obviously, stating the problem in these general terms left much room for disagreement on very important details. This type of problem framing also left out, or made it difficult to justify, a whole range of policies, particularly those relating to certain solar technologies and decentralized energy production, some of which were beginning to develop a constituency.

The issues of conservation and the role of the public versus private sectors also turned up in conflicts between the White House and the CEQ. In a draft report evaluating the ERDA plan, the CEQ emphasized conservation and the public sector too heavily for the White House's liking, making the report an implicit criticism of the administration's budget and policy.[112] Schleede argued that the CEQ should not be allowed to publish the report, even if such action looked oppressive to outsiders, because to do otherwise "would 'reward' CEQ for taking an approach with a proposed public report that is pretty irresponsible . . . we insisted that ERDA get in line with Administration position. . . . (Incidentally, the ERDA report had also leaked and there were ERDA staff charges of heavy-handedness.) Why should we treat CEQ differently?"[113] In this case and others, the White House determined the broad ideology to which others at least had to respond.

As the 1976 election year wound on, Congress did pass a few more energy bills, but President Ford vetoed two of them. In part, he vetoed both bills because they interfered too much, in his view, with the private sector – a battle he fought with Congress during his whole term.[114] In a study published a month after Ford had lost the 1976 election, the Energy Resources Council (an organization forced on the executive branch by the Congress) reviewed the previous several years and reiterated the themes and general ideas of Ford's policies, namely, to stimulate domestic resource development and deregulate energy sources to the extent possible. The report noted that Congress had been hostile to these general goals all along and had frustrated many of them.[115]

The foregoing analysis of administration battles over ideology may make it appear that there was more coherence in the executive branch, or at least among White House aides fighting for their principles, than was actually the case. In summarizing his long chapter on energy in the Ford years, de Marchi emphasizes that, for all of the White House's protestations about the importance of free markets, they were not prepared to endorse them in a wholehearted way.[116] Real deregulation would have resulted in substantially higher prices to consumers and devastation in certain segments of the fuel industries, leading to substantial political costs to President Ford. He had to be wary of such costs, both because he had never been elected and because of the immediate aftermath of Watergate. Watergate seriously, if temporarily, realigned power in American policy making, and the Republican president who had pardoned Richard Nixon as almost his first official act held a substantially weakened office. Congress, on the other hand, had gained influence in the aftermath of Watergate. In addition to being averse as a whole to imposing high costs on constituents, several legislators sought to realize their own goals in energy policy, often trying to push the Ford administration faster and farther than it wanted to go. The administration did in fact increase funding dramatically for previously neglected energy sources, including solar. Nonetheless, the institutionalization of the broad, and sometimes contradictory, normative goals of keeping energy prices low, reducing imports of oil, relying on the free market, and defining the problem in terms of inadequate supply choice, created a policy context in which solar advocacy had a hard time being taken seriously.

Problem Framing and Policy Response: Carter

Programmatic and normative debates over energy policy raged in and out of government during President Carter's term. When he took office in 1977, energy prices were still much higher than they had been prior to the 1973 oil embargo, with natural gas prices still going up in real terms and oil starting to rise again in 1979. Fuel shortages, especially of natural gas, exacerbated the hardships of the very harsh winter of 1977. Numerous private groups were sponsoring energy policy studies, and many of these sought to influence the incoming administration.[117] Much of the energy controversy during Carter's administration focussed on oil and natural gas, the complex histories of which are analyzed elsewhere.[118] This analysis looks at the more general debates about energy policy.

On Inauguration Day, President Carter promised to deliver to the Congress in ninety days a National Energy Plan, a comprehensive set of programs to deal with the energy crisis. He made James Schlesinger head of the Energy Policy and Planning office in the Executive Office of the President. Schlesinger assembled a team of about fifteen professionals, and they worked out the plan on schedule. Team members were mainly from government and academia and, unlike the people who worked under President Ford, were much more positive about the role that government could play in energy policy. Because of the magnitude of the task and the severe deadline, the group worked long hours and largely in isolation. There was no time to try to develop a plan based on a carefully nurtured consensus with public groups, Congress, or even other executive branch agencies. The National Energy Plan process was, as a result, quite technocratic.[119]

The National Energy Plan's overall depiction of the problem confronting energy policy was simple:

The diagnosis of the U.S. energy crisis is quite simple: demand for energy is increasing, while supplies of oil and natural gas are diminishing. Unless the U.S. makes a timely adjustment before world oil becomes very scarce and very expensive in the 1980's, the nation's economic security and the American way of life will be gravely endangered. The steps the U.S. must take now are small compared to the drastic measures that will be needed if the U.S. does nothing until it is too late.[120]

This is a typical narrative of decline and loss of control. The increasing demand and shrinking supply seem like inexorable natural forces, both stated in the passive voice, removing the question of agency. These events just happened, and would wreck havoc unless the country adopted the necessary preventative steps immediately. The policy story had no clearly defined villain.

Also in the National Energy Plan was the concept of a transition. The authors of the plan, and many energy analysts outside government as well, saw the decline in oil production and rise in prices as part of a

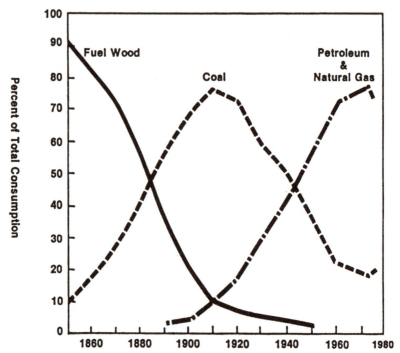

Figure 1. The United States has shifted to different fuel use patterns. (*Source*: U.S. Bureau of Mines and Federal Energy Administration.)

larger historical movement away from oil and natural gas toward some renewable energy system. According to this idea, the United States had made two previous historic transitions in its use of energy – from wood and water to coal, and from coal to oil and natural gas.

A graph like the one in Figure 1 appeared in many analyses. In this view, energy policy was merely a response to the inexorable changes in resources. Through natural processes, demand was exceeding supply, and these constraints dictated that the nation must undergo another transition. The only issue was whether the transition would be orderly and relatively painless or abrupt and costly.[121]

Framed in this way, policy makers' options appeared very circumscribed. Such a framing of the problem did not allow for a status quo, do-nothing approach; if the changes were coming, one might as well manage them. The challenge was guessing which energy sources would come next and thinking about how best to put them into place.

As I will discuss in detail in later chapters, the Carter administration was friendlier to solar energy than its predecessors. Nonetheless, the problem framing that they used and the ideas that they associated with energy policy created large obstacles for solar energy, since they emphasized needs that solar could not, in the short-term, satisfy. Those inherent conflicts would leave the administration frustrated with solar energy and its advocates and the solar movement frustrated with and suspicious of the administration.

6

Solar Advocacy in the Crisis

The energy crisis provided a unique opportunity for solar advocates of all types. The public's and policy makers' loss of confidence in conventional energy policy opened the way for advocates to argue for new ways of looking at energy policy and the role of solar technology in it. Concurrently, the solar movement began to incorporate influences from some of the other social movements of the day, including environmentalism and radical critiques of technological society. Bringing these issues into the debate split the solar movement, as competing elements within it articulated different visions of society and the role of solar energy in it.

PUBLICLY CONSTRUCTING SOLAR ENERGY

During the energy crisis, solar advocates produced a rapidly increasing volume of articles and books that argued for more attention to and resources for solar energy. The multiplicity of solar advocates can again, for our purposes, be divided into two categories. The modest differences that separated solar advocates in the 1950s and 1960s deepened in the 1970s, with the more ambitious advocates tying their advocacy of solar energy tightly to strong environmental values and often to whole critiques of modern industrial capitalism. For this reason I name the more guarded advocates conventional and the more ambitious advocates ecological.[1] Although any such classification scheme does some injustice to the many variations within each category, in the mid-1970s solar advocates began to diverge in the ideas and, particularly, the values that they associated with their technology and with energy technologies more generally. These two groups did share some common ideas. Both groups expressed concern with nontechnical barriers to increasing the use of solar energy, recognizing that economic, institutional, and social barriers stood in the way of a widespread use of solar technologies. Economic barriers encompassed not simply high prices but also factors like difficulties in getting financing for novel technologies. Institutional barriers

116

included, for example, building codes and failures to incorporate sun rights into property deeds. Solar advocates defined social barriers less clearly, often using this catchall category for consumer or vendor resistance to solar that did not fit into other categories.[2]

These groups split over the fraction of the nation's energy that solar could provide in the medium term. For example, in the last month of the Ford administration, the Energy Research and Development Administration (ERDA) released a study that it had commissioned from the MITRE Corp., which claimed that solar was already competitive with electric heating in many parts of the country, although it was still more expensive than oil or gas. In contrast to this positive assessment, at about the same time the ERDA assistant administrator for solar publicly questioned the feasibility of solar technologies for generating electricity and called for a study to see if the government's budget for such technologies should be reduced. Also at the end of 1976, analyses published in respected scientific sources argued that solar energy could contribute very little, at least in the short and medium term, to U.S. energy needs.[3] In contrast, writings by solar advocates, while mixed on the extent to which solar was ready to be commercialized, unanimously argued that it could and should be a large part of the American energy system in the near future.[4]

Conventional Advocates

A number of indicators suggest that the solar movement grew rapidly during the energy crisis.[5] The movement contained groups with diverse ideologies and views on the nature of the energy problem and the role that solar could play in it. The conventional, guarded advocates saw solar as simply another fuel to plug into the existing energy system, carrying no implications for social or political changes, and arguing that the removal of conventional impediments to the diffusion of solar, such as financing or getting high-quality installation on new devices, would lead to substantial growth in the solar energy market. Solar was desirable because it would last forever as a replacement for fossil fuels and could not be embargoed by foreigners (the national security rationale).[6] Similarly, these advocates based their criticism of the government's solar programs on conventional criteria, such as arguing that the government was neglecting important technologies like passive solar or that it was distorting markets by subsidies to conventional fuels.[7]

Less guarded and more ambitious for solar, at least in the long run, were some scientists and engineers promoting their own particular solar technologies. For example, Peter Glaser wrote in 1969 that the future of solar energy could lie with space satellites that collect large quantities of solar energy and beam them back to earth in the form of microwaves to be collected by a receiving antenna and distributed to the electrical grid. This was the highest of the high-tech solar proposals.[8] In another case of large-scale thinking, in 1970 Aden and Marjorie Meinel, both scientists, proposed that part of the Arizona and Southern California desert be turned over to a huge, centralized solar electricity–generating system, a National Solar Power Facility, that would, in due time, supply the entire United States with electric power. They regarded decentralized, roof-top solar as too small to make a significant impact on energy usage and thought that Glaser's ideas of going into space presented other practical difficulties, though they liked his approach of thinking big. Rejecting photovoltaics combined with storage as too expensive and low-temperature collectors as too inefficient and therefore expensive, they proposed high-temperature concentrating collectors coupled with molten salt storage as the way to provide a constant source of heat to drive electric generators. They suggested building the system in units of 1,000 megawatts (electric), eventually accommodating 1,000 such units on the equivalent of a square of land only seventy-four miles on a side.[9]

The Meinels understood the importance of language in depicting their technology and used metaphors skillfully to describe it and the values associated with it:

One must be aware of the degrees to which words polarize people when it comes to sensitive topics. We have become aware that the moment we mention power plants some people cease to hear what we are saying because of the opposition that has been generated to power plants in the past two years. We are tempted to call our proposal for solar farms to reap the energy harvest from the sun since in a very real sense we are not destroying a resource – we are creating one out of sunshine.[10]

These technologically ambitious conventional advocates still maintained a guarded social view of the change to solar energy. While conscious of solar's environmental benefits, they saw no reason to make a large social change in the process of moving to a solar energy system. They assumed the status quo in the basic technological ensemble and in the social and political structures that go with it. They saw their technology as a way of preserving the status quo, albeit with more attention to environmental consequences. They emphasized growth and prosperity, narrowly conceived.[11] All of these proposals conceptualized solar energy simply as a replacement for conventional fuels, and so they implicitly endorsed conventional values about technologies and social systems. As Ford and Kane concluded, "The most satisfactory response to these problems is to find an energy source which is not in short supply and which can provide a major fraction of our energy needs without causing major environmental disruptions."[12]

The scientific trade press – journals targeted broadly to scientists as opposed to narrow technical journals – began paying more and favorable attention to solar energy. For instance, reporters from the Research News section of *Science* published a book on energy that argued that solar could be competitive in only five years and that it should get substantially more R&D money from the government.[13] However, solar's coverage in the mass media, though growing from 1969 to the embargo in 1973, remained scant.[14]

After the 1973 oil embargo this group of solar advocates, some technologically guarded, others more ambitious, continued to accept the social and political norms that went along with conventional energy systems. The virtues of solar to these advocates included that it was cleaner than fossil fuels, it was inexhaustible, and it was not subject to foreign embargos. This group did not, in the main, challenge the fundamental assumptions that the demand for energy would increase inexorably and that the purpose of new technology was to find better ways to meet that demand. They intended solar energy as something that could plug right into the existing technological system, in some cases almost literally. Their main goals for government programs, besides removing institutional barriers, were to bring down the initial costs of the solar energy systems. Repeatedly they averred that solar systems were almost competitive with conventional fuels and that R&D programs could soon make them fully competitive.[15] These advocates were leery of making what they considered extravagant short-term claims for solar energy.[16] This group included a few mainstream politicians and businessmen.[17]

By the mid-1970s, some very large corporations, including some electric utilities, were getting involved in the solar industry. General Motors announced in February 1977 that its radiator division would begin making flat-plate collectors and firms like General Electric, Exxon, Mobil, ASARCO (a mining and metals processing firm), and Grumman were already in the solar business, many having bought out smaller solar equipment firms.[18] These large firms formed a significant and conservative segment of the guarded solar advocates. This group tended to have more restricted views about the potential for solar. Perhaps more importantly, these actors associated purely conventional values with solar technology, principally that of economic efficiency. The energy problem was, to them, simply a question of meeting market demand for energy at the lowest possible price, and solar was interesting insofar as it could solve such a problem.

Similar organizations and individuals, including national politicians, also promoted solar development and associated with it very conventional values. These writings depicted solar as good for a state, region, or industry because it protected the users from future price increases or shortages of fossil fuels – a combination of economic rationality and security goals.[19] Others, particularly politicians, noted that solar was economically more competitive than many people realized, but was being held back by other barriers, such as building codes, bankers' conservatism, and uninformed consumer habits.[20] These conventional solar advocates promoted solar without any intention of changing the fundamental normative orientation of social and political institutions. They took an endlessly growing consumer culture and the ways of life that went with it for granted.

Ecological Advocates

The period from 1969 to the embargo saw the continuing emergence of a different normative idea in the energy debate, that of environmental protection. Several institutional developments, changes in public discourse, changes in problem definitions, and dramatic external events came together to make environmental issues highly salient and link them tightly to energy policy.[21] Environmental groups made their presence felt in numerous policy arenas. President Nixon, in his 1970 State of the Union Address, recognized the importance of environmental protection, and his administration gave its approval to the first Earth Day. The value of protecting the environment rapidly became an important part of the American political discourse, from the grassroots to the presidency, and an issue to be faced when thinking about energy policy.[22]

Solar advocates touted their technology as environmentally benign, and environmentalists came to see solar as an important part of the solution to the structural problem of energy-related pollution. Due to cleavages in the solar community, solar advocates and environmentalists never became a single unified force. Nonetheless, they overlapped substantially, with major figures in the environmental movement playing lead roles in the solar movement by the late 1970s. Solar advocates of all stripes spoke up about the environmental benefits of their technologies, especially compared to conventional energy technologies. For example, the Meinels discussed the potential environmental impact of their ideas for a large-scale system for generating electricity in 1971 and concluded that negative effects would be minimal even though theirs would have been the most environmentally disruptive of the solar technologies.[23] Many authors discussing or advocating more modest-sized applications of solar also mentioned its environmental benefits.[24]

Just as important, environmentalists by this time began to think that solar energy could play a role in leading a more environmentally harmonious life.[25] Organizations such as the Sierra Club, the Audubon Society, and Friends of the Earth began publishing articles and editorials in their organizations' magazines that called for greater attention to and resources for solar energy. They often presented it as the only way out of the environmental disruption caused by the use of conventional fuels. They explicitly criticized the Nixon administration's emphasis on nuclear power and fossil fuels.[26] An article in *Audubon* summed up the thinking of these groups:

How the electricity is generated has been of little concern until recently. The cheapest way was considered the best way, and the environment be damned (or dammed!). We must rethink our whole concept of supplying energy to the nation. ... Solar power offers exciting prospects. ... Although we must not delude ourselves into thinking solar power is a cure-all, we must pursue it because, when all the resources, energy, and ecological balance sheets are tallied up, solar power will almost certainly be the most efficient way. ... We will need massive investments in R&D, but when you can put a man on the moon, there is little you can't do – technologically, that is.[27]

The message of this sort of writing is quite clear: If one were serious about protecting the environment, then one must also think very seriously about solar energy. By this line of thinking, not only was environmental protection an important value when thinking about energy, but solar energy became the very embodiment of that value. These writings also included a direct challenge to the notion that conventional economic measures, particularly short-term ones, should dominate energy policy.

After the 1973 oil embargo, environmentalists increasingly couched their advocacy of solar in a critique of nuclear power.[28] The conflict between solar and nuclear power formed the major axis of cleavage within the solar movement and in the energy debate more generally. Solar advocates of the 1940s, 1950s, and 1960s, with perhaps one exception, would have found such a conflict puzzling at best, as many of them had worked on nuclear power and were sympathetic to it. But by the mid-1970s a substantial antinuclear movement vigorously opposed new power plant construction, and utility executives were concerned about anything that could undercut public support for nuclear power.[29] One such problem was public enthusiasm for solar energy and the broad public perception that it was already available or soon would be. An October 1976 article in the *Solar Technology Report*, a publication for the utility industry, noted with dismay a recent national survey that indicated that the public thought solar was the cheapest form of energy. According to this publication, "Electric utilities, as represented by EEI [Edison Electric Institute], see this perception of solar energy as 'cheap' as leading to an erosion of favor for nuclear power."[30] Clearly, some pronuclear interests had reasons to be hostile to solar energy.

From the environmental and antinuclear movements thus emerged another type of solar advocate, which I call an ecological advocate, who injected explicit and different normative concerns into the debate over solar policy – some related to ecological relationships and others focussing more on social and political matters. The latter were fundamental to the ecologists' critique because they saw alternative modes of living as essential for a sustainable society. Such advocates talked about ecological stewardship, the moral obligation to preserve resources and ecosystems for future generations. They also discussed how solar, done properly, would use more decentralized technology that would enhance communities by giving them more autonomy and control over their most crucial systems.[31] Advocates expressed these sentiments in a variety of ways:

Energy attitudes, both nuclear and solar, are currently characterized by an inordinate concentration upon technological "tricks"... The question of energy choice must be looked at as a LIFE CHOICE. What kind of people do we want to become?[32]

Early Ecological Advocates

From the beginning of the energy crisis, a group of analysts often linked their concerns about environmental degradation to a set of critiques of the broader structures of a modern technological capitalist society. These analysts came from a variety of perspectives but had in common the notion that environmental problems resulted from fundamental incompatibilities between modern political and social structures and living in harmony with the natural world. According to these critiques, modern technological systems were not simply malfunctioning or manifesting inefficiencies; they were in some profound sense unable to preserve the environment, and the social and political structures that had produced those technologies could not make sufficient improvements to prevent a serious ecological disaster. In particular, these critiques asserted that conventional values like economic growth and national security were so deeply embedded in modern technological systems, as in the sociopolitical systems that created them, that acting on other values like ecological preservation required a wholesale transformation of both systems. Shortly after the 1973 oil embargo, these notions began to penetrate the solar movement and to cause serious cleavages within it. After almost thirty years of consistency in the values associated with energy, including solar, these structural, ecological concerns provided an entrance to a whole host of new values, challenging the conventional values that analysts had associated with energy for decades.[33]

These ecological solar advocates put their views of solar technology into a broader framework that had a characteristic analysis of energy policy. Despite some variation, their core idea emphasized that an ever-growing consumption of energy and other materials was not sustainable, no matter what technological breakthroughs society might develop. Moreover, energy efficiency must be taken more seriously if the energy crisis was to have any solution.[34] As David Brower of Friends of the Earth wrote in his foreword to Amory B. Lovins and John H. Price's 1975 book, *Non-Nuclear Futures: The Case for an Ethical Energy Strategy*:

The environmental view, then, is that the sooner the threat of energy addiction is ended, the better. . . . Since extirpatory growth must end sometime, it ought to be stopped by people, while they and the earth still have some roots left. We are pleased with the force of the author's demonstration that there are such strong economic and ethical arguments for a strategy that is in humanity's own self-interest.[35]

While these analysts made economic arguments, they insisted that other values should play a role in energy policy. For example, Lovins wrote in the introduction to *Non-Nuclear Futures*:

Fundamental to any discussion of energy alternatives is a choice – usually tacit but nonetheless real – of personal values. The values that make a high-energy society work are all too apparent today. The values that would make a lower-energy society work are not new; they are in the societal attic, and could be dusted off and recycled. They include thrift, simplicity, diversity, neighbourliness, craftsmanship, and humility. They also include the clear thinking needed to avoid a prevalent confusion between growth and distribution (the "let them eat growth" theory), between movement and progress, and between costs and benefits.[36]

His metaphor for the values that needed to be put into energy choices likened them to old family mementos, or perhaps clothes, that we would find in our attics – nothing new or exotic, still serviceable, and needing nothing more than dusting off.[37] Presented in this way, as a return to traditional values, Lovins's propositions were more appealing than a call for radical change. His arguments could minimize people's fears that they might have to take on situations and ways of life that were foreign to them. But adopting such social norms would in fact have meant a drastic change to the 1970s status quo.

This ecological group of analysts generally opposed nuclear power. Organizations opposed to nuclear power grew in numbers and political sophistication during the late 1960s and 1970s.[38] Such advocates saw solar as the answer to the question of what to do if society did not expand nuclear power.[39] In the most sophisticated versions, they grounded their opposition to nuclear power in the same normative concerns that led to support for solar energy, namely, that energy systems had to function in ways that were ecologically sustainable and socially desirable. Exactly what constituted socially desirable values varied among writers, but some of the items quoted above from Lovins appeared frequently. These writers saw technological systems as putting into place structures and incentives that encouraged certain ways of life and discouraged others. To them, nuclear power, as the extension of conventional energy practices and technologies, would continue to accelerate the negative trends already in evidence, from environmental degradation to the erosion of local, familiar institutions and their replacement by larger, bureaucratic, and insensitive ones. In this sense they considered technology to be like legislation, and they felt that a drastically different society would require drastically different technological systems as well as different laws, indeed that different technologies would constitute new opportunities and constraints, much like new laws.[40]

Contemporaneously, many writers engaged in a broader discussion about what they called appropriate or alternative technology. They called into question the conventional set of technologies used in industrial societies and the social arrangements that had grown up with and around them. All of these works criticized large-scale technological systems and all argued for social values that could be attained only with the use of alternative technologies.[41] The arguments varied among different writers, who did not always fully develop them.[42] Nonetheless, most of them concurred with a critique of conventional technologies summarized in the magazine *AERO Sun Times*:

Continuation of present technologies is neither possible nor desirable. The technologies themselves are proving socially, environmentally, and spiritually damaging, and often uncontrollable. The values they support are no longer desired, and their product no longer seen as the primary wants of our society. And alternative technologies are available.[43]

The appropriate solar technologies would be small, decentralized, labor-intensive, relatively simple, and so forth. The emphasis was to improve people's quality of life while reducing their quantity of consumption.[44]

Some people regarded ecological solar advocates as simply alternative technology (AT) adherents who focused on energy in trying to achieve their broader aims. While it is true that people and ideas overlapped among AT groups and ecological solar advocates,[45] the reality was more complex. Individuals came to the position of ecological solar advocacy from a variety of paths, and they had differing degrees of support for the more general AT movement. In particular, some solar advocates regarded the AT emphasis on the development of small rural communities in both the developing and industrialized worlds as missing the major issue in energy debates, namely, the political and economic conflicts between solar and nuclear energy systems and, more generally, between industrialization and sustainability.[46]

In sum, ecological solar advocates saw technologies as legislation. They explicitly associated technologies with normative ideas, regardless of the direction of causal arrows, and thus they promoted solar energy technologies because they also favored certain ways of life and social and political institutions, such as environmental sustainability or community self-reliance. The line between the AT movement and the ecologically oriented solar movement was often fuzzy, and sometimes it was not clear who was on which side.

Ecological solar advocates began growing in importance in the solar movement right at the time that solar energy began growing in popularity with the public. Congress had increased the budgets for solar R&D beyond the amounts that President Ford had requested his last year in office.[47] A Roper poll taken two months after President Carter took office identified solar energy as the public's favored energy source to replace foreign oil in the long term, and solar was second only to coal in the short term.[48] The solar movement gained strength and grew in size and organization, despite its fragmentation. In addition to the American chapter of the International Solar Energy Society and the Solar Energy Industries Association, by early 1977 organizational solar advocates included environmental groups, such as Friends of the Earth, and public interest groups, such as Ralph Nader's Public Interest Research Group. The movement also encompassed grassroots solar groups and others based in universities.[49] Many of the grassroots groups embraced ecological solar advocacy values in the ways they framed the energy problem and the values they associated with solar technologies. They contrasted their technologies' values with those of conventional technologies, such as those expressed in a statement focusing on "the difference between self-reliance and dependence, self-determination and centralization, cooperation vs. competition and accountability as opposed to exploitation."[50] Debates about the values involved in energy choices were often implicit or carried on in some of the small newsletters or journals cited previously. But they leapt into public prominence in 1976 and 1977 in arguments over the proposals of a young energy analyst, Amory Lovins.

Lovins and the Soft Path

In October 1976, Amory Lovins, a consultant physicist and energy policy analyst working for Friends of the Earth, published an article in the high-profile journal, *Foreign Affairs*, that was later expanded into a 1977 book, *Soft Energy Paths*.[51] These works affected the energy policy debate remarkably, triggering an immediate and furious response from many critics, with Lovins responding in detail to each of them. He presented a thorough critique of conventional thinking about energy policy and the most creative and sophisticated arguments in favor of solar energy to date. His analysis provided a conceptual focus for a group of growing importance in the solar movement – those who based their attachment to solar energy on beliefs about the nature of environmental problems and the relationship of energy technologies to them.[52] Lovins' arguments fit into the cleavage between solar and nuclear power well, as part of his strategy for a soft energy path included a rejection of future central station nuclear power plants, and he had written previous works that had also been critical of nuclear power.[53]

Lovins had two fundamental analytical points that diverged radically from more conventional analyses. First, in estimating the needed energy supply, he started from end-use demand and worked backwards, following the principle that energy supply should be matched to end-use needs in scale and quality. By matched in scale he meant that we should use large energy production facilities for large uses and small ones for small uses, and thus not build a large power plant to heat a house when passive solar design and solar hot water heaters will do the job. By matched in quality he meant that we should not use expensive forms of energy, such as electricity, to perform low-grade jobs, such as domestic space heating and hot water. Electricity should be used for tasks for which it is uniquely suited, such as lighting and telecommunications. His second analytical point was that the costs of energy from different sources should be compared in terms of their long-run marginal costs, not their current average costs, since the latter for fossil fuels were often artificially low.[54] Based on these analytical principles, he argued that over the next fifty years the United States should move toward an energy system characterized by reliance on very efficient energy technologies combined with a variety of renewable energy resources, many of which would be more decentralized than was then the case. In particular, he argued that the United States should not build more large, central station power plants.[55]

Lovins defended his technical claims at length. Just as importantly, he understood that debates over energy policy were political and ethical, debates over the kind of society in which one wants to live, and said so. "In my view, on the other hand, the energy problem is chiefly a social, political, and ethical one of how to accomplish our society's diverse goals by meeting its heterogeneous end-use needs with an elegant economy of energy."[56] He regarded his soft path superior to the hard path (conventional energy policy) in many ways, including on the basis of a traditional value, economic efficiency. The soft path energy system would be cheaper in the strict microeconomic sense than the hard path, assuming that the accounting was done properly. He also emphasized that the soft path would better promote pluralism, another value important in American political culture that had been little evoked in energy discussions. People could live a variety of lifestyles, if they were willing to pay for them, under a soft energy path, but certain lifestyles would be curtailed under a hard one. "In my view of the future, people who want to live [in a manner that uses a great deal of energy] can do so, but those who don't needn't: there is room for diverse lifestyles, including those representing post-industrial values."[57]

While the soft path was consistent with ecological values, Lovins argued strongly that it did not require them, that it could co-exist with more conventional values like economic rationality. Nonetheless, the ecological side of the solar movement embraced his work with enthusiasm, and supporters and critics associated those values with him and his work. The split within the solar movement deepened, and these ideological arguments provided the backdrop for debates during the Carter administration over solar policy.[58]

Critiques of Lovins

Lovins' work prompted a flood of editorials, articles, reports, and photocopied papers that circulated quickly in energy policy communities, including fierce criticisms written by both nuclear and some solar advocates in academia and industry. A set of senate hearings collected many of these, along with Lovins' responses to them. The final documents ran to over 2,200 pages.[59] The critiques published in this report often attacked Lovins on a variety of arcane technical grounds, and he responded to them in kind. One of his contentions that had made the soft energy path argument so important and provocative was that it was optimal from a narrow economic point of view.[60] However, a reading of the record makes it clear that the often vituperative tone in Lovins' critics was not a mere disagreement over data or calculations. The criticisms often turned ad hominem, ridiculing and nasty. These people were upset.

For example, Dr. Ralph Lapp, an energy and nuclear consultant, wrote that "Mr. Lovins has authored a very irresponsible article." Later in his critique he said, "By the same token he [Lovins] suffers from the Aladdin Syndrome; he apparently believes that non-existent energy sources can spring forth from an R&D lamp, fully developed and economically viable." Perhaps most revealingly, he said, "Mr. Lovins here seems incapable of understanding that the trend to electrification in an industrial society does have its own logic and that the trend is now intensified by the necessity to shift from fluid to solid fuels."[61] This last comment revealed a conception of the energy problem reminiscent of those since the 1950s, where human agency vanished entirely. The energy problem derived from some deterministic "logic" instead of government policies, business decisions, and the actions of other human institutions. This type of policy narrative depicts the energy problem as an accidental cause, like the weather or an earthquake, one in which unguided actions, the logic of electrification, result in unintended consequences, the rapid growth in demand for fuels.[62] This lack of agency also implies a lack of responsibility and control. If no one or no institution caused this electrification, then no one was responsible and nothing could be done about it except to supply the electricity that was needed. This problem framing could only reject Lovins' notions that the United States could change the path of its energy system.

Many other Lovins critics argued in similar ways about nontechnical issues. They clearly associated normative values with certain technological choices, and they reacted vigorously to what they perceived as Lovins' challenges to some deeply held values. Ian Forbes, a consultant who had numerous exchanges with Lovins, written and oral, said,

Even if Lovins' path were feasible and non-coercive, it is not clear that it is axiomatically a desirable goal. It flies in the face of centuries of human transition and the desire for less individual physical effort. In fact, it is in many ways a re-run of the protracted debate over industrialization in 19th century England.[63]

Equally vehement and vituperative critiques came from some conventional solar advocates. Sheldon Butt, then president of the Solar Energy Industries Association, wrote a furious article, reprinted in the hearings, in which he described Lovins as possessing the "arrogance of a self-appointed Messiah." Claiming that the social and political implications of an energy strategy are the most important, he said,

In summary, Chapter X of Lovins' article truly identifies his goals as being those of creating a "new society" founded upon the concept of "elegant frugality" – in short, a society of peasants and craftsmen. The promises made earlier in the article that we can abandon much of our present energy capital stock and replace it with "soft" energy without giving up the material benefits which we have received from our present system are revealed by Chapter X as purposeful falsehoods.[64]

Aden and Marjorie Meinel, who had worked on the development of central station solar power plants in the desert Southwest, wrote yet another strong ad hominem attack on Lovins:

We are chilled at the actions advocated by this seductive and well-written article and appalled that a person claiming to be a physicist could resort to what appears to us as distortions of technical reality. . . . Should this siren philosophy be heard and believed we can perceive the onset of a New Dark Age.[65]

Previously implicit values in debates about solar energy and energy policy came out into the open. Lovins was accused of being Messianic, elitist, a liar, and a zealot who intended to turn modern democracies into feudal dictatorships. Can one be the Antichrist just for developing a novel approach for calculating dollars per BTU? Obviously not, but Lovins had hit on some very sensitive nerves, challenging directly the fundamental values and technical beliefs that dominated conventional thinking about energy policy, and he had done so credibly and in an important forum so that defenders of the status quo felt the need to respond quickly and vigorously. The debate reached the White House, with some of Lovins' critics from the nuclear industry sending their comments to Katherine Schirmer, President Carter's chief aide for energy. By the end of October 1977 even Lovins' critics realized that they were getting nowhere attacking his technical arguments, so detailed and ready were his responses, and that he was besting them in debates.[66] These debates were never resolved in any simple sense. They instead became rallying points for those on different sides of the issues. Interestingly, some of Lovins' claims about energy efficiency that critics branded as outlandish in 1977 became part of conventional wisdom not many years later.

RECONSTRUCTING ENERGY POLICY

Solar advocates of all stripes did more than promote their technology; they also tried to present a view of energy policy more generally that was congenial to their view of their technology. The growing energy crisis provided conventional and ecological solar advocates an opportunity to reconstruct energy policy in important ways.

Conventional Solar Advocates

Even before the oil embargo, conventional solar advocates sounded an alarm of imminent shortages. They framed their arguments in terms of an impending crisis: Only by beginning the change to solar energy immediately could society avoid disastrous shortages in the near future. In his 1972 book, B. J. Brinkworth stated dramatically in his first sentence, "Our grandchildren will live in a world without oil."[67] Metaphorically, conventional solar advocates depicted all energy as a physical entity, and they believed that society was using a finite source in fossil fuels that was running short. As Daniel S. Halacy put it:

Of importance is the fact that while there *is* still fossil fuel left, we have already gone through the cream ... and are now working on the skimmed milk, with the bottom of the bottle embarrassingly visible. Surely there is more coal and surely there is more oil. We just have to dig deeper, or haul farther, or process more. But it takes energy to mine a ton of coal, and when that energy approaches what is contained in the coal itself, we are in trouble and had better leave the stuff in the ground.[68]

Conceptualizing energy as a set of distinct physical goods leads to very different conclusions than, for example, the concept of energy as an economic good whose scarcity is indicated by price.

By 1971–1972 solar energy received good press in journals read by a wide segment of the scientific community, as well as in specialized segments of the lay media. All of these accounts tended to depict solar as necessary because of the eventual exhaustion of fossil fuels, and as desirable because of its limited environmental impacts. Those concerned with the end of fossil fuels used a language of crisis. An article in the *Smithsonian* declared that,

This is the energy crisis, a crisis which has little to do with the summertime difficulties of power companies or the political considerations of importing Mideastern oil. It requires recognition of the fact that our energy resources are dwindling, the bitter realization that at some not-so-distant hour the party will be over.

This meant that, in the words of the Washington editor of the *New Scientist*,

even the nation's politicians – President Nixon among them – have begun to cast around in some desperation for energy technologies that will see the United States through to the next millennium. Power from the Sun, while even on the most optimistic of forecasts is not expected to provide more than a small fraction of these needs, is suddenly no longer regarded as a quaint, if intellectually appealing, technological backwater.

These articles, and others like them, typically reviewed several solar technologies, noting recent developments and that all or most of them were not yet commercially competitive. The articles usually ended by stating that solar received only a tiny fraction of federal funding on energy. Presenting solar energy this way, especially in the scientific trade press, as a neglected but developing technology, built a case for it as a legitimate topic deserving of more research funds.[69] All of these authors, while indicating a strong sense of crisis, accepted as inevitable and unremarkable the technological, social, and political arrangements that led to that crisis. Perceiving that the country is "running out" of fossil fuels, they responded by seeking technologies that could deliver the same quantities of bulk energy to keep those very technological, social, and political arrangements functioning. The crisis, they hoped, had a technological fix.

After the oil embargo and price increases of October 1973, conventional solar advocates sounded the same themes, this time with an acute crisis to give their points more salience. For example, Paul Fannin, a senator from Arizona and long-time supporter of solar energy, framed United States energy policy as starkly dichotomous choices:

Thus, the United States seems to be faced with two choices: reduce the nation's consumption of energy, with a parallel reduction in the standard of living; or take steps, including intelligent conservation programs, to ensure a continuing ample supply of energy for this country and for other nations as well. Most Americans would agree that the second choice is the wiser, assuming that it is possible.[70]

The rest of the article talked about the potential of various solar technologies and the barriers to their adoption. Senator Fannin sought to preserve the existing arrangements that constituted contemporary society, arguing that the absence of solar could lead to social change.

This view of the energy crisis led conventional advocates in particular policy directions. They tended to be broad in their support of solar, arguing for all kinds of solar technologies.[71] Many of them had an especially strong orientation to large solar projects. The Meinels, discussed earlier, were quite explicit in preferring large projects, in their case solar farms in the desert Southwest. Since the energy system required large quantities of electricity, it made sense to them to build large projects that enjoyed economies of scale.[72] Another popular concept throughout the 1970s was ocean thermal energy conversion (OTEC). The sun heated the top layer of sea water, but deeper waters remained very cold. By exploiting this temperature difference, huge floating power plants could generate large amounts of electricity.[73] All of these large technologies would be expensive undertakings, and their proponents acknowledged that their costs, at least for the initial few plants, would be greater than for conventional plants. But they claimed that the acute crisis and environmental constraints made the investment a wise one in the long-term:

There's no doubt that bulk power can be made through solar energy conversion. We've got the technology. The problem is cost. But the expensive conversion of sunlight into electricity is becoming more attractive as our fossil fuels run out or become too dirty to burn.[74]

Most of these conventional advocates had no opposition to other long-term energy sources, such as nuclear power, though they thought that solar was better. Many thought solar to be only one part of the future energy mix, one that included breeder reactors. "It is necessary to continue to use all these [other energy sources], and to develop such follow-on sources as the breeder reactor and fusion power plants."[75] While these advocates argued that solar was not getting its fair share of social resources, almost none of them were associated with the antinuclear movement.

A key policy point for these advocates was the notion of barriers; solar needed governmental help to remove financial, institutional, or other barriers that impeded its adoption, even when it was economically competitive. For example, solar technologies required a large up-front investment that could dissuade potential buyers, even if the long-run cost was favorable. This feature became an economic barrier without easily available financing mechanisms to enable consumers to realize the long-term cost savings. Some barriers were questions of habit and custom. Consumers, utilities, and banks were not familiar with using these new technologies and so might prefer those that they knew better.[76]

Ecological Solar Advocates

Ecological advocates had a different approach to energy policy. They shied away from the view that the new technologies, such as solar or fusion, could simply plug into the existing energy system and would require no changes in the economic, social, or cultural context of which the energy system was a part. To the contrary, many of these advocates saw the roots of the energy crisis in precisely such nontechnological factors, and so their prescriptions for change ranged more widely.

A common theme in these advocates' writing was that of a transition. The principle sources of energy had changed in the past from wood to coal and, later, to oil and natural gas. As oil and natural gas became scarce, society would have to make a transition to some new energy source. The question was, which one?

The notion of a transition was not unique to ecological solar advocates. Energy policy analysts of many stripes used the same word. Indeed, the very same graph began appearing in diverse government energy policy documents (see Chapter 5). For example, during the Ford administration the Energy Research and Development Administration (ERDA) released a major planning document for energy R&D. To justify the government's accelerated R&D program, the document talked about the transition to "unlimited energy supplies" as part of a longer historical process. It included a graph showing the sequential rise and decline of wood, coal, and petroleum, and the possible rise of nuclear power. The report acknowledged that, in addition to technological problems, "Of equal importance will be the difficult institutional problems which transition will impose." However, other than this cryptic sentence, the rest of the report read as if the only problems were technological.[77] Three years later, a DOE report on the status of solar energy used the exact same graph, minus the nuclear part, to talk about the coming transition and the need for new energy technologies. Again, the transition appeared mainly technological.[78]

The ecological advocates thought that the impending changes in the energy system would bring with them large social, political, and economic changes:

Just as in the past cases, the coming transition to sustainable energy will entail far more sweeping changes than simply the shift from one energy source to another. The transition will entail radical transformations in the panoply of technologies involved in the production, conversion, and consumption of energy; in the structure of institutional, economic, group, and individual relationships; and in the theory, philosophy, values, and goals that define the direction of social behavior.[79]

Moreover, this transition was one of choice. There was not a single, inevitable next energy system, but rather a competition between solar energy and breeder reactors or nuclear fusion. According to these analysts, different technological choices would lead to very different social futures:

But energy sources are not neutral and interchangeable. Some energy sources are necessarily centralized; others are necessarily dispersed. Some are exceedingly vulnerable; others will reduce the number of people employed. Some will tend to diminish the gap between rich and poor; others will accentuate it.[80]

These social and political concerns, as well as environmental ones, led ecological advocates to promote certain types of government policies and solar technologies.

For some analysts, the implications of the transition also lent urgency and danger to the choices of future energy technologies. As David Orr put it:

Historical evidence indicates that the shift can involve great turmoil leading to social and political disintegration. We might reasonably assume that the greater the dependence on nonrenewable energy sources (e.g. fossil fuels) and the greater the demand for energy, the more difficult the change will be. . . . Because of the high capital costs of the renewable energy options, they are to a large extent mutually exclusive.[81]

In this view, energy policy did not possess the luxury of trial and error. Since the new energy system would utilize inexhaustible fuel and consume most of the available capital, a bad choice would produce very long-lived bad consequences.

Note that, for the purposes of analyzing what drove various solar advocates, it does not matter whether the ecological advocates were correct in their assessment that certain political and social consequences would in fact flow from the preferred technologies. What matters is that they believed that their preferred technologies – in this case small-scale, decentralized solar energy – would produce the society and politics they desired. One could criticize this approach as a naive technological determinism, which in some instances it was, and one that solar advocates shared with their critics. For our purposes, however, it is more useful to see this advocacy as something different. A pervasive energy system would, in their view, erect powerful incentives and constraints affecting social actors, that is, technology would act as a form of legislation. In particular, these advocates claimed that small-scale solar energy would encourage a society more environmentally benign, less hierarchical and bureaucratic, and with greater social justice.[82] Given the tight linkage that they perceived between technological choices and these social norms, it seems clear that these normative values drove this debate, creating a serious cleavage with more conventional solar advocates and most senior government officials. Those officials were, in a profound sense, seeking different goals and solutions to different problems.

ECOLOGICAL ADVOCATES CRITIQUE GOVERNMENT SUPPORT

These normative concerns also led ecological advocates to oppose large-scale alternatives to solar, such as breeder reactors and nuclear fusion. While both would be almost inexhaustible, the breeder was controversial in terms of safety, and its use of plutonium raised concerns about weapons proliferation. A workable fusion reactor did not (and does not yet) exist, and so its costs, availability, and environmental problems were still speculative. Yet, while these problems were part of the ecological advocates objections, they were also concerned with the normative issues associated with those technologies.

These normative commitments also led ecological advocates to favor certain types of government policy support, not just support for particular technologies. Ecological advocates were very critical of government programs that favored traditional linkages with large corporations and more centralized technologies, even centralized solar technologies. For example, in a 1977 series of articles Allen Hammond and William Metz critiqued the government's solar program, arguing that it was modeled on the nuclear power program, which looked mainly to large centralized electric power plants and which sought to choose a technology early and build large-scale facilities very quickly. The driving assumption of such a program was that only large-scale facilities could expand supply quickly, and there was considerable pressure on government officials to do something about the energy crisis.[83] Such a policy, they warned, would make the same mistakes that the nuclear program had made, choosing a technology too early and so possibly missing a superior technology that was in an earlier stage of development. Just as important, the development model of the nuclear program, whatever its virtues, was singularly inappropriate to a solar program. Hammond and Metz argued that solar was qualitatively different from other energy sources:

Solar energy is democratic. It falls on everyone and can be put to use by individuals and small groups of people. The public enthusiasm for solar is perhaps as much a reflection of this unusual accessibility as it is a vote for the environmental kindliness and inherent renewability of energy from the sun.[84]

This quote demonstrates an explicit recognition of the value content of energy policy choices that was still uncommon in the mainstream scientific media. Instead of starting the article with a criticism that federal policy was not going to minimize costs, Hammond and Metz went directly to a normative issue. Federal policy did not recognize the normative properties of solar energy technologies, their "democratic" and decentralist character, and so the solar programs would fail to develop solar in the best way, that is, they would fail to develop it as a qualitatively different kind of energy source.[85] This conception of the energy policy problem frames the issue quite differently than does the conventional one. Solar is more than simply a replacement for declining fossil fuel supplies. One is doing more than simply unplugging conventional supplies and plugging in solar. Rather, in this view, solar energy, if developed in a way that acknowledges its normative properties, brings with it the prospect of changes in social and political institutions as well as energy sources.

Hammond and Metz understood that much of the debate over the feasibility of solar energy, that is, how much it could replace fossil fuels and by when, was in fact a hidden normative debate:

Assessments of this question [potential for solar market penetration] tend to get swept up into what has become a highly charged debate between environmental advocates and the defenders of coal and nuclear power – a debate whose terms are more nearly philosophical or ethical than economic.[86]

Coming on the heels of the furor raised by Lovins' work, this conclusion may not seem surprising. But its publication in *Science*, a widely read and respected mainstream journal, gave the ideas both exposure and legitimacy. Policy makers, including White House aides, who were at all informed on the issue probably knew about it.

7

Limited Access: Solar Advocates and Energy Policy Frames

A key question for any government institution is whether and how citizens can influence its policies. The pluralist model of American government suggests that its institutions are highly permeable, that most organized groups, assuming they can mobilize the necessary political resources, can press their views and affect policy. A more complex view analyzes how institutional rules, practices, and structures deeply influence who can have access to the institution and what kinds of access they can have. In executive branch agencies the White House staff could limit solar advocates' access to top decision makers by appointing officials not friendly to those advocates. On the other hand, the discussion in Chapter 5 of the conflict between the White House and both the Energy Research and Development Administration (ERDA) and the Council on Environmental Quality (CEQ) in the Ford administration suggests that the staffs in those agencies, particularly below the political appointee level, often thought about energy problems quite differently than did the White House and may have been a channel of influence for advocates who could not get access to the White House.

In addition to the agencies, the administrations sometimes operated ad hoc policy studies and processes. These activities often got much press and advocates' attention. I analyze one of them at length, the Solar Domestic Policy Review (DPR) of the Carter administration, examining how it provided outsider access to the policy process, to whom it did so, and the effect of such access. I have chosen the solar DPR because it resembles a critical case; if you expect solar advocates to influence policy anywhere, you expect it there. Other ad hoc policy exercises, such as Project Independence under Presidents Nixon and Ford, provided little or no access for solar advocates. For example, Project Independence did have an outside advisory committee, but most of the members were presidents of coal, oil, and utility firms, and none of them was associated with the solar movement. They also held a series of ten hearings around

136

the country, most of which targeted regional fuel sources and none of which focused on solar energy.[1] In addition, the Nixon and Ford White Houses were not easily accessible to solar advocates or alternative conceptions of energy policy, as discussed earlier. Greatly increased access for solar advocates during the Carter administration provided a strong contrast to earlier administrations and also demonstrated starkly the limitations of that access when advocates are unable to change the concepts, values, and problem frames under which top officials formulate energy policy.

ACCESS FOR SOLAR ADVOCATES UNDER CARTER

Government support for solar energy rose rapidly in Jimmy Carter's administration, but then began to fall even before he left office. Solar advocates enjoyed their greatest success as a pressure group during his presidency, but they failed to change the way top policy makers framed the problem of energy policy and the normative and technical ideas associated with it. They could not institutionalize a new set of values in key segments of the policy process, suggesting the limitations both of pluralist pressure group tactics in affecting long-term policy changes and of institutionalizing values only in organizations that are peripheral to the policy process. Hence, despite the ecological solar advocates' prominence in the solar movement during the Carter years and their substantial public support and access to policy makers, they could not make changes in the problem frames of either the Department of Energy or key parts of the White House. As a result, support for their technology foundered.

The focus of this chapter will be two instances of advocates' access, one with the president and one with DOE officials during the solar DPR. These cases provide instances of, first, direct access to the president and, second, prolonged and intensive interaction with DOE officials. Another important policy exercise, the National Energy Plan, also had a public participation process, which, in principle, could have been a channel of access for solar advocates. But the NEP was done in such haste and the public response to its work was so massive that the officials working on the plan could make no use of it. For instance, a request for public written comments on the NEP received 27,898 responses, more than a staff writing a report in ninety days could manage.[2]

White House Access: Lovins Meets Carter

On October 18, 1977, President Carter met with Amory Lovins. Originally only the president, Lovins, Stuart Eizenstat, who was the chief of Domestic Policy Staff in the White House, and Katherine "Kitty" Schirmer, Eizenstat's chief aide for energy issues, were going to attend.

At the last minute Secretary of Energy James Schlesinger and Science Advisor Frank Press received invitations. Scheduled for ten minutes, the meeting went on for thirty, suggesting that the president took considerable interest in the conversation.[3] Lovins remarked later that Carter had read *Soft Energy Paths* and seemed quite knowledgeable about its concepts, more so than any of his aides.[4] Lovins was by this time solidly identified with the ecological wing of the solar movement, even though his arguments were, in part, grounded in conventional economics. Carter's preparatory briefing paper suggested a discussion that focused on the competing economics of different energy technologies and did not encourage him to get into a discussion of normative issues with Lovins.[5]

The effect of the meeting on policy is impossible to gauge, but President Carter took Lovins seriously enough to irritate some nuclear power advocates. Ian Forbes, an opponent of Lovins, wrote to Eizenstat, complaining that the president, the day after meeting Lovins, had quoted some of Lovins' numbers at a meeting of international experts on the nuclear fuel cycle. Forbes was upset that the experts would know where the numbers came from and claimed that the numbers were not credible, and so would discredit the president. Referring to Lovins' numbers as "amateurish miscalculations," Forbes said that the president had only to ask and he could get much better advice from other experts, such as Forbes.[6]

Obviously, by itself a single half-hour meeting with the president is not likely to affect large changes in policy. But the meeting indicated a more extensive level of contact and visibility for Lovins among senior White House officials. This meeting took place within the context of a raging, highly visible, debate over Lovins' ideas in the energy policy community, as I detailed in Chapter 6. White House staff concerned with energy were certainly aware of that debate.

In addition, one does not get an appointment with the president by just calling his secretary and asking for one. Lovins' meeting with the president could have happened only if the president and some of his staff were aware of Lovins' work. The meeting would have been preceded by some level of contacts between the president's staff and Lovins. In short, the meeting was important not just as a thirty-minute encounter, but also as a reflection of a higher level of visibility for Lovins and his ideas among White House staff. The ecological solar advocates could well begin to feel that they had growing access to powerful decision makers.

Ad Hoc Policy Exercises: The Solar DPR

The Carter administration devised the Domestic Policy Review (DPR) system to conduct interagency reviews of nonclassified issues. Presidential staff had to rely on agency expertise for many issues, and getting advice from a variety of agencies was a way of avoiding dependence on a single agency, and hence a single source of expertise and its possible biases.[7] The administration conducted DPRs on only a small number of issues, and getting such a review meant that high-level officials, as well as outside constituencies, would devote substantial attention to that issue.

In September 1977 officials at the Council for Environmental Quality (CEQ) proposed a solar DPR and lobbied the Domestic Policy staff for it.[8] For some months the Domestic Policy staffers resisted and denied publicly that the White House would conduct a solar DPR.[9] Those denials soon ceased. On April 6, 1978, Energy Secretary James Schlesinger and CEQ Chair Charles Warren sent a memo to Eizenstat formally requesting a solar DPR. In their request they depicted solar as inexhaustible, environmentally benign, and becoming increasingly competitive economically.[10] This depiction reflected the traditional value of economic rationality, with a bit of environmentalism added, and was roughly consistent with the values expressed in the Ford and Nixon administrations.

At the same time, Congress had been pressuring the administration to show that it was serious about solar energy. Several legislative aides had formed the Solar Coalition, a group promoting solar legislation and an increased DOE solar budget. The coalition was determined to push an aggressive solar program, regardless of administration desires.[11]

Partly as a result of these and other pressures, Eizenstat and Schirmer sent a memo to the president recommending the solar DPR. They noted that "undertaking this review is not designed to commit the Administration to larger solar budget expenditures." Next to this comment Carter wrote, "I agree."[12] These comments reflect a technocratic and naive image of the role that policy analysis plays in policy making, one that sees analysis simply as a way to inform policy makers' decisions. In fact, such a large undertaking as a DPR is also a political activity, one that involves the building of coalitions, providing channels for access, and the opening up of new policy arenas for debate and advocacy. By involving officials from a variety of agencies and engaging in an extensive public participation program, discussed later, the officials running the DPR could not help but encourage solar advocates, despite those advocates' skepticism toward the administration's solar policies. President Carter announced the solar DPR on Sun Day, a privately organized, nationwide celebration of solar energy.[13] Solar advocates in and out of government were pushing for more resources, and Sun Day demonstrated a growing public constituency for solar energy. Implementing the solar DPR coupled with the growing public enthusiasm for solar put more pressure on the administration than the mere decision to undertake the DPR might have otherwise entailed. Simply going ahead with the study would make it very hard to contain its effects to that of merely advising the president.[14]

A Solar Energy Policy Committee, a cabinet-level group chaired by the secretary of energy, formally headed the DPR. They delegated their responsibilities to a Coordinating Committee that was made up of senior officials from the various agencies involved in the study. The members of this committee then designated lower level officials as their representatives to the Integrating Group, which, chaired by a DOE official, actually carried out the study. Six substantive panels divided up the work of the study into such subjects as the impacts of solar technologies, financing of solar, institutional incentives and barriers, and so on. The Integrating Group then coordinated the panels' work and put its results together into a final report.[15] The most controversial panel was the impacts panel, which estimated how big a contribution solar energy would make to the nation's energy system by the year 2000 and "the investment, employment, social, and environmental impacts of the estimated levels of solar penetration."[16]

Stuart Eizenstat made the charge to the study very broad, asking the study about the magnitude of the potential solar contribution to energy demand; whether all federal solar programs, "taken as a whole," were optimal for accelerating solar commercialization; and what kind of federal strategy could best unite public and private efforts to achieve this accelerated use of solar. In explaining why solar use was important, Eizenstat said,

The national security and economic problems posed by our increasing dependence on imported oil establish a clear need for the rapid development and use of alternative domestic energy sources. Continued economic growth can occur only if we prepare now to make the transition from oil and natural gas to energy sources we have in abundance.[17]

This rationale for the study, along with the formal structure, showed clearly that top-level officials espoused the traditional values of economic rationality and national security when discussing solar energy. How could solar, in a cost-effective way, replace imported oil? Despite the study's charge, most of the panels were concerned with narrow, pragmatic problems in developing solar technologies. In addition, the concerns that motivated ecological advocates, those who had alternative conceptions of the issues, such as the social impacts of energy technology, were relegated to one part of one panel. Given the DPR's very tight deadlines, the impacts panel was not going to be able to consider these alternative issues in much depth, and the traditional values shaped this framing of energy policy as they had shaped earlier ones.[18]

The DPR staff had to perform a wide-ranging analysis under very severe deadlines, quickly becoming conversant with the technologies and issues. To help them, the DOE prepared a background report that reviewed the technologies and issues related to solar, and summarized eleven recent studies of solar energy. This report, while of great help to the DPR staff, could also influence how they would think about solar policy. For example, in summarizing all of the recent studies on solar, the report emphasized that each of them made estimates of the fraction of primary energy that solar might provide in the future.[19] A section entitled "Key Issues" listed assessing the goals for solar energy as the first issue, with evaluating the research, development, and demonstration program as the second. These issues framed the solar policy problem as a set of highly technical problems, for which there were strongly conflicting answers in the literature. This problem framing dominated the high-level discussions about the DPR and solar policy, despite the attempts of many people to interject other issues and problem frames.[20]

The DPR could have framed the problem differently. The Congressional Office of Technology Assessment (OTA) released a solar energy study just as the DPR was getting started. The OTA study, though mindful of the economic and national security issues, recognized that other concerns may be more important, especially given the uncertainties of economic forecasts. The OTA began by criticizing federal programs for too great an emphasis on central solar electric power plants. The study recognized from the start that decentralized solar technologies were not just a value-free substitute for fossil fuels or nuclear plants:

If energy can be produced from onsite solar energy systems at competitive prices, the increasing centralization which has characterized the equipment and institutions associated with energy industries for the past 30 years could be dramatically altered; . . . Given the increasing fraction of U.S. industrial assets which are being invested in energy industries, tendencies toward centralization of many aspects of society could also be affected.[21]

The report contained a great deal of economic analysis of the different solar technologies. However, its authors acknowledged that the economics were so uncertain that they probably should not drive policy. The possible range of solar costs overlapped the possible range of conventional fuel costs, which meant that other criteria were legitimate in making energy policy decisions.[22] The OTA's alternative problem frame eliminated the need to attempt a precise estimate of how much solar energy would come online how quickly, the issue that would tie up the DPR both substantively and politically, and showed that mainstream government sources provided alternative problem frames if executive branch policy makers were interested in them.

In the Issue Definition Memorandum, Eizenstat stated that the DPR would have a public participation program but left all of the details up to the staff running it. The staff implemented a diverse and extensive program, going well beyond perfunctory participation. They engaged the public from an early stage in the study and used both formal and informal methods of getting input from citizens. Moreover, the Solar Lobby, an advocacy group, was very involved in the DPR. The public solar constituency was growing and becoming better organized. The Solar Lobby helped organize the National Solar Congress, a citizen conference held in Washington while the DPR was in progress. These activities kept pressure on the DPR to be an open process and ensured that people interested in solar would participate in its activities. In addition to hearings and other outreach programs, the DPR staff worked with solar activists on a daily basis.[23] The DPR staff appeared to take the hearings seriously and commissioned outside analyses of them.[24]

However, this participation program did not change the way officials framed the problem. Despite early and in-depth public involvement of some ecological solar advocates, the values of national security and economic rationality remained paramount in conceptualizing the issue. The problem frame did not entirely determine the outcome, as there were other forces at work as well, such as the growing importance of the ecological advocates as a pressure group. Nonetheless, the frame did constrain the outcome of the study, and its authors had to stretch considerably to stay true to their initial values and please this vocal constituency. Moreover, the ecological advocates who were most closely involved with the DPR had to try to work within a framework defined by values that for them were not paramount.[25]

The DPR, though behind schedule, had a draft document ready for public review by late August 1978. The document served to inform the public about the current state of the DPR staff's thinking. A paragraph of caveats immediately after the title page claimed that, because of the severe deadlines:

Many of these options may *not* be good public policy and may *not* be ultimately recommended for Presidential approval. Their inclusion here does *not* constitute an endorsement of their soundness or appropriateness.[26]

The draft contained much description of different solar technologies and existing federal programs for them. It also presented an analysis of how much solar energy could, under three different scenarios, be in use by the year 2000, while acknowledging that all such estimates were very uncertain. It presented the most analysis of the middle scenario, the "maximum practical case," in which solar provided 18.1 quads of primary energy in 2000.[27] The final section of the draft discussed federal policy for solar and a rationale for supporting it. It could contribute to "national and international energy needs." In doing so,

> The pace of solar development also will affect progress toward other national goals such as a clean environment, a prosperous economy, an expanding job market, improved national security, flexibility in foreign affairs, and decreased reliance on foreign resources.[28]

These goals are, with the partial exception of a cleaner environment, all traditional ones associated with energy policy since the Truman administration. Despite all the participation, the draft DPR document reflected no influence of those with alternative normative conceptions of the problem.

The DPR staff aggressively sought comments on its draft, and they received 119 by their deadline, with the largest number coming from industry (including utilities) and public interest groups. Many comments expressed concern over the economic analysis, with utilities and nonsolar industries expressing the most caution about solar potential. Public interest groups and the general public argued, to the contrary, that the draft DPR document was too pessimistic in its evaluations of various solar technologies, and they criticized the federal government for lacking serious commitment to a strong solar program. The public interest groups in particular stressed that the DPR should pick a strong overall goal of the United States getting 25 quads (q) of solar energy by the year 2000, while the individual public respondents were less concerned about that more abstract issue.[29] The public interest groups emphasized the importance of small-scale solar technologies, while the public respondents criticized the draft for inadequate attention to the social effects of different energy technologies, including those on low incomes, such as the elderly, minorities, and so on. In short, the comments from both of these groups reflected some of the ideas of the ecological advocacy perspective on solar energy, providing yet another opportunity for those ideas to influence the policy discussion. There were some differences between the groups, reflecting the greater sophistication at policy debates of the public interest groups, but both emphasized a conceptualization of solar issues that still had not penetrated policy discussions at the top staff and policy-making levels.[30]

Media coverage of the draft DPR noted the discontent of many solar advocates with it.[31] Ecological solar advocates published their own critiques, arguing that the DPR did not do its economics right and, at a more political level, that the draft did not reflect the comments that

citizens made at the DPR public hearings. They claimed that it promoted
solar policies that would fail to expand decentralized solar and would
maintain or expand large solar projects geared to utility companies
and large manufacturing firms. In short, the policies in the DPR would
not do much for community-oriented solar, the critics charged, and
the process itself had been less than democratic, despite the widespread
public interest in solar.[32] The DPR staff would have disputed this
last point, as they felt very committed to the public participation
program and staged an extensive one despite the very tight deadlines
under which they were operating. Nonetheless, many participants in
those programs claimed that their views were not reflected in the final
DPR document.[33]

From the release of the draft DPR document to the president's
announcement of his final decision the following June, solar advocates
and government officials engaged in an extensive debate, some of it
private, over what the president would adopt as the government's solar
policy. The final product of the DPR study, the Response Memorandum
to the President, made it clear that the original framing of the DPR's
problem thoroughly dominated its analysis and conclusions. The charge
had been to assess the contribution that solar could make to the U.S.
energy supply, meaning the replacement of conventional fuels, and the
best comprehensive solar strategy for enlisting public and private
resources to accelerate solar's use. No other issue seems to have been of
any importance, despite all that the DPR staff might have heard in the
participation program. Solar was deemed important for standard economic and national security reasons, and even the obligatory nod to its
environmental desirability got very little play – none in the Executive
Summary.[34]

The Response Memo outlined three scenarios: a Base Case, a
Maximum Practical Effort, and a Technical Limits Case. Building on the
then-current use of 4.8 q of solar, mostly hydropower and woodburning,
the different scenarios led, by the year 2000, to 10–12 q, 18 q, and 25–30
q, repsectively. The memo stressed that these levels of solar penetration
assumed action at the federal, state, local, and private levels.[35] The memo
then went on to describe three sets of policy options: continue present
policies, expand them, and radically expand them. These options were
not tied explicitly to the earlier scenarios, but the way they were presented made it seem that they should be. However, these policy packages
would result in drastically less use of solar than what was anticipated in
the three scenarios, except that the radical expansion policy would
supply the amount of solar energy envisioned in the middle, Maximum
Practical scenario.[36] This inconsistency would be the target of much criticism and debate over the final solar policy.

Solar advocates tried to press their case to the administration in several ways. In mid-December 1978, five members of the Solar Lobby got a meeting with Stuart Eizenstat. The group consisted of Denis Hayes, Tom Hayden, a solar advocate from California and organizer of the Campaign for Economic Democracy, and the presidents of three different unions – Lloyd McBride of the steel workers, William Wimpinsinger of the machinists, and Edward Carlough of the sheet metal workers. The unionists had requested the meeting, and the composition of the group made it clear that solar advocates had connected to a constituency that earlier environmentalists often had not. In preparation for the meeting, the White House staff developed arguments that the solar advocates should not measure the administration's commitment to solar by the size of its budgets. The aides anticipated that the solar group would ask for larger budgets and a solar bank, an institution to make subsidized loans for solar purchases. The final draft of the DPR had been sent to the White House by this time, though it had not been released publicly, and it contained some policy initiatives that could be very costly.[37]

In late February individuals from the Solar Lobby and the Solar Energy Industries Association (SEIA) got a meeting with President Carter.[38] White House aides knew that these two groups had their differences but realized that they were coming to present a united front for stronger support of solar energy. High on their list was the Solar Bank, more solar tax credits, more federal use of solar energy, dramatically increased federal solar R&D, and a Solar Policy Council at the White House level to coordinate solar programs. The staff recommended that the president not commit to any of the specific programs, but listen and use their arguments later to help justify whatever policies he did choose. They noted that he would have to decide soon whether or not to set a quantitative solar goal, and that the Solar Lobby had just released its own study calling for a goal that twenty-five per cent of the nation's energy come from solar by the year 2000.[39]

The advocates' alternative conceptualization of the problem led to very different conclusions and associated a different set of values with energy technology. The DPR demonstrated convincingly that none of the advocates' values had managed to penetrate the thinking, or at least writing, of the officials who drafted the final DPR documents that went to the president. For the DPR, the only questions were how much oil solar could displace, assuming that oil prices went up to about $25 per barrel by the year 2000, and how much such displacement would cost in terms of new budget expenditures, assuming that everything else, in terms of institutions and lifestyles, stayed the same. In contrast, for the Solar Lobby's *Blueprint* study, the question was how to think about energy in the context of what prices ought to be and what was required to protect the environment, acknowledging that large-scale energy choices had serious implications for many aspects of modern life, and that the end of oil was drawing near. The actual level of the budget was less important than the net cost to the government and society, that is, a billion-dollar federal solar budget that led to two billion dollars in social benefits was a good policy.

The solar advocates did not confine their lobbying to individual meetings and publishing booklets. Denis Hayes sent a memo to some of Carter's main political advisors, summarizing the findings and recommendations of the *Blueprint* and urging them to see this as an opportunity for Carter akin to President Eisenhower's "Atoms for Peace" speech. He later wrote to Carter directly, promoting the study and making an economic pitch, arguing that solar and conservation could "place an absolute lid on soaring energy prices."[40] Moreover, the Solar Lobby was not the only solar advocacy group trying to reach the president. Members of the House of Representatives and the Senate, as well as state and city officials, all wrote to him or his aides, urging, almost uniformly, that he adopt the twenty-five per cent solar goal for the year 2000 and start the Solar Bank, among other policy initiatives. A group from an association of mayors added that such a policy would be quite popular, that during a time when most news on the energy and environmental front was bad, he could take the lead in developing a positive policy supporting a popular technology and so benefit politically.[41] A March 1979 Roper poll showed that solar remained the public's favorite long-term energy source, by almost two to one over nuclear power, and that it was in second place just behind coal in the short-term.[42]

Administration officials began debating solar policy internally soon after the release of the DPR Response Memo. Secretary of Energy Schlesinger urged the president to choose the second of the three options in the DPR and repeated his view that growing public interest in solar required the president to take a leadership role.[43] By May 1979, the White House staff began drafting a decision memo to go to the president, which would lay out his options for a final decision. An early draft noted the advantages of solar as "reducing our balance of payments, reducing dependence on oil imports, strengthening national security, improving the environment, and creating jobs." The ecological advocate concerns about scale, decentralization, promoting self-reliant communities, and so on, were absent from this list. The draft gave as the advantage of the Solar Bank that "It is a major priority of the Solar Lobby which regards it both as a rallying point and as a desirable means for providing a visible form of subsidy." It also noted the disadvantage that it would do little for the poor, and that the agencies were split, with only the Domestic Policy Staff, the DOE, and the EPA approving of it.[44]

The draft memo also recommended that the president announce a solar goal for the year 2000 to demonstrate his leadership in what could be a popular issue in the upcoming election. The president needed a popular issue. Oil prices had been going up since the Iranian revolution and the fall of the Shah in late 1978. In March came the Three Mile Island accident, which further impeded the development of nuclear power. The president's April 5, 1979 energy message announced oil price decontrol, which started shortly thereafter, and a windfall profits tax, which was delayed in Congress. The spring and summer saw more gasoline shortages. Overall, the public was growing increasingly hostile to the government and the president, largely for energy-related reasons, and there was a sense of crisis in the White House as staff felt that the Carter presidency was in serious political trouble.[45]

The process of the DPR itself had raised expectations among solar advocates, another pressure on the president, and the draft decision memo recommended that the president adopt the twenty per cent solar goal that corresponded to the Maximum Practical Scenario outlined in the DPR, the middle of the three scenarios. The memo noted that this goal "does not correspond to any option examined by the DPR." Next to this statement Eizenstat wrote in the margin, "Then how can it be recommended w/ any intellectual honesty?" The memo went on to argue for the goal as a national goal, one for both the public and private sectors, and so not one that would damage the budget. Next to this argument, Eizenstat wrote, "OK, but let's talk."[46]

A later draft of the decision memo gave the same rationales for solar, and recommended that the president adopt option two of the DPR but also a solar goal of twenty per cent, along with the Solar Bank and a few other policies. The memo noted that the goal did "not correspond directly to any option proposed by the DPR," but that no longer seemed to bother Eizenstat.[47] The final draft of the memo said the same thing, and Eizenstat attached a cover memo urging the president to adopt both the Solar Bank and the twenty per cent goal:

In large measure, the public response to your solar message will be determined by the reaction of the leading outside solar advocates and the members of Congress who have identified themselves with this issue ... proponents of solar would renounce any program, no matter how solid in other areas, which did not contain these two elements [20% goal and Solar Bank].

The president approved both the Solar Bank and the goal.[48] Thus the policy that came out of the DPR contained some things that the Solar Lobby and like-minded advocates wanted, but it would do so without even discussing at the highest levels the reasons those advocates gave for supporting solar – the social and political values that they saw in a solar future. The president and his staff made it clear that they wanted solar energy to help them with their immediate problems of making the status quo work better and bolstering the values of economic rationality and national security, both narrowly conceived.

Eizenstat's memos also made it clear that the policy coming out of the DPR had to be the way it was or risk the political wrath of a growing constituency. Solar advocates had arrived as a pressure group. But the task set for solar energy, to reduce quickly dependence on imported oil, was daunting. Since the advocates' values and reasoning for supporting solar had not been accepted by the White House, they ran the risk of losing their influence rapidly. Thus the government officials and solar advocates were constructing this problem, and energy technologies, differently. In the DPR, energy technologies were simply a way of providing a certain set of goods and services and of protecting the nation from foreign influences. For the ecological advocates, they were also a way of preserving the environment and encouraging a different type of society. The *Blueprint* claimed that certain types of solar technologies "tend to foster self-reliance, political and cultural pluralism, and a favorable balance of payments" and that the alternatives, particularly nuclear, entailed environmental problems. The *Blueprint* trod fairly lightly on the social implications of nuclear power, but its authors cited in their footnotes studies that argued for severe political implications of the widespread use of nuclear power, such as the need for secrecy and the infringement of civil rights in a society in which plutonium would be in routine commerce.[49]

While the Solar Lobby had an alternative set of values that shaped its approach to energy policy, it did not own this issue. It could not get its definition of the issue accepted as the official definition. Despite the Solar Lobby's frequent interaction with the DPR staff, despite having one of its employees on loan to the DPR, despite its ability to be recognized as a significant pressure group and get meetings with the president and his top aides, it could not change the fundamental framing of the issue or the values that were inherent in that framing. So far, their success as a pressure group had not led to the institutionalization of their values.

The president announced his solar policy at the dedication of the solar hot water heating system on the West Wing of the White House, which I described in the Introduction. The previous fall the White House had announced plans to install the solar system, and its high cost had received much negative publicity. Unhappy solar advocates argued that the collectors were much more expensive than they had to be due to the special problems of doing construction on the White House. The White House itself emphasized that the collectors were not intended as a demonstration of the technology but instead as symbols of the president's commitment to solar. The system was finished at the end of April 1979 and dedication scheduled for June 20.[50] The form as well as the substance of the presidential solar policy announcement became contested issues in the White House. Gus Speth, acting chair of the CEQ and a strong supporter of solar energy, argued for it being a prime-time televised address. Failing that, he wanted a major speech, not just "low-key, off-the-cuff remarks."[51]

Speth lost. The president announced the new solar policies at the dedication of the White House solar system in a brief speech. The White House also released a twenty-six-page Fact Sheet to go with the speech and to accompany his solar message to Congress and, two days later, a background report for the press.[52] Both documents discussed the Solar Bank, the goal, tax credits, and other programs. They stressed that all of the programs, spending and tax credits, would add up to a $1 billion solar program. In describing why solar energy was important, the background report reiterated all of the conventional arguments that had appeared in the internal memos: the need to replace foreign oil, work against the day when fossil fuels would be depleted, protect the environment, hedge against inflation, and so on. In one sense, the background report put a great deal of emphasis on solar, but only in conventional terms. "True energy security – in both price and supply – can ultimately come to this nation only through the development of solar and renewable technologies."[53] The administration paid no more attention to the values of the solar advocates in public than they did in private. The advocates present at the speech, as mentioned in the Introduction, began complaining to the press immediately after the ceremony about the lack of depth in President Carter's commitment to solar.[54]

Access Denied: Solar Advocates in Carter's Last Years

Ecological solar advocates' and environmentalists' relations with President Carter deteriorated rapidly after the June 20 speech announcing the solar DPR results and policy. The president gave a major speech on energy on July 15 in which he proposed, in part, an Energy Mobilization Board, which could override environmental regulations to get energy production facilities built, and the Energy Security Corporation, to produce subsidized synfuels. Environmentalists strongly opposed both measures. In a five-page memo, Gus Speth of the CEQ spelled out the situation for the president. He pointed out that there were about 50 national and 2,500–5,000 local environmental groups in the United States, and he reminded the president that they had been "among your earliest and strongest supporters." This latest administration proposal had deepened a growing rift with environmentalists.

The reaction to your July 15 energy program and subsequent related Administration actions is fundamentally different. *The environmental community's split with us on that program is apparently deep and pervasive. Relations are now at a low ebb. A major rebuilding effort is essential if we are to patch things up to a satisfactory point for 1980.*

Speth pointed out that some environmentalists had already started working for Carter's Democratic rivals, and then set out actions that the administration should take to win them back to the fold, including compromises on the Mobilization Board and Security Corporation, followed by a strong environmental record for the rest of the term, including filling several environmental vacancies in the administration. Carter's reaction to the memo seemed positive, as he wrote on it:

To Stu and Gus –
a) Plan mtg to discuss w/ environmentalists key issues.
b) Have staff screen my public statements (& others) & distribute pertinent comments to key groups.
c) Marshall admin. support.
d) Advise me on further action.
JC[55]

President Carter did take Speth's advice on appointments. He appointed Speth himself and Denis Hayes, both well-respected environmentalists, to chair the CEQ and to head the Solar Energy Research Institute (SERI), respectively. On the same day that Speth sent the aforementioned memo to the president, he also sent one to Hamilton Jordan, Carter's closest aide, about "upgrading CEQ's Role in the EOP [Executive Office of the President]" and argued that the CEQ should be made more a core organization in White House decision making, both through formal procedures and by giving the CEQ more perks and visibility to increase the respect with which its staff was treated. The memo made its way to Carter, who wrote on it, "To Al – Environmentalists are important to me. Talk to Gus and assess best role for CEQ. J.C."[56] As head of the CEQ, Speth continued to try to influence the administration in proenvironmental ways.[57]

Denis Hayes' appointment as the director of SERI upset some people outside the environmental movement because he was such a well-known ecological solar advocate. The environmental community, however, could only praise appointing the organizer of Earth Day and Sun Day to head SERI. There was some resistance at SERI to Hayes' appointment, but within a year he seemed to have won over the staff and raised its morale. He was also attempting to redirect the institute toward smaller technologies and away from the larger ones.[58] Neither of these appointments, however, were enough to win back the environmentalists who were so upset over the July 15 speech and subsequent programs. They still thought that the administration was turning against their values. And even the environmentalists within the administration had little influence over policy. By a year after his appointment as the CEQ chair, Speth had lost most of his battles within the White House.[59] Subsequent developments in solar policy would not heal the rift.

CONGRESS AS A LIMITED ALTERNATIVE VENUE

Congress is often an attractive policy venue for advocates who have lost in other places. The diversity of its membership meant that solar advocates could often find sympathetic members to champion their policies. The fluidity of its committee structure, especially in times of crisis, meant that advocates could search for a committee dominated by solar supporters if the more traditional committees lacked such support. And in fact numerous members did support solar. Congress as a whole passed numerous solar bills and, as discussed in earlier chapters, often provided solar programs with more money than the Executive Branch requested, creating a "bidding war" that frustrated the White House staff.

Prior to the oil embargo, much of the support for changes in energy policy, and for solar in particular, came from Congress.[60] The White House often either had to enlist the support of important legislators for its initiatives, or it had to propose programs to preempt congressional initiatives. As the energy policy debate expanded to involve more groups and constituencies with diverse values and definitions of the problem, these actors looked to a variety of congressional committees and subcommittees when they found the Executive Branch closed to them.

The same held true after the oil embargo. In the first fourteen months following the oil embargo, Congress passed thirty-two bills related to energy, only one of which the president vetoed. Legislation covered all kinds of energy issues, including environmental. Solar sometimes showed up as parts of larger bills, such as the Housing and Community Development Act (PL93-383), which promoted solar and conservation in housing, as well as in exclusively solar bills.[61]

Democrats controlled both the House and the Senate during the energy crisis, and they developed energy strategies different from the Nixon and Ford administrations. For example, during the Ford administration, Senator John O. Pastore and Representative Jim Wright cochaired the task force that drafted such a strategy, and they intended it to challenge the president's in fundamental ways. Their plan argued that energy policy had to be consistent with broader economic policy and that the most important economic tasks were to reduce unemployment and inflation. They claimed that President Ford's plan would only exacerbate each. "We reject the fundamental premise of the President's program that the only way to achieve energy conservation is deliberately to raise the price of all petroleum products to all American consumers by heavy indiscriminate additions in taxation." The congressional task force emphasized conservation in the short- and medium-terms and the development of new supplies in the longer term (into the 1980s) as the way to achieve energy independence.[62] This approach rejected one of the basic ideological premises of the administration's program, namely, the reliance on free markets as the solution to the energy problem. The White House saw this ideological difference over the market versus government intervention as one of the largest gaps between it and congressional plans. They also claimed that the congressional plan simply would not work, in part because it did not allow enough freedom for market forces to act to cut consumption.[63] While the normative ideas that drove this congressional energy strategy were quite different from those of ecological solar advocates, the plan suggests that Congress might have been an institutional venue in which different values and actors could get involved in and influence policy making.

Congressional solar advocates experienced the same normative divisions as the solar movement itself. For example, Representative Michael McCormack, a Democrat from Washington and an early supporter of solar energy, had worked as a research chemist at the Hanford nuclear facility and became the only scientist in the House at the time of his election in 1970. Assigned to the House Science and Astronautics Committee, he sought aggressively to make energy his issue. However, fossil fuels were the turf of the Interior Committee and nuclear energy of the Joint Committee for Atomic Energy. So McCormack chose solar energy and conservation. He came to advocate much greater funding for solar R&D. Yet he was a most unlikely candidate for championing solar energy in the 1970s. For just as solar was becoming more associated with the environmental movement and its criticisms of nuclear power, one of its main champions in Congress was zealously pronuclear and a harsh critic of environmentalists.[64]

McCormack sponsored the two most important solar bills in 1974: the Solar Heating and Cooling Demonstration Act (PL93-409) and the Solar Energy Research, Development, and Demonstration Act (PL93-432). McCormack was strongly pronuclear and saw solar as a complement to nuclear, not a competitor. In promoting his bills, McCormack emphasized that solar was abundant, clean, secure from foreign influences, and nearly competitive economically – all of the conventional values associated with solar for decades.[65] Yet by 1976 he spoke as the voice of restraint, arguing against extra appropriations for solar, in large part because solar became increasingly associated with antinuclear leg-islators. He reemphasized that the country needed both the breeder and solar energy.[66]

Environmentalist legislators, such as Richard Ottinger of New York, formed a second category of congressional solar advocates. Ottinger got involved in energy policy immediately, acquiring an appointment to McCormack's Energy Subcommittee. He often had a critical perspective on the way ERDA was handling solar energy. He questioned ERDA wit-nesses in the Solar Heating and Cooling Demonstration Act oversight hearings about his concerns that the research components of the solar demonstration program would make the cost of solar look higher than it had to be.[67] He was also antinuclear, which incurred McCormack's hostility, and his growing leadership in the solar area was one of the factors that associated solar technologies with values attributed to its ecological advocates, which in turn led McCormack to pull away in his support of it.[68] The split in the broader solar movement was reflected in the split among solar advocates in Congress, and is one of the things that limited Congress as an effective alternative point of access for solar advocates.

8

Solar Policy in Crisis

Solar energy policy was part of energy policy for all three administrations during the energy crisis. All three hoped that new technologies in general could solve at least some of their problems in dealing with the crisis and could do even more in preventing worse crises in the future. Each administration harbored ideas about solar energy and the way it fit into energy policy, which constituted their problem frames. Those ideas, interacting with their institutional settings and interested actors, led to battles over the solar budget, which exhibited all of the volatility that one might expect from a technology burdened with great uncertainty and an unstable policy environment.

THE ENERGY CRISIS AND THE TECHNOLOGICAL FIX

Every administration sought a technological fix to the energy crisis, at least in the long-term. Policy makers did not like the implications of solving the energy crisis by doing less, so wedded were they to the ideas that using less energy meant stagnation, decline, and so on. Locked in as a core assumption in their problem frame was the need to find ways to deliver large blocks of bulk energy, and to increase that level of energy consumption into the indefinite future. Given that problem frame, consistent since the Truman administration, they all sought technological fixes.

The Nixon administration put a heavy emphasis on increasing energy R&D, including substantial increases for nonnuclear R&D. Thus began a rapid run-up of the energy R&D budget that would last for the rest of the decade. The administration proposed $772 million for FY 1974, a twenty per cent increase over FY 1973. That increase looked modest compared to Senator Henry (Scoop) Jackson's proposal for a $2 billion energy R&D in the FY 1974 budget. These proposals came six months before the oil embargo.[1] Nixon later upped the ante even more when, on June 29, 1973, still well before the embargo, he announced a series of new policies:

America faces a serious energy problem. While we have only 6 per cent of the world's population, we consume one-third of the world's energy output. The supply of domestic energy resources available to us is not keeping pace with our ever-growing demand, and unless we act swiftly and effectively, we could face a genuine energy crisis in the foreseeable future.

As part of that swift action, he announced a five-year, $10 billion energy R&D program to begin in FY 1975. He also announced an additional $100 million in R&D for FY 1974, at least half of which was supposed to go to coal research. He immediately initiated a study of where to spend the money, suggesting that the White House did not have any specific plans for the money but felt that it had to take the lead in championing energy R&D.[2] By mid-October, already into FY 1974, the R&D numbers rose again. The new budget, including a few congressional add-ons, totaled $1.002 billion, a whopping thirty-seven per cent increase over the recalculated FY 1973 budgets. Roughly sixty-two per cent was to go to nuclear research, fission and fusion, about seventeen per cent to coal, and about ten per cent for research on mitigating environmental effects of energy production, leaving eleven per cent for everything else put together. Solar received an enormous percentage boost, rising from $2 million in FY 1973 to $13.2 million in FY 1974, but that still left it at about one per cent of the total. Conservation fared little better, at $15.5 million.[3] Thus, on the eve of the embargo, the Nixon administration's energy R&D program established a set of priorities by investing substantially in two classes of new energy supply technologies, nuclear and coal, technologies that could, in the administration's view, deliver bulk supplies of electricity or fluid fuels. This policy identified nuclear and coal as the energy sources of the future, with a nod to environmental protection, and loose change to solar and conservation.

This emphasis on the technological fix and these priorities among technologies continued under President Ford, though with a longer time frame. In the short- and medium-terms, President Ford put a heavier emphasis on deregulating energy markets, especially price deregulation for oil and gas, and environmental deregulation for coal and nuclear power. In reports and memos, top officials clearly stated that new technologies were years from solving America's energy problems.[4] Despite this conviction, they continued to increase investments in R&D. Their proposed FY 1977 energy R&D budget was $2.24 billion, a thirty-five per cent increase over FY 1976. Solar shared in that increase, with its R&D funds going up thirty-five per cent to $116 million. That said, the proportions of the energy R&D budget changed only a little. For FY 1977 nuclear energy R&D, including fusion, would get sixty-two per cent of the total, fossil fuels twenty per cent, and solar five per cent, a larger piece of the pie than three years before, but still only a small slice.

Both Nixon's and Ford's aides claimed that in the short run oil and gas deregulation was the key to solving the crisis, the presidents believed them, and Ford himself argued for it publicly. Nonetheless, they talked and acted as if they believed that in the longer term the country would require a technological fix, that the existing energy system was not sustainable. The emphasis on deregulation embodies the normative idea of economic rationality – that government policies should act so as to let the market function in as unfettered a manner as possible. Note that this is a more refined notion than the emphasis on economic growth that we saw in the Truman administration. The emphasis on the technological fix in the longer run shows two things. First, both presidents accepted the notion, common among economists, that private firms, if left to themselves, would underinvest in R&D, and so the government should step in to provide this public good.[5] The energy crisis was simply a signal to speed up the government investment in this particular branch of R&D.

The emphasis on the technological fix also tells us something about their implicit notions of technology and its effects on social and political life. The very idea of the technological fix is that one can use new technologies to avoid making social or political changes in societies that are in some sense under stress.[6] New energy technologies were supposed to enable American society to continue as it had in the recent past, with no concessions to problems of energy supplies. The technological fix shored up the status quo, and so policy makers saw new technologies as ways of avoiding any serious social or political changes. This notion excludes the idea of using new technological systems to encourage new ways of life and social organization.

President Carter's administration kept this focus on a technological fix for the long-term. His short- and medium-term policies varied a bit from Nixon's and Ford's, still stressing price deregulation for oil and natural gas but also including a larger role for government in encouraging greater energy efficiency and the production of synthetic fuels. The National Energy Plan, his administration's first energy policy statement, listed the development of new energy technologies including solar, as the key to solving the long-term energy problem.[7]

ADMINISTRATION IDEAS ABOUT SOLAR ENERGY

While all of the administrations of the 1970s focused on energy policy, they paid very different levels of attention to solar energy. What becomes clear from the following analysis is that none of the administrations took solar to be the solution to their energy problems, and so in that sense never took it as seriously as its advocates wanted. We need to examine solar policies from two different perspectives – solar as a long-term technological fix and solar's relationship to the short-term energy crisis. These ideas and policy frames did not, of course, exclusively determine policy, but instead interacted with the institutional structures and interested actors involved in the issue. This chapter pays close attention to solar advocacy within government. Such advocacy was not merely the result of prosolar persons within government, but also derived from institutional structures and practices that gave such people the opportunity to advocate for solar and ties those government advocates had to solar advocates outside of government.

Solar Potential Identified Under Nixon

Throughout President Nixon's administration officials made references to solar energy as a promising long-term technological option for helping to cope with energy shortages, but only one among several, including the breeder reactor. In his June 1971 energy message to Congress, he included one short paragraph on solar. After noting the immense potential of solar, he said that the "National Aeronautics and Space Administration and the National Science Foundation are currently re-examining their efforts in this area and we expect to give greater attention to solar energy in the future."[8] That reexamination turned out to be a joint panel established by NASA and the NSF in January 1972, which reported its findings in December 1972. The panel concluded that the importance of solar, if it could make a substantial contribution at all, came from two properties – it was both environmentally clean and inexhaustible. The report's authors accepted conventional projections that energy demand would continue to rise and that fossil fuels would face depletion at some point. In contrast to fossil fuels, the resource potential for solar appeared to be huge if it could be harnessed economically.[9]

The panel's assessments were remarkably positive, asserting that there were no substantial technical barriers to the use of solar and that it could be economically competitive within a very few years. Solar, they claimed, could provide thirty-five per cent of building heating and cooling, thirty per cent of gaseous fuels, ten per cent of liquid fuels, and twenty per cent of electricity by the year 2020, despite projections of very high energy consumption by that year. As they understated, "On close examination, the possibilities for the economic use of solar power, given reasonable R&D support, appear much better than generally realized."[10] In terms of public R&D resources, the report put its heaviest emphasis on solar electric technologies, mainly solar thermal power plants and photovoltaic panels. This emphasis on electricity was controversial in the solar community, though very much in keeping with what some of the most visible solar advocates had argued. Solar advocates split in their reactions to this report, which reflected a growing divergence of opinions in the solar community, discussed in earlier chapters as the differences between the conventional and ecological solar advocacy.[11]

The NASA/NSF Solar Energy Panel devoted only a few paragraphs to environmental concerns, industrial issues, and "sociological" issues. They noted that, if done right, solar energy could be very environmentally benign, thus imbuing solar with the environmental values that were growing in importance at that time. Indeed, they thought that solar would be more economically competitive than was commonly realized because the costs of generating electricity in the future would have to include the substantial costs of pollution abatement for conventional fuels.[12] The industrial problem was one of creating circumstances that would induce industry to invest in a risky venture with a long-term payoff. A single paragraph addressed the possible social implications of developing solar energy:

Research on the social conditions which foster solar energy technology protects against the truncating of a technological policy by the social responses it engenders. . . . There is a need for more social scientific work to define the social (including economic, political, and cultural) problems presented by solar energy utilization. The establishment of National priorities for the use of solar among other energy forms should recognize the social impacts of the utilization of each energy form.[13]

Thus the panel explicitly recognized, however briefly, that developing and diffusing energy technologies were more than just technical or economic acts. The social or political response that the panel cautioned against was a negative one that could "truncate" a policy. Aggrieved social groups could organize to stop technological developments that government policy sought to promote, as was happening then with nuclear power. The panel suggested that such protesters could be headed off at the beginning by working to address their concerns at early stages of policy making. This view of the sociopolitical implications of a technology saw them as problems of encroaching on people's interests and getting strong negative reactions. Nonetheless, the NASA/NSF panelists' recognition that *any* political and social implications followed from favoring a certain set of technologies over others moved a substantial step beyond the conventional technical and economic assessments of the ties between a technology and society.

Despite its visibility, the NASA/NSF report did not become the official problem frame for solar energy. Presidential policy makers in the Nixon White House perceived solar quite differently than did the panel. The fundamental conclusions of the NASA/NSF panel never affected the thinking of senior White House aides or President Nixon. In fact, prior to 1972, solar hardly appeared on the White House's energy map at all. In his 1971 summary memo, John Whitaker described to President Nixon thirty-seven possible actions the president could take in response to fuel shortages, including long-term actions that he did not consider to be particularly efficacious. Not one of the possibilities listed included solar energy development.[14] Firms and interest groups made some effort to alert White House aides to the discussions of solar going on outside the government.[15] Peter Flanigan, the chief White House aide for energy in Nixon's early years, explained the administration's lack of interest in solar energy to an academic solar energy advocate:

There are undoubtedly many reasons why solar energy is not receiving attention as a major power source, but perhaps the most fundamental is the dearth of imaginative technological proposals suggesting that solar energy can, in fact, produce electric power at prices competitive with alternative sources. Neither the product – electricity – nor the basic scientific theory is new, so one is immediately involved in a commercial engineering venture unlike the exploration of space and the development of atomic weapons. . . . In order to justify a major new program or an agency devoted to solar energy, I feel there must be a real technological breakthrough in thinking about the means for making a practical system. Without such a spark, I am afraid it will be difficult, if not impossible, to get any effort started.[16]

Flanigan's argument shows the supply orientation in White House thinking. By assuming that the U.S. energy system would always consume large quantities of bulk energy, especially electricity, he defined the issue in terms of what kinds of technologies one could plug into the system to keep delivering that energy. Moreover, Flanigan clearly did not think that solar would ever become such a source. He conceptualized new technologies as ones that had made substantial breaks with the past, that were qualitatively new and based on new, exotic, science. According to these criteria, nuclear power, particularly breeders and fusion, could make a claim on the future, but solar could not. The basic solar technologies had all been in existence for some time, and Flanigan did not see incremental developments as adequate to bring solar to the point where it could be a major power producer. Solar did not offer excitement; in Flanigan's terms, it had no "spark," much less an explosion, to propel it into the policy makers' imaginations. Cautions about pollution did not suffice to induce the White House aides to take solar seriously before 1975. Concerns had not yet become fears.

Despite administration skepticism, legislative hearings prior to the 1973 oil embargo led to increased funding for solar research. Six months after the mid-1972 hearing on energy R&D policy, the House Committee on Science and Astronautics released a staff report on solar energy research. It defined the energy problem as the difficulty in providing "adequate, clean energy." The report stated that long-term energy needs would probably depend heavily on solar and that federal R&D funding levels were very low, about five to six million dollars in FY 1973. It recommended increasing federal funds to about $150 million per year or more, spending three billion dollars over the next fifteen years.[17] The amount finally appropriated for FY 1974 was about $12 million, a substantial increase in percentage terms over FY 1973.[18]

Despite this surge in spending, congressional action did not change the terms in which officials discussed the energy problem and solar energy. Congress and the White House continued to see the problem as economic efficiency and, to a lesser extent, national security. Environmental values had entered the official discourse, but in the narrow way of just seeking cleaner fuels. The more profound critiques of the production and use of energy that had begun to take hold among environmental organizations had made no impact on official discussions in either branch of government. Executive branch reorganizations that might have given such groups more chances to be heard in the policy process had not yet materialized, and the creation of new policy venues in Congress still confined participation to groups that had always been represented in such places.

Skepticism Prevails Under Ford

Early in the Ford administration, top officials saw questions of cost and commercial feasibility as the greatest barriers to the diffusion of solar technology. These officials did not believe that the technologies could yet compete, and they also believed that commercializing the technologies too quickly with government programs would only damage solar's long-term development. For them, it was still a technology of the future, and reducing the capital cost of solar was the issue.[19]

Other officials, lower down in the government hierarchy, began developing conceptualizations of energy policy more favorable to government support for solar technologies. For example, in November 1974 the Federal Energy Administration released the final reports of Project Independence. The report's solar volume promoted solar technologies on the grounds that they could soon be commercially feasible and were environmentally benign. However, they also argued for the use of life-cycle costs when comparing two different energy systems, including assessing environmental impact costs, instead of simply comparing capital and fuel costs. Such costs did not enter into standard commercial calculations, that is, the environmental costs of energy systems were not usually internalized into their market prices. For that reason the government would need to provide financial incentives to producers and consumers of solar technologies. The recommended incentives included things such as tax credits, low-interest loans, direct subsidies, and mandated solar use in certain circumstances. While the report acknowledged the impossibility of estimating quantitatively the effects of the various incentives, they did estimate the maximum future contribution from solar technologies at 12.7 q by 1995 and 38.8 q by the year 2000.[20] This particular study gave solar a substantial long-term role in producing the nation's energy.

The concepts of life-cycle costing and internalizing environmental costs into prices represented different normative ideas than were in the conventional problem frames, and gave the value of environmental protection greater emphasis. If the administration had adopted these ideas for the official problem frame for energy, solar would have fared much better. But the emphasis at the top of the Ford administration was to deregulate energy markets, not impose further requirements on them. In this case both approaches would have had a similar effect, since deregulating prices and internalizing environmental costs both would work to raise energy prices, though with the revenue going to different places. The important differences were normative.

The president and his advisors also saw little potential for solar as a short-term solution to the energy crisis. An Energy Resources Council study reiterated these sentiments:

Emerging technologies will not play a significant role in stabilizing our energy situation in the next ten years. Solar, geothermal, and synthetic fuels will make only a small contribution to domestic energy supplies by 1985 – about 1 per cent of total use. While the technology for these sources exists, they must be proven economically viable on a commercial scale.[21]

This official skepticism about solar's short-term potential and view of energy in general played out in a set of constantly changing institutions under Nixon and Ford.

Solar advocacy began to increase within the executive branch during the Ford administration because in part of the creation of institutional homes for such advocacy. The National Science Foundation ceded its solar program to the newly created Energy Research and Development Administration (ERDA), which commissioned three studies of the commercial potential for solar technologies, one each from General Electric, Westinghouse, and TRW. The studies produced such an unmanageable volume of material that ERDA then commissioned Battelle Laboratories to summarize the results of the previous studies. The purpose in assigning the task to four different contractors was to receive a diversity of views by which to define future research needs.[22] Yet the list of contractors and subcontractors included no environmental groups or other industries that specialized more heavily in solar technologies.

Nonetheless, the Battelle report identified social, political, and philosophical analyses as one category of research needs. Battelle mostly conceptualized such research as understanding why consumers would or would not buy solar technologies. Nonetheless, some of the proposed research would investigate the indirect or higher order effects on communities of adopting solar technologies, explicitly recognizing that widespread use of solar energy systems would affect communities in ways not directly related to energy use.[23]

However, these broader social concerns did not penetrate to the highest levels of ERDA or the White House. According to Administrator Seamans's early report to the president, ERDA's goal for the solar program should be "to develop at the earliest feasible time those applications of solar energy that can be made economically attractive and environmentally acceptable as alternative energy sources."[24] An interagency task force on solar reached a similar conclusion a few weeks later.[25] Thus, only conventional interpretations of energy goals or concerns filtered into White House discourse from this report. The ideas that did not fit administration preconceptions and ideologies received no hearing.

The Ford administration's choices of top personnel for ERDA also helped to exclude solar advocates. Robert Seamans headed the agency, having worked formerly in NASA and as Secretary of the Air Force. Seamans had no ties to the old AEC, a White House attempt to alleviate concerns that ERDA would be the AEC in disguise.[26] But the selection of the assistant administrator for solar and geothermal energy sources shows the exclusion of solar advocates from top administration positions.

On January 14, 1975, Senators Hubert Humphrey and Henry Jackson, both senior senators on committees important to energy, wrote to President Ford about the pending appointment of the assistant administrator for solar and geothermal. They made their wishes quite clear: "A special effort is needed to ensure that this position is filled by an experienced advocate of solar and geothermal energy. We cannot afford to continue our present reliance on fossil fuels and nuclear systems to the neglect of solar and geothermal energy."[27] Two days later a deputy assistant to the president replied with perfunctory assurances that their letter would be brought to the attention of the president and his assistants supervising the hiring. The letter said that the director of the personnel office was "presently reviewing recommendations for these positions."[28] In fact, the administration had made its choice five days before Humphrey and Jackson had even written to the president.[29] Dr. John Teem received the appointment as solar assistant administrator. Trained as an elementary particle physicist, Teem was in charge of research for fusion, high-energy physics, materials, and other physical sciences at the AEC. His only background in solar was a short stint with the small firm of Electro-Optical Systems, Inc., which made photovoltaic cells for the space program. Xerox bought the firm, and Teem moved up the ladder in Xerox until he went to the AEC.[30] While he had experience with one solar technology, he was by no means a solar advocate. This was precisely the sort of appointment that solar advocates had feared – someone from the nuclear bureaucracy in the AEC. It suggested that, while the government had created a new policy venue in the form of the ERDA, new constituencies had little voice in it, and that both the form and magnitude of solar programs would continue to reflect the old AEC bias. ERDA's General Advisory Committee also contained no solar advocates.[31]

About one year later, Dr. Teem resigned, and his replacement, Robert L. Hirsch, was someone even further removed from solar technologies. The full name of the solar division referred to solar, geothermal, and advanced energy systems, also encompassing fusion research. The new assistant administrator came from a fusion background, having concentrated on fusion and other nuclear topics for his entire career. The president's aides recognized his lack of expertise in solar, and one of them commented on the recommendation in a memo to President Ford:

Hirsch's background appears to be almost entirely in the nuclear field. This could raise a question as to his qualifications under the statute. It also could be made the basis for criticism by opponents of nuclear energy that these alternative sources of energy will not receive sufficiently vigorous leadership under someone whose background is in the competitive field of nuclear energy.[32]

Despite these questions, Hirsch got the appointment, reflecting a lack of concern among top administration officials for the solar division of ERDA.[33]

In June 1975, ERDA delivered to the president and Congress, as required, its first national plan for energy research, development, and demonstration (R,D&D). This plan listed the twenty-one categories of technologies that ERDA intended to support and estimates of the future energy contributions of each of them. It expected solar heating and cooling to make a "substantial" contribution (the middle of three rankings) by the year 2000 and solar electric and biomass to make "moderate" contributions by 2000, the lowest of the impact ranks.[34] Solar was in the program, but not at its center. The document stated explicitly that the highest priority technologies were those that would come online the soonest, would substitute for oil and gas, were near to being marketable, and would make the largest contribution to the energy system – difficult criteria for solar to meet.[35]

The ERDA plan received heavy criticism from Congress. The Congressional Office of Technology Assessment (OTA) report released in October 1975 contained a sharp and detailed critique of the ERDA plan. The OTA criticized it for proposing a program that could not meet its own goals and for putting too heavy an emphasis on supply technologies, especially for electricity, relative to conservation technologies, which only got two per cent of the ERDA budget. The OTA also questioned ERDA's solar program because it heavily emphasized solar electric applications, although the best near-term results would come from the heating and cooling of buildings. Such technologies required more than research to promote them, and the OTA criticized ERDA for giving short shrift to nontechnical barriers to solar in particular and energy in general.[36]

The OTA study incorporated a greater diversity of views than did ERDA or the executive branch more generally. The panel that advised the OTA on the solar chapter had much wider participation from the academic community and the solar community, including the scientist George Löf and the head of the Solar Energy Industries Association, Sheldon Butt. In addition, OTA invited critiques of the ERDA plan from twenty-three organizations, such as firms, trade associations, and interest groups, including four environmental groups. Those environmental groups' access was growing and was already greater in Congress than in the executive branch.[37] Thus OTA, the analytical arm of Congress, was becoming a new institutional venue in which actors shut out of the executive branch could argue their case and interject new values into the policy debate.

These concerns did not get very far in the White House. In late 1975 a top White House aide advised against the president's attending Solar Expo '76 the following January. "Solar energy," he wrote, "has very little near term (pre-2000) potential, based on current knowledge. . . . Presidential participation in the Expo would lend credence to the claims of the far out advocates."[38] In early 1976 an official at the OMB, commenting on a draft speech by someone in the Consumer Affairs Office, also reacted negatively to a positive assessment of solar's potential. "We've reviewed Virginia Knauer's draft speech and found it overstated the case for solar and understated the case for coal and nuclear. (She didn't mention nuclear at all!)"[39] The Ford White House perceived solar and nuclear as competitive, antagonistic energy choices, and the staff clearly did not favor solar. The revised ERDA national plan of April 1976 reflected the criticism of both the White House and the OTA. In deference to the normative values dominant in the White House, the plan gave much greater prominence to the private sector. Responding to the criticism of OTA, the plan argued for a big boost, especially rhetorically, for conservation. Solar heating and cooling, as well as solar electricity, numbered among the technologies slated for support. While the major problem with solar was still its cost, ERDA's new plan recognized other barriers to its adoption, all of which related to the difficulty of getting the building industry to accept a new technology.[40]

In a speech to the Illinois Solar Energy Conference, Frank Zarb, Administrator of the FEA, displayed senior officials' thinking about the technological possibilities for solar, and why those officials were skeptical about near-term reductions in solar prices. Consistent with the views of the Nixon administration, Zarb argued that solar's high cost would not come down much because the necessary technology already existed and its simplicity made it harder to reduce the costs.

But the very simplicity of the technology is one of the impediments to reducing its cost to the very low levels needed to make solar electric power competitive. It will be very difficult to reduce the cost by simplification. The answer lies in expanding markets and – perhaps – different technological approaches.[41]

Despite his caution, Zarb ended his speech affirming the administration's commitment to developing solar energy and their belief that it could be a major energy source in the next century.[42]

Zarb's speech suggested the same model of technological development as the previous administration. He assumed that incremental improvements in existing solar technologies could not produce a dramatic drop in price. If such technologies were little more than mirrors, glass, and plumbing, we already knew how to make those things, and so the price could not come down in a very rapid way. Large price reductions only come, in this way of thinking, via "breakthroughs," the creation of entirely novel technologies, which then have the opportunity to mature and simplify into an inexpensive commodity item. Zarb's model is at odds with the history of many technologies, but the point is that the model's prevalence in policy makers' minds in the 1970s led them to downplay the chance that solar could make a near – or maybe longer – term contribution to the energy problem. Yet, running counter to the White House perspective, an ERDA economic analysis of solar heat and hot water systems in 1976 concluded that they could be competitive with electric heat in a very short time, given some assumptions about the future price of fuel and the costs of collectors going down to twenty dollars per square foot.[43] The higher one went up in the administration, the darker appeared solar's future.

In funding for R&D the Ford administration maintained its commitment to freer markets. These policy makers saw technological innovation moving along a continuum from basic research through development and demonstration to the final marketing of a product.

From their perspective, the government had a strong role to play on the research end, but its proper role declined as an innovation moved toward the market end of the continuum. Therefore, officials gave more support to research and development than for demonstration, which they viewed as better left to markets. Nonetheless, President Ford sometimes signed demonstration legislation even though he and his staff considered them bad policy. For example, the administration had opposed the modest Solar Heating and Cooling Demonstration Act of 1974, but decided to sign it anyway because they feared a larger one. Furthermore, the bill passed the House 253–2 and the Senate by a voice vote, and so would have easily survived a veto attempt.[44] The ERDA National Plan for R,D&D released in 1976 reemphasized the importance of the private sector and the need for the federal research effort to fit in to it. The federal job was to "establish an appropriate policy climate for private sector action, share risks with the private sector, and conduct a complementary RD&D program."[45]

Despite substantial solar energy R&D funding increases after the embargo, some members of Congress and solar advocates regarded the executive branch as indifferent or hostile to solar energy. One senator alleged that the administration was suppressing an AEC report on solar. Another raised concerns about press reports that, at an early meeting of the R&D Advisory Committee of the Federal Energy Office, the members of the committee laughed derisively at a presentation on solar and wind energy.[46] In fact, most of the top officials in the White House did not consider solar a solution to energy problems in the short- or medium-term.[47] To counter this general perception of his administration's reticence, President Ford and his aides asserted continuously in public that they very much did support solar energy and pointed to increasing budgets as proof. On one such occasion, April 2, 1976, Ford went so far as to claim that he had "increased in next year's budget the research and development funds in solar from about $80 million to $120 million – all that they asked for and more, too."[48] This last claim was not true.

President Ford's February 28, 1976, energy message to Congress outlined his view of the energy situation and the appropriate next steps. The accompanying Fact Sheet devoted a few paragraphs to solar energy. The problem with solar was "its high cost and the abundance of inexpensive alternative fuel sources." His policy for solar contained announcements of the forthcoming request for proposals for siting SERI plus a sharp increase in the solar R,D&D budget for FY 1977.[49]

In terms of budget authority, President Ford proposed a solar energy R&D budget that would increase from $41.9 million in FY 1975 to $160 million in FY 1977, a factor of four in two years.[50] Most of the money would be spent on four groups of technologies. The largest amount,

$45.3 million in FY 1977, went to solar heating and cooling of buildings, the technologies most often associated with solar. The second largest amount, $43.4 million in FY 1977, went to solar thermal electric applications. These large technologies usually concentrate the sun's rays to achieve high temperatures and drive a steam boiler to generate electricity, a form of central station solar electric power plant. The third technology, photovoltaics (PVs), often called solar cells, got $32.8 million in FY 1977, and wind power received $17.1 million.[51] An assortment of other technologies got the rest of the funds.

Note two important points about this distribution of funds. First, ERDA spread its funds widely. With no clear favorite, all technologies received some money. The proportioning of funds differed little from that recommended in Dixie Ray Lee's Atomic Energy Commission (AEC) 1973 report to President Nixon on energy R&D.[52] Second, roughly equal funding went to the types of solar technologies associated with different ideologies. Typically, windpower and heating and cooling of buildings could be installed in a decentralized fashion and were therefore favored by the ecological advocates. Solar thermal electric and PVs were associated more with large industry and high technology, and so sometimes fell under the ecological advocates' attacks. It seems that the government was trying to cover all of the bases in its funding.[53] Nonetheless, this apparent equality of treatment can be deceiving. Both during the Ford and later in the Carter administrations, critics claimed that most of the ERDA solar money went to large corporations. They protested that the many small firms in the solar industry did not have the staffs, sophistication, or other resources to get money from the government, and that the larger corporations were wired into the agencies both by long habit of association and representation on study panels, advisory councils, and the like.[54] These issues caused the schism in the solar movement to grow wider in the coming years.

The Ford administration fought both Congress and ERDA over the solar budget. Congress sought to spend more money, and spend it in a different way, than did President Ford and his advisors. For example, several senators urged Ford to seek supplemental funding for the Federal Energy Administration to start an aggressive solar commercialization program. The administration declined, in part taking the usual tack that the technology was not ready, and so a commercialization program would be premature. It also asserted that the government should not, in any case, seek to "overtake" the private sector – commercialization was none of the government's business.[55] This response showed White House and Congressional disagreement over the status of solar technology and reiterated Ford's normative commitment to keeping the government out of private markets.

In other budget battles, Congress tried, and often succeeded, in adding funds to the energy R&D budget. The appropriations bill for ERDA for FY 1977 passed Congress in early July 1976 with $130 million more for solar energy than President Ford had requested, for a total solar budget of $290 million. OMB officials strongly urged the president to veto the bill (which also contained some unwanted water resource projects), arguing again their two fundamental points. First, the solar program was already amply funded and larger budgets would simply be wasteful, as ERDA already had "large unobligated balances in this program." Second, as always, they argued that such budgets would infringe on the private sector too much, distorting the free market. Even if Ford's veto were ultimately overridden, the OMB saw it as desirable to set the stage for the budget battle the next time around.[56]

The White House also had an ongoing conflict with ERDA over its budget, including its solar budget. Neither the administrator, Robert Seamans, nor his assistant administrator for solar, John Teem, were by any means part of the solar movement. But soon after taking office, they began arguing for larger solar budgets than the White House wanted to give them. In July 1975, the beginning of FY 1976, the White House did not budge, turning down Seaman's request for supplemental appropriations for the solar heating and cooling demonstration program, explaining that such an increase would be premature because there had been no cost-effectiveness study done of the optimal size of the demonstration program.[57] Although it lost that battle, ERDA continued the fight, submitting a FY 1977 budget to OMB that was $1.1 billion in budget authority over the planning target that OMB had set for it. In his cover letter Deputy Administrator Robert Fri was not the least bit apologetic:

The OMB target leaves no room for growth in key programs, many of which are in their initial stages and require substantial increases to develop into effective programs.... Nearly all ERDA programs involve high priority Presidential commitments and objectives.... The timely accomplishment of these program objectives is fundamental to the Nation's energy independence, economic well-being, and national security.

Among the items for which ERDA was fighting was an increase in the solar budget.[58] The conflict took a toll, and John Teem resigned. He said publicly that his disagreements with OMB had affected the timing of his resignation, an allegation that the White House denied.[59]

One Step Forward, Two Steps Back with Carter

Solar energy got top billing in President Carter's first National Energy Plan's (NEP) list of long-term possible sources.[60] The description of solar energy was the same since the 1940s, as having massive potential, possibly great importance, but always a day away, in this case after the year 2000. Nonetheless, the plan described solar space and hot water heating as "ready now for more widespread commercialization" and proposed a set of tax credits to encourage market growth. About a month before the NEP was released, ERDA had chosen a site in Golden, Colorado, for the new Solar Energy Research Institute (SERI), a process that had begun with solar legislation in 1974. The creation of SERI gave solar R&D much more visibility, despite controversy over its operation.[61] The NEP also called for the use of solar in federal buildings as a way to stimulate the market and for increased R&D on technologies that were not yet commercial, such as photovoltaics.[62] This plan depicted solar energy as it had been traditionally by policy makers – as a replacement for fossil fuels that one could simply plug in to currently existing political and technical systems. The plan did not hint that adopting solar energy implied any drastic shift in social or political institutions, or that using solar energy on a wide scale was a means for importing other values into society or politics. Outside of government circles, however, such debates were raging. Government policy toward solar may have been positive, though not as much so as the advocates wanted, but it seemed unaware of the ideological battleground that solar was becoming.

Allen Hammond and William Metz reported in 1977 on the perception that solar was not regarded seriously by important government energy officials. "Indeed, the potential of solar energy is still regarded with skepticism by many government energy officials and publicly discounted by spokesmen for oil and electric utility companies." The budgets for solar were as high as they were because of strong popular and congressional support. Evidence for this skepticism was the relative size of the solar budget compared to the much larger fossil and nuclear budgets. In part, Hammond and Metz attributed this skepticism to solar programs' structure. Government solar energy programs were being done in the nuclear model in the sense that they were funding research aimed at large solar centralized power plants. This approach made solar look bad, according to Hammond and Metz, because solar centralized power plants were not the task for which the technology was most suited.[63]

A group of solar advocates organized a celebration of solar energy, called Sun Day, scheduled for May 3, 1978. President Carter agreed to make a speech on Sun Day. The debate in the White House over his Sun Day speech took place against a backdrop of growing interest in Congress and among numerous constituencies, as well as widespread suspicion that the Carter administration had a weak commitment to solar energy programs, despite their favorable mention in the NEP. Just before Sun Day, an article in the *National Journal,* a publication respected by Washington policy makers, reiterated these themes, particularly that the new Department of Energy was not giving a very high priority to solar and was perceived as hostile by solar advocates:

Inside and outside the Administration there is some dissatisfaction over the Energy Department's treatment of the solar option. The new department seems to be ranking solar among the also-rans in its still-evolving energy supply strategy. [64]

Within the administration, the advice going to the president was mixed. The chair of the Council of Economic Advisors, Charlie Schultze, was strongly opposed to a new solar initiative and generally negative on solar's potential to contribute to the nation's energy supply. He claimed that its costs would remain high and that it would not be an important source of energy in this century:

The exotic sources are a bottomless sink for budget resources and have questionable payoffs. Many of the CEQ proposals (a solar farm in each state) sound romantic, but do not make good budgetary or energy sense. *We should continue to pursue basic research in this area but avoid further unnecessary commitments to unproven exotic sources.*[65]

These and other similar comments framed the solar issue in the way that solar advocates opposed. Schultze called solar technologies "exotic," a term that advocates claimed was no longer accurate and that made them seem distant from commercialization. He branded the CEQ proposals as "romantic," a derogatory appellation in policy circles, and claimed that solar was not important because it did not satisfy economic rationality criteria. The other negative comments on the solar initiatives came, not surprisingly, from the Office of Management and Budget (OMB), which often resists programs that would increase budget expenditures.[66]

In contrast, some White House aides, such as Charles Warren and Gus Speth of the Council on Environmental Quality (CEQ), strongly supported an increased solar program. They urged the president to increase the solar budget, begin a wide-ranging study of solar policy (the Domestic Policy Review of solar energy discussed in Chapter 7), use replacement cost pricing when judging energy investments in federal buildings, and put a solar hot water system on the White House. In addition to conventional criteria, Warren and Speth argued for these initiatives in normative terms:

Not since Earth Day, eight years ago, has there been such a massive, popular statement of support for a new direction in American life. Earth Day marked the acceptance by this country of a new set of values, and Sun Day promises to evoke a similar reappraisal.[67]

This memo began to frame the solar issue in an entirely different way, but it did not spell that frame out completely. Warren and Speth never articulated specifically which values they thought might gain public acceptance due to Sun Day, though clearly they were related to environmental values. They did not mention problems of cost or competitiveness, except for arguing for a new way of calculating such things, and they did not emphasize the value of economic rationality. They simply stated that additions to the FY 1979 solar budget, which the administration had submitted to Congress long ago, were justified "on their merits" and

are essential to a convincing demonstration of Administration commitment. Moreover, budget increases in the solar area are probably inevitable, given Congress' initiatives both to assert its leadership and to ensure consistency with existing programs and goals.[68]

Thus Warren and Speth urged the president to champion a strong solar program to gain leadership in the issue and credibility with an important and growing constituency. This kind of argument does more than try to shift the normative basis of policy debates. If the president accepted Warren and Speth's line of argument, the ownership of this issue would change. Environmentalists, particularly ecological solar advocates, would set the terms of debate, giving them ownership of the issue and making it possible for substantially different values to be pursued as a result of government energy policy. The energy crisis had thrown old problem frames into question, and new ones, along with their accompanying empirical and normative ideas, were competing for top policy makers' attention.

Two other important advisors tried to influence the Sun Day speech. Frank Press, the president's science advisor and the head of the Office of Science and Technology Policy (OSTP), sent the president a memo encouraging him to accept many of the individual program elements proposed by the DOE for the solar initiative, despite OMB opposition. Some of the new proposals would have answered earlier criticisms that the solar program neglected smaller technologies. Press did not suggest that the values that drove solar and energy policy should be changed in any way, though he recognized that criteria other than narrow technical or economic efficiency were important in these decisions. In discussing a dispersed renewable energy technology initiative, he said, "This program has little technological value, although it may be important politically. The program is small. A political call."[69]

Secretary of Energy James Schlesinger also suggested to the president specific new solar programs. Schlesinger supported not only his department's program, but also much of what the CEQ wanted, especially the use of marginal cost pricing in making energy decisions for federal buildings. Schlesinger's memo did not argue that the public was making a radical shift in its values. Instead, he based his decision on the value of economic rationality combined with the need to accommodate a rapidly growing political constituency that had substantial support in Congress.[70]

President Carter delivered his Sun Day speech at the newly chosen site for the Solar Energy Research Institute (SERI) at Golden, Colorado. The final message reflected particularly the advice that he had received from Schlesinger, Schirmer, and Speth.[71] He emphasized the importance and magnitude of the solar tax credits as a way of answering charges that the NEP had little for solar. He also announced plans to put a solar hot water system on the White House, as well as solar energy technologies on some federal buildings. He announced a $100 million boost in the solar budget, the minimum that Schlesinger had said would be credible with solar advocates. In addition, he officially launched the domestic policy review of solar energy, the DPR. He said nothing about Sun Day itself, and made it clear that the driving forces of energy policy were economic and security concerns related to reliance on imported oil, though he also briefly extolled the environmental virtues of solar energy. This speech delivered much that the solar constituency wanted, but made no mention of the values that they championed and gave no hint that the president intended to change the normative basis of energy policy. The ecological solar advocates had begun to come into their own as a political pressure group, but they did not define the energy issue, and hence did not own it.[72]

The events on Sun Day, including the president's speech, received front-page coverage in the national media. Many solar advocates, including some in Congress, had used Sun Day to take the administration to task for having too much emphasis on synthetic fuels and nuclear power in its energy policy. The papers noted that the House Science and Technology Committee had added $150 million onto the administration's original request for FY 1979, more than the president's $100 million.[73]

At about the same time as Sun Day, both the CEQ and the Congressional Office of Technology Assessment released reports on solar energy, both of which argued that solar energy could play a much larger role in the nation's future than conventional wisdom suggested. The CEQ report claimed that the United States could get twenty-five per cent of its energy from solar sources by the year 2000 and half by 2020. Implicit in these claims was a criticism of the administration's policies, which had much more modest goals.[74] Thus, while President Carter participated in and embraced Sun Day more than any of his predecessors had earlier solar events, the growing solar constituency used it to argue that the administration still lacked sufficient commitment to this new source of energy.

Members of the Carter administration debated solar energy policy vigorously throughout Carter's term. The June 1979 dedication of the White House solar hot water system, with its announcement of the twenty per cent solar goal and other results of the solar DPR, marked a zenith in the administration's solar policy. Environmentalists in and out of the administration suffered numerous reversals after that time, beginning with the July 1979 malaise speech that came only a few weeks later. Before that time, administration officials focused on how to build a solar program. After that, solar advocates fought a rear guard action trying to prevent cuts in solar programs.

Prior to July 1979, most of the relevant senior officials in the administration favored building a solar program, associating it with thoroughly conventional values and even suggesting that solar technologies could have a significant impact on energy supplies in the near-term. For example, within the White House, the head of the domestic policy staff and his chief assistant for energy, Stuart Eizenstat and Katherine Schirmer, urged the president to sign a photovoltaics R,D&D bill. The legislation was ambitious and its level of funding was, in their view, excessive. They depicted photovoltaics as just another way of producing electricity, with no normative implications attached to their use. The only problem with photovoltaics was their cost. Eizenstat and Schirmer urged the president to sign the bill because it would do no harm and, more importantly, because signing it would signify the administration's support for the technology, while vetoing it would signal the opposite, and antagonize solar advocates in Congress and the public.[75]

Frank Press, the head of the Office of Science and Technology Policy in the White House, gave the president similar advice, with a heavier emphasis of relying on the market. In a review of assorted DOE and CEQ solar energy initiatives, he recommended accepting many of them, emphasizing research and education and discouraging government commercialization activities.[76] The Department of Energy likewise proposed a package of solar energy initiatives in this period, including research, development, and demonstration projects in photovoltaics, wind, biomass fuels, and small hydropower facilities, along with education and other outreach programs. They also supported "small-scale technology grants" and "a decentralized technology demonstration program," without any indication that these programs might have unconventional normative ideas associated with them. They also claimed that their program would "accelerate commercialization of *renewable* technologies which can pay off in the near term." This remarkable last claim set up solar to fail in the eyes of the president.[77]

The CEQ articulated the only alternative normative vision within the administration, arguing that moving to a solar economy was much more than simply changing technologies. They grounded their argument in the notion that solar was associated with a normative as well as technological transformation, that adopting solar technologies meant putting into place a system that encouraged a different kind of political, social, and ecological life. The CEQ officials were trying to define this issue as one of accepting and encouraging new political, social, and environmental norms instead of simply making an economic calculation. Senior White House officials in previous administrations had never articulated this sort of argument.[78]

CEQ lost the argument. No one else picked up their framing of the issue, and it appeared to play no part in the final presidential decisions. Debates within the administration over solar energy increased during the period of the solar Domestic Policy Review, as described in the previous chapter. Those debates began to change after the president's announcements on the DPR in June 1979 and his "malaise" speech a few weeks later. This latter speech was a turning point in his administration with regard to energy.

Midway through his term, and after repeated setbacks in the energy crisis, including recent shortages stemming from the Iranian Revolution, President Carter began to emphasize factors other than economics in thinking about energy policy. By July 1979 the administration was very unpopular and, in the view of the White House staff, in a crisis. The president cancelled an energy policy speech scheduled for July 5 and instead went to Camp David, where he held a domestic summit, calling in advisors from the government and elsewhere. The president and his top advisors felt the need to redefine his presidency and regain leadership over the crucial issues of the day, especially energy policy.[79] The July 15 speech itself had both normative and programmatic parts. The president spoke of his own failures of leadership, and of the failure of spirit that seemed to be gripping the country. He then posited the energy crisis as the arena in which America could regain its mastery over its destiny, and listed six points as his program for doing so.[80]

He mentioned the twenty per cent solar goal and the Solar Bank as part of his overall program, but that was the only good news for solar advocates. He called for an immediate cut in oil imports and for the creation of two new governmental entities discussed in Chapter 7, the

Energy Mobilization Board and the Energy Security Corporation. The Mobilization Board would be set up to steamroller over any delays in siting crucial energy facilities, including delays caused by environmental regulations. "We will protect our environment. But when this Nation critically needs a refinery or a pipeline, we will build it." These were not sentiments that would appeal to environmentalists. The Energy Security Corporation would be funded by the government to develop synthetic fuels from coal and oil shale, abundant resources but much disliked by environmentalists.[81] In short, the speech repudiated the environmentalists' values. It defined the most crucial problem as importing too much oil and the president asserted his leadership by declaring that the United States would reduce its imports quickly and sharply. This goal bode ill for solar advocates, for there was little that their technology could do to reduce imports in the short-run. The Carter administration was not waiting for the long-term technological fixes, and no longer believed that the emphasis on conservation and efficiency that undergirded the first National Energy Plan was sufficient.

Much attention to the followup to the speech focused on the dramatic way in which Carter fired some of his Cabinet and staff, including the secretary of energy, Schlesinger, whom he replaced with Charles Duncan.[82] However, White House aides were also working on the president's new energy strategy. Patrick Caddell, a private pollster who was also a strategist for the president, sent him a long memo, drafted with the aid of some other unofficial advisers, detailing what such a strategy should look like. In the section on building allies, Caddell listed eight types of groups that the White House should seek as part of its coalition, including governors, mayors, business groups, and labor leaders. Environmental groups were not on the list.[83] White House staff reacted favorably to Caddell's ideas, adding some of their own, emphasizing the need for action, and suggesting that they develop a more detailed plan. A month after Carter's speech, he must have been feeling very frustrated with the time that it was taking to get something off the ground. He wrote in hand on a memo that the staff sent to him: "To Jack and Ham – We seem to be going backward from more specifics to generalities. Let Fritz, Charles, Al, Jack, Ham, Stu, Pat, Larry or someone develop a plan and ACT. Kirbo can help with oil co. support, etc. Enough W.[hite] H.[ouse] memos. J.C."[84]

The administration continued to push its solar program after the July 15 malaise speech, with letters to important legislators and with a meeting with members of the Solar Energy Industry Association (SEIA).[85] The composition of the meeting suggests how far the administration was from the environmental side of the solar movement. The meeting was only for the SEIA, with no one from the Solar Lobby or other environmental solar groups invited. The reasoning for the meeting was that industry would have to push solar heavily, both in terms of investment and marketing, to reach the president's solar goal, and particularly to displace fossil fuels as quickly as possible. The organizations represented were the large firms that had bought or were suppliers to solar businesses, including Libbey-Owens-Ford, Olin Brass, Grumman, and Exxon. "Our agenda is to get the industry to go out and sell solar." This was also a group that was not so averse to the synfuels and Energy Mobilization Board parts of the program of the July 15 speech.[86]

Despite this meeting and other ongoing administration programs, solar energy had become a low priority for the administration. The agenda seemed to be set by events that the president could not control. On November 4, 1979, the Iranians took the American diplomats in Iran hostage, beginning a crisis that would last until President Reagan's inauguration day. That event also signaled the end of Iranian oil sales to the United States, and by December oil prices on the spot market reached $40 per barrel.[87] Events in the White House and the agencies suggested that solar also was being neglected by a range of policy makers, not just at the presidential level. For example, as part of his June 20, 1979, solar speech, the president announced the creation of a Solar Subcommittee to the Energy Coordinating Committee, an interagency organization that included White House staff and was intended to monitor and coordinate solar policy. Despite pressure from the White House, the subcommittee was not even able to schedule a meeting until May 23, 1980, almost a year after the president had announced it.[88] Another blow came when someone leaked to the Solar Lobby a May 17, 1980, confidential memo from Charles Duncan, the secretary of energy. The memo outlined spending plans for a five-year period, from FY 1982 to FY 1986, and called for cuts in solar and conservation spending and increases in nuclear and fossil fuel budgets. Environmental groups called the memo an "outrage" and cited it as evidence that the administration had abandoned solar energy and energy conservation. The DOE acknowledged the memo but denied that it constituted an abandonment of solar, arguing that it was taken out of context and failed to give the larger picture.[89]

The administration's solar program had, by the summer of 1980, come under severe criticism by reports from the Congressional Office of Technology Assessment (OTA) and the General Accounting Office (GAO). In a July 18 memo Speth urged that the White House form a small, high-level group of officials from DOE and the White House staff to recommend responses to these criticisms. However, it was late September 1980 before Eizenstat formed such a task force, which, to my knowledge, never met. In a matter of weeks the issue was moot.[90]

Sources on solar spending in the Carter administration are difficult to interpret, due both to variable reporting conventions and other unexplained inconsistencies among them. Nonetheless, the broad trends are clear and indicate one reason why solar advocates were growing disenchanted with the administration by 1979 and 1980.

When President Carter took office in January 1977, the government was already several months into FY 1977; thus FY 1978 was the first year in which he could have a significant impact on the budget. That impact was dramatic. Research and development budgets leapt up for all solar and renewable energy technologies, including wind and biomass. By one estimate, budget authority increased by fifty-two per cent from FY 1977 to FY 1978. The administration was less generous with solar heating and cooling demonstration programs, cutting them by fourteen per cent.[91] President Carter would not propose such a large jump again. About the time of Sun Day – May 1978 – the administration was considering only a five per cent increase in solar R&D funding for FY 1979 and a further forty-five per cent cut in heating and cooling demonstration funds. They did try to sweeten the deal by proposing a $100 million solar tax credit for FY 1979, and argued that solar hot water and space heating were so close to being commercially viable that the tax credit would do more good than additional demonstration projects.[92]

In May 1979, just before President Carter released the solar DPR, the Department of Energy published the second National Energy Plan. In that document the DOE proposed to increase substantially R&D funds for FY 1980, raising the budgets for photovoltaics, solar thermal electric technologies, and biomass by about twenty per cent or more over FY 1979 levels. The first two technologies were of most interest to electric utilities and large hi-tech firms. Other solar technologies received more modest increases, some less than inflation, and residential heating demonstration programs were once again slated for large cuts. The plan proposed to cut all of the "Solar Applications" programs, such as demonstrations, market research, and training programs, by about eight per cent overall.[93] The ecological advocacy wing of the solar movement could find much to dislike in these proposals, though the more conventional wing, such as firms associated with SEIA, could find more to please them. Since the ecological wing had, in 1979, a larger public presence than SEIA and published its own studies critical of the administration's solar programs, the overall public impression was that the solar movement was growing disillusioned with the Carter administration. The June 20, 1979, speech dedicating the White House solar collectors included the announcement of increases in some solar budgets, but as we saw in the Introduction, it was not enough to mollify the solar advocates attending the ceremony.[94]

The July 1979 malaise speech further eroded relations with environmentalists in general and ecological solar advocates in particular, as detailed earlier. When the DOE sent its FY 1981 budget request to Congress in January 1980, the amounts proposed for solar were not enough to heal the rift. Solar R&D got only a five per cent increase overall, less than inflation, though solar applications got a twenty-eight per cent increase, targeted mainly at training and market testing programs.[95]

Like his predecessors, President Carter had numerous conflicts with Congress over energy. In particular, Congress kept trying to raise the solar energy R&D and applications budget beyond the administration's request. For example, the Senate recommended increasing the DOE's FY 1981 solar budget by twenty per cent more than the administration requested.[96] This congressional intervention meant that DOE officials could consistently look forward to more generous budgets than the OMB wanted to give them.

These solar budget and policy battles, together with the actions of solar advocacy analyzed in Chapters 6 and 7, demonstrate that the White House set policy within a serious set of constraints. The administration had to develop its policies in response to pressures from outside groups, internal advocates, and congressional solar champions. The solar movement as a successful pressure group had arrived in the Carter administration, and considering that some of the very same people had been successful as part of the environmental movement, it seemed that the values they advocated were finally becoming a force to be reckoned with in policy making. And yet their influence declined precipitously well before President Carter left office, and catastrophically once President Reagan moved into the White House. The analysis here shows that the values they advocated and the narratives they used to frame the energy policy issue never penetrated the most senior levels of policy making. Even when members of the group got senior appointments in the Executive Office of the President, they were put into a marginalized office, the CEQ, and had no discernible effect on the way the president and his top advisors framed and decided on policy. Conventional values of economic rationality and national security held sway, and even environmental values crumbled when they came into conflict with them, as demonstrated by the administration's attempt to create the Energy Mobilization Board. If solar advocates saw their technology as a way of encouraging the creation of a new society, they quickly discovered that top policy makers had no interest in those sorts of changes. The durability of institutionalized ideas and the deep conflicts over the meaning of energy technologies go a long way in explaining the fate of solar energy policy during the energy crisis, as discussed in the next chapter.

9

New Technologies, Old Ideas, and the Dynamics of Public Policy

U.S. energy policy makers held remarkably consistent normative and technical ideas (sometimes called values and beliefs) about energy technologies for over three decades. Both types of ideas shaped the problem frame that officials used in thinking about energy policy. Policy elites who thought about the future and about new energy sources conceptualized their problems in terms of economic benefits and national security. Notions of economic benefits changed over time, from the idea that energy should be cheap to promote maximum economic growth to more refined notions that energy markets ought to be efficient to get optimal economic performance. Nonetheless, both notions point to getting energy at the lowest possible price. Discussions of national security emphasized importing oil from sources that would not be interrupted by political acts.

Precisely how policy makers expressed their values and beliefs depended on the contingent circumstances in which they found themselves, but both sets of dominant ideas made for a problem definition that greatly disadvantaged solar advocates. Because of its high market prices, solar was hardpressed to compete with fossil fuels, and because of its diffuse nature, it did not fit into the existing energy production system the way nuclear power promised to do. Although policy makers began to include an assortment of environmental protection values into their frames, that did little to alter the situation.

In addition, normative and technical ideas interacted in complex ways, and the boundary between them was ambiguous and contested.[1] For example, consider the apparently empirical notion held by a White House aide about the infeasibility of solar energy as a major energy source. As cited in the previous chapter, this aide took from a discussion with Congressman Mike McCormack what the aide called a "*Solar* fact" that getting one percent of the country's total energy from solar would require converting ten percent of all houses to solar, and would cost

$70–105 billion.[2] The aide called this a "fact," the most solidly empirical of appellations. And yet, contained within this alleged fact were a number of normative and questionable empirical assumptions. It assumed empirically that the price of solar systems would not go down much. It also assumed normatively that the United States should remain a very high-consumption society, which in itself contains assumptions about the technological possibilities for energy efficiency and the normative desirability of ever-increasing material consumption. Changes in any of these underlying ideas would change this apparently simple "fact."

At a more aggregate level of policy discussions, the normative and empirical ideas became just as enmeshed. As I showed in Chapter 5, Nixon administration officials regarded high levels of energy consumption as normatively desirable, as indicators of a good and progressive society.[3] The empirical fact of high energy consumption became a normative standard. Thus the official energy policy frame made sustaining and enlarging that consumption more than just preserving the empirical status quo; growing energy consumption was a valued social goal, not just an empirical fact. This problem frame stacked the odds against solar energy in normative as well as empirical terms. By this normative standard, the sorts of technological changes that would most enhance solar energy's prospects, particularly large improvements in energy efficiency, look normatively undesirable, whatever their technical feasibility. Conventional energy policy analysts held these intertwined empirical and normative goals deeply, as shown by their bitter attacks on Amory Lovins when he challenged that problem frame, as detailed in Chapter 6.

For thirty-five years solar advocates presented their technologies that used a variety of renewable energy sources as a way to exploit a vast, inexhaustible, but diffuse, resource. Most of them for most of the period did not think that creating a solar society entailed significant social or political change. Hoyt Hottel, Maria Telkes, Farrington Daniels, and the other early solar pioneers of the 1940s and 1950s all sought to make solar affordable, largely with the assumption that it would plug into the existing energy systems, replacing fossil fuels, and enabling society and polity to continue functioning as before, with greater security and, perhaps, less pollution. Most of them saw no contradiction in promoting research and development in both solar and nuclear power, or solar and synthetic fuels, and their only complaint was that nuclear got an unfairly large portion of federal subsidies. A few of them, such as Daniels and Eugene Ayers, sometimes hinted that a substantial change in such a major technological system would affect more than how one heated a room or lit a lamp. But for most of these advocates, solar energy technology offered just another way of securing the status quo against the end of fossil fuels. They sought a new technological system to prevent the social changes that would accompany scarcity.

By the 1970s a new type of solar advocate emerged. These activists came to the technology from a part of the environmental movement that believed that the fundamental structures of society and politics – those concerned with industrial and agricultural production, housing, settlement patterns, and transportation – were, in some deep sense, flawed.[4] These ecological advocates did not simply want any and all solar technologies. They sought technologies that would reinforce and be more compatible with a qualitatively different society and politics, one in which ecological sustainability and local community self-reliance would displace increasing ecological damage, bureaucratic centralization, and anomie. For them, making a drastic change in the energy technology system would be akin to making a legislative change for all of society.[5] Whether the technologies they sought would have given them the society that they desired is not the point here. Rather, the point is that their social goals and ideas about technology as a social force led them to a very different framing of the energy problem and solar's role in it. Within their problem frame, solar was not only a feasible solution to the energy problem, it was the only desirable solution, the only energy technology ensemble that would encourage and strengthen the sort of society that they desired. In their frame, issues such as high initial costs and an immature industry were problems to be solved, not barriers to policy. This shared meaning of solar energy technologies bound together ecological advocates as a social group and drove their choices, leading them to champion smaller, more decentralized solar technologies and to reject schemes like the solar-powered satellites.[6] The problem frame that came out of this meaning led them to regard problems like costs as secondary considerations, just the opposite of conventional frames.

Top-level policy makers never shared that framing of the problem or the normative values that went with it. Their public pronouncements and written internal debates show no hint that they ever even considered this alternative problem frame and set of values. The presidents and their top aides – in every administration – talked about energy almost exclusively in economic and national security terms, with occasional references to narrowly construed environmental values. Even in the Carter administration, no one outside of the Council on Environmental Quality (CEQ) gave any sign that they even thought about some of the more radical alternatives, and they never committed them to paper, suggesting that such ideas were not welcome in policy deliberations.

These facts suggest a new interpretation of solar energy policy, particularly its rapid rise and fall in the 1970s. The conventional explanations for energy policy and solar's failure to establish itself within it do not explain all of the events recounted here. It was not enough that solar was expensive and its future costs were uncertain. That could be said of all future energy technologies, including nuclear energy. And it was not enough that the Reagan administration was ideologically hostile to solar energy. Solar advocates began losing their battles for support while President Carter was still in office, and the ideological explanation begs the question of why Reagan and his people evinced such hostility to solar energy. The association of solar energy with the ecological wing of the solar movement was a phenomenon of the 1970s, not what one might have predicted in the 1950s or 1960s. Perhaps most importantly, the events analyzed here require us to reexamine the pluralist account of solar energy policy. Pluralism must, to explain events adequately, incorporate the importance of ideas, normative and empirical, being institutionalized into official problem frames.

SOLAR ADVOCATES' LIMITED INFLUENCE ON POLICY

Standard notions of American pluralism claim that any organized interest group can influence public policy by mobilizing the appropriate political resources, such as votes, money, public opinion, and the like.[7] From this perspective one can evaluate a group's influence or effectiveness by the extent to which it gets those policy outcomes that it desires. By that measure, the solar movement, particularly the ecological wing of it, appeared very powerful and effective for a brief period in the late 1970s. The question is why it both rose and then fell with such speed. The advocates pushing solar energy did not suddenly lose public support or their ability to argue their case.[8] Instead, the values that ecological advocates associated with solar energy and the solar movement were in stark contrast to the conceptualization of the energy policy problem by top-level decision makers. The official problem frame, and the values that drove it, did not change, despite the considerable efforts of the solar movement to argue for an alternative.

Thus the history of solar energy policy presents anomalies to pluralism. Prior to the energy crisis, prominent scientists, engineers, and businessmen advocated for solar energy, beginning after World War II and continuing for over twenty years. Well-placed within the technical, government, and business community, these advocates should have been influential among important policy analysts and makers. On numerous occasions they were able to make their case to legislative and executive branch officials, including some cabinet secretaries, members of the House and Senate, and, in a few instances, to the president via his top aides. Many of the advocates spoke with the authority of impeccable technical credentials, exemplified by Farrington Daniels, a veteran of the Manhattan Project, member of the National Academy of Sciences, and president of the American Chemical Society. By the middle 1950s such advocacy became formalized with the creation of the Association for Applied Solar Energy (later becoming the International Solar Energy Society and the American Solar Energy Society), broadening solar's constituency to include business people, bankers, and so on.

So why were these groups not more successful? Part of the explanation certainly lies in unfortunate contingent circumstances, such as President Truman's firing Interior Secretary Julius Krug only weeks after Krug had decided to launch a very large solar energy research program. Part of the explanation lies in unpropitious structural circumstances, such as the steady decline in energy prices in the 1950s and 1960s. And part of the explanation lies in traditional interest group analysis. Solar energy did not have the same level of business, scientific, military, or congressional support that nuclear power enjoyed.

But these factors do not constitute an adequate explanation. To develop a better one I have focused on recent policy literature that argues for the importance of ideas, both empirical and normative, in shaping and changing public policy. The case study itself – the history of solar energy policy – demonstrates the importance of ideas, particularly the importance of institutionalizing new problem frames and the technical and normative ideas that go with them. Absent institutionalizing new ideas, substantial, sustained changes in policy remain unlikely.

Prior to the energy crisis, most energy policy concerned disputes between different fuels and the different regions of the country that produced and consumed them. With policy makers accepting a problem frame based in such disputes, solar energy had little to offer except as a possible alternative in the distant future. However, since analysts and policy makers expected future energy demand to be immense, it seemed that future alternatives needed to produce large quantities of bulk energy, a task for which most people considered nuclear power to be better equipped. Policy advisors did frequently note that the government underfunded solar R&D, especially compared to nuclear power, but, absent a pressing crisis, nuclear's better fit with existing problem frames, along with its greater political resources, kept the subsidies flowing, while solar only got research targeted to auxiliary goals, such as NASA's funding for the development of photovoltaics for use on its satellites.

The beginnings of the energy crisis in 1970–1971 coincided with the rise of institutionalized environmental protection values in the form of new legislation and the Environmental Protection Agency to implement that legislation. Those ideas had some effect on energy policy, but not enough to put solar energy at center stage. Nonetheless, Presidents Nixon and Ford began pouring money into all alternative forms of energy, including solar, quickly increasing solar R&D budgets, sometimes as a response to Congressional initiatives. That said, the definition of the energy problem, the way it was framed, as discussed at length in earlier chapters, changed little, merely acquiring a sense of urgency from the energy crisis.

Solar energy policy in the Carter administration shows the difference between successfully pressuring for a policy and successfully institution-alizing a new set of beliefs and values associated with some technology. Those years marked the time when the solar movement was the closest it ever came to being a mainstream movement, claiming to provide a feasible solution to an urgent problem. At the very time that solar technologies were commanding increasing resources, the ecological wing of the solar movement became increasingly influential in policy circles. The Solar Lobby and related groups began to form a very effective pressure group for solar energy, and they clearly got most of what they wanted out of Carter's solar Domestic Policy Review process. But it is equally clear that high-level policy makers never took the advocates' values or framing of the problem seriously. The advocates' political and social issues were never part of official discourse or debate. Even advo-cates' particular conceptions of environmental concerns never penetrated discussions in the White House. Policy makers simply never accepted, at least not in writing or in policy, the notion that the environmental prob-lems related to energy suggested a deeper critique of existing energy, social, and political systems.

The ecological advocates also argued their case in economic terms, but their economic frame of reference, too, was different.[9] They argued, unsuccessfully, for the long-run marginal cost pricing of all fuels, and, in addition, including within the market prices for energy the social costs of consuming it, such as environmental damage. Policy makers had much shorter term concerns on their minds, such as reducing imports and the inflation caused by rising oil prices. If those were the most important questions, then ecological solar advocates had nothing useful to con-tribute. In the short-term, their proposed solutions would have raised prices even more and would not have quickly or significantly reduced oil imports. Solar advocates did not, for all their temporary influence, own this issue, and could not affect the official framing of it. Had the Solar Energy Industries Association (SEIA) wing of the solar movement been the dominant one in policy making, the outcome during the Carter administration would have been little different. They too depended on long-run marginal cost pricing as part of the problem frame to be taken seriously, and they wanted many of the same policies as the ecological wing. However, they had nothing more to offer the administration, even when it reached out to them in July of 1979.

Policy makers could and sometimes did take a longer term perspective, as they did with nuclear power in the 1950s and 1960s. But the pressing nature of the energy crisis in the 1970s made that perspective more difficult to use as a guide for policy, since the existing crisis put great pressure on policy makers for immediate solutions. Moreover, part of a long-term solution linked to solar, such as increasing energy prices to their long-run marginal costs, would have exacerbated the economic impacts of the OPEC-driven price increases. The long-term solution would have made the short-term problem worse. Herein lies a conundrum: Policy makers were most able to establish the conditions for a long-term transition to solar energy when energy policy was not in crisis, but that was when they were least motivated to do so.

Public opinion was also quite limited as a tool for supporting solar policies. As many researchers point out, solar energy enjoyed great public popularity during the last half of the 1970s and into the 1980s. Both Carter's and Reagan's cuts in the solar budget, and their bolstering of other energy technologies, came in spite of strong and consistent public opinion that supported solar energy as preferable to all other alternatives to oil and gas.[10] This fact suggests that public opinion is not related in any simple way to policy outcomes. The first reason is that not all issues are of equal importance to the public. Energy is often not a high-salience issue, compared to crime, inflation, taxes, and similar problems. In survey data taken during the energy crisis, it was not the most important issue, even then falling only somewhere in the middle of people's concerns.[11] Moderately salient issues such as energy have a complicated relationship to public opinion. Often policy makers can ignore public opinion because many of the individuals who may support solar energy, for example, care more about other issues. The attentive public that follows energy policy closely is only a minority of the general public, and only part of this attentive public is trying to influence policy. Thus, while there was broad support for solar energy, that support was not very deep, so solar supporters could only mobilize modest political resources on their behalf.[12] Although President Carter may have been hurt by the loss of environmentalists' support, President Reagan seemed unharmed by antagonizing that same constituency. As a result, the electoral politics of solar and environmental issues did not favor solar advocates at the end of the 1970s.

Failure to redefine the energy issues and inject new values into the debate harmed solar advocates in another way. The limited data from the time suggest that, while a large percentage of the public favored solar, many of those prosolar persons did not share the values that underlay those beliefs for the ecological solar advocates. The public may have liked solar, but they did not widely share the critique of industrial society that went with it. They supported the technology but not the values that the leading advocates promoted. Thus public support for solar energy was not support for the overall positions of the solar advocates.[13]

That policy makers associated solar with the ecological advocates was, from a historical perspective, anomalous. Solar had been promoted by very mainstream people from the end of World War II to the 1970s, and still was, in the form of the Solar Energy Industries Association. That it was, by 1980, generally associated more with ecologically oriented values was a result of a set of complex events detailed in earlier chapters. Solar energy advocacy could have been popularly associated with a different constituency and its values, and so constructed differently. But, as I have argued, that would not have made the biggest difference in the short-run. The real problem was solar advocates' inability to change the official problem frame for energy, leaving both the ecological and conventional solar advocates with a problem definition to which they could contribute little. The ecological advocates may have seized ownership of the solar energy issue, but they never owned the more general energy issue. That is, their definition of the issue never became the official definition of it.[14] They had been unable to institutionalize their values into the top policy-making organizations in the federal government, and so top executive branch officials never took their framing of the energy problem seriously.

THE LIMITATIONS OF ALTERNATIVE POLICY VENUES

This role of ideas and problem framing suggests another limitation of pluralism as an explanatory scheme. Baumgartner and Jones argue that stability or slow incremental change in policy comes from policy monopolies, stable arrangements of executive, legislative, and private sector institutions that agree on interests, values, and problem definitions and allow little or no outside participation. Substantial policy change requires disturbing this monopoly. Usually such change occurs when new policy venues, in the form of different institutions for making policy, take jurisdiction over an issue. The new venue is open to new actors, which means that new values and problem frames can dominate policy making and authoritative actors can take new policy solutions seriously.[15]

The policy history of solar energy presented here makes the case that all policy venues are not equal. Chapter 7 shows the difficulties of using Congress as an alternative venue. For certain types of policy change, it may be necessary to change the values and problem frames in a few highly placed institutions, such as the Executive Office of the President, and in a key executive branch agency. It is not enough to find a few receptive institutions, like the Council on Environmental Quality (CEQ) or new congressional committees, though those certainly help.

My analysis suggests that it was extremely difficult to make major changes in problem frames and institutionalized ideas in the highest levels of the executive branch. As fragmented as the American government is, and as many points of entry as there are to the policy process, the top level of policy making is not permeable by a wide variety of ideas about the nature of and solution to policy problems. While diverse beliefs and values may float around and find a home somewhere in the government, those values have little chance of penetrating key institutions except under special circumstances. Solar advocates thought that they had such circumstances in the form of the energy crisis, but even as President Carter announced the results of the solar Domestic Policy Review (DPR) and the accompanying increases in solar programs, they knew that they had not changed the way the administration thought about the energy problem, and that the new programs were simply the result of the pressure they had brought to bear within a crisis setting. Those successes proved very fragile.

The new institution of energy policy, the Department of Energy (DOE), did largely centralize energy decision making within the executive branch after 1977, a goal of every energy study since the President's Materials Policy Commission of 1952. But the DOE was wedded sufficiently to the legacy of its predecessor, the Atomic Energy Commission, that it was not a brand new institutional venue in which new constituencies could promote their causes on an equal footing with the old ones.[16] In contrast, the agencies and organizations in which solar advocates had more success in institutionalizing such new ideas, mainly the CEQ, exerted little influence on policy.

THE PUBLIC'S ROLE IN IMPROVING ENERGY POLICY

During much of its history, energy policy has been highly exclusionary, comprising systems characterized by very limited participation, as one would expect in a stable policy subsystem.[17] The history of solar energy policy, and attempts to influence the government to take solar seriously, also exhibit this lack of participation. Until the 1970s, the only way that solar advocates could be heard in any part of government was through informal and contingent channels. When Palmer Putnam wrote his solar chapter for Truman's President's Materials Policy Commission, he consulted with as many solar experts as time and funds allowed. In the Eisenhower, Kennedy, and Johnson years solar advocates tried to interest government officials through conferences, speeches, and other forms of publicity about solar, and we have seen how they would sometimes succeed in getting the attention of someone, though never the top officials. In the Nixon and Ford administrations we saw solar advocates slowly gaining greater access to a wider range of government officials, often first through congressional committees and later through agencies like the CEQ and the Energy Research and Development Administration. These contacts reached higher levels and became more formalized in the Carter years, when major solar advocates were able to schedule meetings with the president himself and his top aides, and when some of these advocates became administration officials. Also in the Carter administration, the solar Domestic Policy Review developed a program for extensive public participation, both formal and informal, that reached out broadly to the general public and reached deeply for repeated contacts with key individuals in the solar movement.

However, as I discussed earlier, the public participation program even in the Carter administration was flawed. It did provide a way for solar advocates to apply pressure on the administration, and to get something in return, but the durability of the official energy problem frame made the advocates' job very difficult and prevented their making a lasting change in policy. By allowing new groups into the policy process, the Carter administration did open up parts of the government to new ideas and ways of thinking about energy and changed the dynamics of policy making. And the new programs that the president put in place moved ahead even without his strong support in the last year of his administration. But they were unable to survive the active hostility of the Reagan years. Public participation did not lead to the institutionalization of new ideas relevant to energy policy in key policy-making parts of the government, but rather activists saw those values ignored or relegated to institutions that were not crucial to high-level policy, such as the CEQ. As I have argued elsewhere, a participation program that is truly democratic must include the ability to debate and influence the definition of the problem. Absent such influences, the participation programs achieved only a modest part of their potential and failed to create as democratic a process as they might have.[18]

Another difficulty resulting from the lack of participation, which was historically the case in solar energy, is that it impedes low-cost learning. Woodhouse has argued that the inevitable uncertainties in developing any new technology, or even in controlling an old one, make desirable that the policy process have learning built in, preferably at a low cost. Some types of participation can serve at least part of this policy learning function. Participation can potentially deliver a wealth of both good and bad news about new policies and technologies to citizens and policy makers, if the process is set up to receive and use it. Such participation needs to be fairly profound, including allowing arguments that an entire problem frame is misconceived and needs changing – one of the requirements of democratic theory as well.[19] While participation increased in the Carter years, and some of it did provide some important feedback to policy makers, the nature of that feedback and the ability to interpret and incorporate it into policy decisions was clearly very limited.

Winner's notion of technological citizenship comprises first and foremost political and institutional spaces in which citizens can debate and discuss future technological developments in a broad sense, including the normative goals that they seek to attain by changing and adapting the technological systems around them. Absent such a "moral community" that can make, or at least influence, policy, people are deprived of technological citizenship, even if they have some success as interest groups.[20] Ecological solar advocates at least began the debates appropriate to technological citizenship. They argued intensely over the most desirable forms of society and the relationship of their technological choices to them. Amidst talk of BTUs and thermal efficiencies also arose discussions of ecological stewardship, social equity, decentralization of power, and alienation. Winner's concept of technology as legislation enables us to interpret the linkage of technological choices to social and political structures; solar advocates saw their preferred technologies leading to their preferred social arrangements, which explains why and how they argued for solar energy. That linkage formed the core of their energy problem and its solution.

Solar advocates published their debates as widely as they could, with the issues bursting onto a wider stage with the congressional hearings held on Amory Lovins's work. As those hearings demonstrated, solar advocates' opponents also joined in that wider debate, disputing their social claims as well as their technical ones. Both sides argued as if they saw technology as legislation and were trying to play the role of technological citizen to influence new technological systems and to defend their preferred form of society.

My argument makes no claim about whether the various sides in this debate were correct in their views, or even if their arguments were thought out well. Some of those arguments have since been persuasively critiqued, sometimes by analysts sympathetic to the ecological solar advocates.[21] The key point is that they at least formed the linkages and began the discussion.

Despite these efforts, solar advocates never achieved technological citizenship. A sufficiently open, influential, and authoritative forum eluded them, or perhaps they did not have enough time in the arenas that were available to them. Either way, the values dominant in energy policy remained consistent from the Truman to the Carter administrations, and there was never adequate political space in which alternative visions of society and polity could be articulated and associated with the choices of energy technologies. Solar, when it was discussed at the highest policy levels, was interpreted through those traditional values, and such a problem definition made the task of solar advocates quite difficult. Existing institutions responsible for energy policy showed no interest in changing the policy problem frame or the values associated with it, and new institutions, such as the Department of Energy, also failed to provide a place for such normative debates. Brief appearances at agency or congressional hearings did not enable advocates to change problem frames or policy narratives. Neither did occasional meetings with White House staff or even a sympathetic president.

Changing problem frames means getting a new policy narrative accepted at many levels of society and is a long-term project. A democracy should develop the institutions that provide opportunities for discussing problem frames. Those discussions might well challenge the normative and empirical ideas that shape policy problem frames, for energy issues as for any other. Advocates of different technological systems will need to argue their case at the grassroots as well as the White House levels, and to do so consistently for years, to have their normative and empirical ideas thoroughly considered.

While no crises currently confront energy policy, governments still need to create policies for the future. New technological systems emerging in the coming decades will engender as profound changes in society as such systems have had in the past two centuries. All too often those changes have been wrenching, and all too often they have left us with deep social, political, and environmental problems. The history of solar energy policy shows us that doing better requires a critical examination of all parts of a policy problem, including deeply entrenched institutionalized ideas. Forms of low-cost learning and technological citizenship may be as important to such an enterprise as the technical expertise that we also require. We have only glimpsed the means for accomplishing such lofty goals, but that is no excuse for neglecting them. Our growing technological power requires increasingly democratic and intelligent policies for the future.

Notes

INTRODUCTION

1. Eliot Marshall, "Carter Hails Solar Age in Presolstice Rite," *Science* 205 (6 July 1979): 21–24.
2. Ibid., p. 21.
3. Peter M. Haas, *Saving the Mediterranean: The Politics of International Environmental Cooperation* (New York: Columbia University Press, 1990). For a broad survey of the field, see Peter M. Haas, "Introduction: Epistemic Communities and International Policy Coordination," *International Organization* 46 (Winter 1992): 1–35.
4. John W. Kingdon, *Agendas, Alternatives, and Public Policies* (New York: HarperCollins Publishers, 1984), esp. pp. 75–82, 123–128, and 131–134.
5. Deborah A. Stone, *Policy Paradox and Political Reason* (Glenview, IL: Scott, Foresman, and Co., 1988). Quote is from p. 7.
6. Donald Schön and Martin Rein, *Frame Reflection: Toward the Resolution of Intractable Policy Controversies* (New York: Basic Books, 1994).
7. Hugh Heclo, "Ideas, Interests, and Institutions," in *The Dynamics of American Politics*, Lawrence C. Dodd and Calvin Jillison, eds. (Boulder, CO: Westview Press, 1994), p. 375.
8. Ernst B. Haas, *When Knowledge is Power: Three Models of Change in International Organization* (Berkeley: University of California Press, 1990), pp. 11–14.
9. This has been a staple of the critical policy literature for over twenty years and is now part of the mainstream, yet it is often forgotten or ignored when it comes to analyses of policy arguments. See Harvey Brooks, "The Resolution of Technically Intensive Public Policy Disputes," *Science, Technology, and Human Values* 9 (Winter 1994): 40; Charles E. Lindblom, "The Science of Muddling Through," *Public Administration Review* 19 (Spring 1959): 81; Laurence H. Tribe, "Technology Assessment and the Fourth Discontinuity: The Limits of Instrumental Rationality," *Southern California Law Review* 46 (1973): 635; Kristin S. Shrader-Frechette, *Science Policy, Ethics, and Economic Methodology* (Hingham, MA: Kluwer Academic Publishers, 1985), pp. 73–74.

10. Sheila Jasanoff, *The Fifth Branch: Science Advisors as Policy Makers* (Cambridge, MA: Harvard University Press, 1990), esp. chaps. 1, 5, and 11.

11. Trevor Pinch and Wiebe Bijker, "The Social Construction of Facts and Artifacts: Or How the Sociology of Science and the Sociology of Technology Might Benefit Each Other," in *The Social Construction of Technological Systems: New Directions in the Sociology and History of Technology*, Wiebe Bijker, Thomas P. Hughes, and Trevor Pinch, eds. (Cambridge, MA: The MIT Press, 1987), pp. 18–50, esp. 30–40.

12. For an extended treatment, see Langdon Winner, *Autonomous Technology: Technics Out-of-Control as a Theme of Political Thought* (Cambridge: The MIT Press, 1977), pp. 317–325. The quote is on p. 325, emphasis in original. See also Langdon Winner, "Technologies as Forms of Life", chap. 1 in idem, *The Whale and the Reactor: A Search for Limits in an Age of High Technology* (Chicago: University of Chicago Press, 1986).

13. Edward J. Woodhouse, "Sophisticated Trial and Error in Decision Making About Risk," in *Technology and Politics*, Michael Kraft and Norman Vig, eds. (Durham, NC: Duke University Press, 1988), pp. 208–223; Edward J. Woodhouse and David Collingridge, "Incrementalism, Intelligent Trial and Error, and the Future of Political Decision Theory," in *An Heretical Heir of the Enlightenment: Politics, Policy, and Science in the Work of Charles E. Lindblom*, Harry Redner, ed. (Boulder, CO: Westview Press, 1993), pp. 131–154; Charles E. Lindblom and Edward J. Woodhouse, *The Policy Making Process*, 3rd ed. (Engelwood Cliffs, NJ: Prentice Hall, 1993), pp. 131–134.

14. For detailed justification for participation in technology policy, and a discussion of some of the mechanisms for it, see Frank N. Laird, "Participatory Analysis, Democracy, and Technological Decision Making," *Science, Technology, and Human Values* 18 (Summer 1993): 341–361 and Frank N. Laird, "Participating in the Tension: A Response to Guston," *Social Epistemology* 7 (January 1993): 35–46.

15. Daniel Lee Kleinman, *Politics on the Endless Frontier: Postwar Research Policy in the United States* (Durham, NC: Duke University Press, 1995), esp. pp. 13–14.

16. Schön and Rein, *Frame Reflection*, chap. 2.

17. For example, see John B. Robinson, "Apples and Horned Toads: On the Framework-Determined Nature of the Energy Debate," *Policy Sciences* 15 (1982): 23–45; Irwin C. Bupp, "Energy Policy Planning in the United States: Ideological BTU's," in *The Energy Syndrome: Comparing National Responses to the Energy Crisis*, Leon Lindberg, ed. (Lexington, MA: Lexington Books, D.C. Heath and Co, 1977). The role of normative ideas is perhaps most obvious in the case of controversies over civilian nuclear power plants. See Dorothy Nelkin and Michael Pollak, *The Atom Besieged: Extraparliamentary Dissent in France and Germany* (Cambridge, MA: The MIT Press, 1981) and Spenser R. Weart, *Nuclear Fear: A History of Images* (Cambridge, MA: Harvard University Press, 1988).

18. See, for example, Ian G. Barbour, *Technology, Environment, and Human Values* (New York: Praeger, 1980), esp. pp. 225–231 for a discussion of solar energy and values. A more extended discussion of values and energy technologies is in Ian Barbour, Harvey Brooks, Sanford Lakoff, and John Opie, *Energy and American Values* (New York: Praeger, 1982). For a quantitative discussion based on survey data of values and energy, see W. David Conn, *Energy and Material Resources: Attitudes, Values, and Public Policy*, AAAS Selected Symposium 75 (Boulder, CO: Westview Press, 1983).
19. Langdon Winner, "Building the Better Mousetrap: Appropriate Technology as a Social Movement," in *Appropriate Technology and Social Values: A Critical Appraisal*, Franklin A. Long and Alexandra Oleson, eds. (Cambridge, MA: Ballinger Publishing Co, 1980).
20. Stone, *Policy Paradox*, and Joseph Gusfield, *The Culture of Public Problems: Drinking-Driving and the Symbolic Order* (Chicago: University of Chicago Press, 1981) both provide analytical tools for parsing policy debates. As noted previously, I will combine those tools with the framework from Winner.
21. Schön and Rein, *Frame Reflection*, p. 29.
22. Judith Goldstein and Robert O. Keohane, "Ideas and Foreign Policy: An Analytical Framework," in *Ideas and Foreign Policy: Beliefs, Institutions, and Political Change*, Judith Goldstein and Robert O. Keohane, eds. (Ithaca, NY: Cornell University Press, 1993), pp. 3–30.
23. Frank R. Baumgartner and Bryan D. Jones, "Agenda Dynamics and Policy Subsystems," *The Journal of Politics* 53 (November 1991): 1044–1074, quote from 1044–5. These ideas are elaborated at much greater length in their book, *Agendas and Instabilities in American Politics* (Chicago: University of Chicago Press, 1993).
24. Maarten Hajer, "Discourse Coalitions and the Institutionalization of Practice: The Case of Acid Rain in Britain," in *The Argumentative Turn in Policy Analysis and Planning*, Frank Fischer and John Forester, eds. (Durham, NC: Duke University Press, 1993), pp. 43–76. Quote is from p. 45 and discussion of discourse dominance is from pp. 47–48.
25. See Hajer, "Discourse Coalitions," pp. 69–70, for a more extensive discussion of the importance of top-level political support for significant changes in dominant discourse coalitions.
26. For an introduction to pluralism, the mainstream variant of interest group theory, along with some important critiques of it, see Charles E. Lindblom, "Another State of Mind," *American Political Science Review* 76 (1982): 9–21; Theodore Lowi, "The Public Philosophy: Interest Group Liberalism," *American Political Science Review* 61 (1967): 5–24; John F. Manley, "Neo-Pluralism: A Class Analysis of Pluralism I and Pluralism II," *American Political Science Review* 77 (1983): 368–383; and Albert Somit and Joseph Tannenhaus, *American Political Science: A Profile of a Discipline* (New York: Atherton, 1964).
27. When energy efficiency is left out of the choices, solar or renewable energy is the top choice, and has been at least since 1977. For surveys of such polls, see Barbara C. Farhar, "Public Opinion About Energy,"

Public Opinion Quarterly 58 (Winter 1994): 603–632 and idem, "Trends in US Public Perceptions and Preferences on Energy and Environmental Policy," *Annual Review of Energy and Environment* 19 (1994): 211–239. A more recent poll shows the same results. See Vincent J. Breglio, "Energy: Post-Election Views," December 1994, available from the Sustainable Energy Budget Coalition, 315 Circle Ave, #2, Takoma Park, MD 20912–4836.

28. On the need for historical context, see Loren Graham, "The Specter of Whig History: Why Historians are Suspicious of STS." in *The Outlook for STS: Report on an STS Symposium & Workshop*, Sheila Jasanoff, ed. (Ithaca, NY: Dept. of Science and Technology Studies, Cornell University, January 1992), pp. 35–44.

29. For fossil fuel prices, see U.S. Department of Energy, Energy Information Administration, *Annual Energy Review, 1988* (Washington, DC: USGPO, 1988), p. 65. For solar R&D data for FY 1980 and later, see U.S. Department of Energy, Office of the Comptroller, "Budget Request," Vol. 2, various years.

30. For some of this history see John G. Clark, *The Political Economy of World Energy: A Twentieth Century Perspective* (Chapel Hill, NC: University of North Carolina Press, 1990).

31. Lewis M. Branscomb, "The National Technology Policy Debate," in *Empowering Technology: Implementing a U.S. Strategy*, Lewis M. Branscomb, ed. (Cambridge, MA: The MIT Press, 1993), pp. 1–35, esp. pp. 5 and 15.

32. Stuart W. Leslie, *The Cold War and American Science: The Military-Industrial-Academic Complex at MIT and Stanford* (New York: Columbia University Press, 1993).

33. James J. MacKenzie, "Heading Off the Permanent Oil Crisis," *Issues in Science and Technology* 12 (Summer 1996): 48–54.

34. See, for example, Nancy Cole and P. J. Skerrett, *Renewables Are Ready: People Creating Renewable Energy Solutions* (White River Junction, VT: Chelsea Green Publishing Co., 1995); The Energy Project, Land and Water Fund of the Rockies, *How the West Can Win: A Blueprint for a Clean and Affordable Energy Future* (Boulder, CO: Land and Water Fund of the Rockies, 1996); Christopher Flavin and Nicholas Lenssen, *Power Surge: Guide to the Coming Energy Revolution* (New York: W.W. Norton and Co., 1994); U.S. Congress, Office of Technology Assessment, *Renewing Our Energy Future*, OTA-ETI-614 (Washington, DC: U.S. Government Printing Office, September 1995); Jesse S. Tatum, *Energy Possibilities: Rethinking Alternatives and the Choice-Making Process* (Albany, NY: State University of New York Press, 1995); and John Douglas, "Renewables on the Rise," *EPRI Journal* (June 1991): 17ff.

35. Richard H. K. Vietor, *Energy Policy in America Since 1945: A Study of Business-Government Relations* (Cambridge: Cambridge University Press, 1984) esp. pp. 130–133; James L. Cochrane, "Energy Policy in the Johnson Administration: Logical Order Versus Economic Pluralism," in *Energy Policy in Perspective: Today's Problems, Yesterday's Solutions*, Crauford D.

Goodwin, ed. (Washington, DC: The Brookings Institution, 1981), esp. pp. 381–392.

36. Laird, "Participatory Analysis"; Laird, "Participating in the Tension." For the most sophisticated and extensive defense of democratizing technological decision making, see Richard E. Sclove, *Democracy and Technology* (New York: The Guilford Press, 1995).

37. Hajer, "Discourse Coalitions."

38. Langdon Winner, "Citizen Virtues in a Technological Order," *Inquiry* 35 (Fall 1992): 341–361. Quote is on pp. 354–355.

CHAPTER 1

1. Craufurd D. Goodwin, "The Truman Administration: Toward a National Energy Policy," in *Energy Policy in Perspective: Today's Problems, Yesterday's Solutions* (Washington, DC: The Brookings Institution, 1981), p. 2.

2. Richard H.K. Vietor, *Energy Policy in America Since 1945: A Study in Business-government Relations* (Cambridge: Cambridge University Press, 1984), p. 43.

3. On off-shore oil leases see Vietor, *Energy Policy*, pp. 16–19. See also David Howard Davis, *Energy Politics*, 3rd ed. (New York: St. Martins, 1982), pp. 76–77. On public power and the TVA see Goodwin, "Truman Administration," pp. 180–186. See also Martin V. Melosi, *Coping with Abundance: Energy and Environment in Industrial America* (New York: Knopf, 1985), pp. 200–204.

4. Abstract of Statement by Ralph K. Davies, June 5, 1947, emphasis in original, folder Anglo American Oil treaty #7, Box 14, papers of Ralph K. Davies – Subject File, HSTL. Davies was a consultant to the Department of the Interior and had been a petroleum administrator during the war.

5. Statement by the President, June 30, 1948, folder Public Power, box 50, Democratic National Committee Library Clippings, HST file, HSTL.

6. See the notes on Cabinet meetings for various dates, such as February 4, 1949, and July 14, 1950, box 1, Notes on Cabinet Meetings – White House File, Set 1, Papers of Matthew J. Connelly, HSTL. Discussions of coal in these meetings tended to see it differently, mainly as a labor relations issue.

7. Robert Stobaugh, "After the Peak: The Threat of Imported Oil," in *Energy Future: Report of the Energy Project at the Harvard Business School*, Robert Stobaugh and Daniel Yergin, eds. (New York: Random House, 1979), pp. 17–18.

8. Vietor, *Energy Policy*, p. 43.

9. *New York Times*, January 16, 1948, p. 44.

10. Task Force on Natural Resources, "Resource Policies for a Great Society," November 11, 1964, box 2, Task Force Reports, LBJL.

11. Task Force Committee, "Report to the Cabinet Committee on Energy Supplies and Resources Policy," November 24, 1954, folder Cabinet Committee on Energy Supplies and Resources Policy, box 10, WHCF-Confidential

File, DDEL. The quote is from p. III-4 and the argument about war mobilization is from p. III-12.

12. For the Senate study and industry testimony, see William J. Barber, "Studied Inaction in the Kennedy Years," in *Energy Policy in Perspective: Today's Problems, Yesterday's Solutions*, Craufurd D. Goodwin, ed. (Washington, D.C.: The Brookings Institution, 1981), pp. 319 and 293, respectively. For the FCST study, see Federal Council on Science and Technology, "Research and Development on Natural Resources," May 1963, Oversize Attachments near cover memo June 21, 1963, WHCF, JFKL, pp. 6–7.

13. A detailed discussion of the Interdepartmental Energy study is in James L. Cochrane, "Energy Policy in the Johnson Administration: Logical Order versus Economic Pluralism," in Goodwin, ed., *Energy Policy in Perspective*, pp. 353–54. The Hornig speech is in Address to National Petroleum Council, July 13, 1967, folder Addresses and Remarks by D. Hornig 1967, box 8, Papers of Donald F. Hornig, Dir., OST, LBJL, p. 3.

14. See Goodwin, "Truman Administration Policies Toward Particular Energy Sources," in idem, *Energy Policy in Perspective*, pp. 168–69.

15. See Task Force Committee, "Report to the Cabinet Committee," 1954, p. III-7 and chart 5. See also Vietor, *Energy Policy in America*, p. 163 and Barber, "Studied Inaction," 1981, p. 319.

16. Price data come from U.S. Energy Information Administration, *Annual Energy Review 1988* (Washington, DC: U. S. Government Printing Office, 1988), p. 65. Exactly what the price of energy is at any given time is a complicated question because different fuels have different prices and even the same fuel can vary in price depending on where one buys it. I simply accept the EIA conventions.

17. The price data come from U.S. Energy Information Administration, *1980 Annual Report to Congress*, Vol. Two (Washington, DC: U.S. Government Printing Office, 1981), p. 169, Table 73. Prices are for a residential consumer using 500 kWh per month, inflation calculated using GNP implicit price deflators, 1972 = 100. For a detailed discussion of the strategies and actions of the utility industry, see Richard F. Hirsh, *Technology and the Transformation in the Electric Utility Industry* (Cambridge: Cambridge University Press, 1989).

18. Davis, *Energy Politics*, esp. chap. 3. For the Kennedy and Johnson administrations, respectively, see Barber, "Studied Inaction," and Cochrane, "Energy Policy."

19. Task Force Committee, "Report to the Cabinet Committee," 1954, p. IV-19, recommends an R&D program to help coal become more competitive. For more extensive description and analysis of the various government programs that affected the coal market, see Barber, "Studied Inaction," pp. 316–320, Cochrane; "Energy Policy," pp. 380–392; and Vietor, *Energy Policy*, chap. 8.

20. Samuel P. Hayes, *Beauty, Health, and Permanence: Environmental Politics in the United States, 1955–1985* (Cambridge: Cambridge University Press, 1987), esp. chaps. 1–2. Robert Gottlieb, *Forcing the Spring: the Transfor-*

mation of the American Environmental Movement (Washington, DC: Island Press, 1993).

21. "Energy Resources Study," 11/23/66, p. 2, folder Natural Resources, box 363, White House Aides – Gaither Papers, LBJL.

22. Address by Dr. Donald F. Hornig, Director, Office of Science and Technology, to the National Petroleum Council, July 13, 1967, Papers of Donald F. Hornig, Director, OST, box 8, folder Addresses and Remarks by D. Hornig 1967, LBJL, and Address by Dr. Donald F. Hornig, Special Assistant to the President for Science and Technology, at the 36th Annual Convention of the Edison Electric Institute, Philadelphia, PA, June 4, 1968, Administrative History, OST, box 1, folder Vol. II – Documentary Supplement (2 of 3), LBJL. The latter talk was entitled "Future Energy Needs vs. the Environment."

23. The President's Materials Policy Commission, *Resources for Freedom: Volume I, Foundations for Growth and Security* (Washington, DC: U.S. Government Printing Office, June 1952), pp. vii–viii.

24. Ibid., pp. 2 and 13.

25. Ibid., pp. 1 and 3. Emphasis in original.

26. Ibid., vol. I, chaps. 5 and 25.

27. Ibid., pp. 18–21.

28. Phil Coombs to Staff, August 3, 1951 plus attached paper, folder Memo to staff Aug. 3, 1951 from Mr. Coombs, box 9, President's Materials Policy Commission, Record Group 220, HSTL. Quote is on p. 9 of the paper.

29. The quotes are from Task Force Committee, "Report to the Cabinet Committee," 1954, pp. III-10 and V-1. Many of the most interventionist programs in the Kennedy and Johnson administrations were inherited from the Eisenhower years. See Barber, "Studied Inaction," and Cochrane, "Energy Policy in the Johnson Administration," as well as Vietor, *Energy Policy in America*, chaps. 6–8.

30. Deborah A. Stone, *Policy Paradox and Political Reason* (Glenview, IL: Scott, Foresman, and Co., 1988). See Chapter 4 for her discussion of the various meanings of security.

31. Goodwin, "Truman Administration," pp. 10–16.

32. National Security Resources Board, "A Recommendation to the President on Steps and Measures Essential to the Fulfillment of the National Security Program," folder Agencies – National Security Resources Board, box 146, President's Secretary's Files – Subject Files, HSTL.

33. Ibid., pp. 2–3 and 5–8.

34. Robert L. Dennison to the President, October 17, 1949, folder Agencies – National Security Resources Board, box 146, President's Secretary's Files – Subject Files, HSTL. Petroleum was not one of the resources that would be inadequate in supply, but it was one of the ones considered, indicating its importance.

35. For the latter, see Harold L. Ickes, "An Oil Policy: An Open Letter to the Members of the Congress of the United States," May 30, 1947, folder #7 – Anglo-American Oil Treaty, box 14, Papers of Ralph K. Davies: Subject

File, HSTL, esp. pp. 23–24. For an example from Truman see Statement by the President, June 30, 1948, folder Public Power, box 50, Democratic National Committee Library Clippings, HST file, HSTL.

36. See John McCormick, *Reclaiming Paradise: The Global Environmental Movement* (Bloomington, IN: Indiana University Press, 1989), pp. 25–27 for the history of the origins of the conference.

37. *Proceedings of the United Nations Scientific Conference on the Conservation and Utilization of Resources*, 17 August–6 September, 1949, Lake Success, New York, Volume I, Plenary Meetings (Lake Success, NY: United Nations Department of Economic Affairs, 1950), doc. E/CONF. 7/7. Quotes are from p. vii. Numbers of attendees are discussed on pp. ix–x.

38. Ibid., p. 2. For another example, see Fairfield Osborne's plenary speech, p. 13. Osborne was the president of both the New York Zoological Society and the Conservation Foundation.

39. Task Force Committee, "Report to the Cabinet Committee," 1954, p. V-1.

40. Task Force Committee, "Report to the Cabinet Committee," 1954, pp. III-8 to III-9.

41. *United Nations Scientific Conference*, 1949, vol. 1, p. 4.

42. PMPC, *Resources for Freedom*, vol. 1, p. 1 for both quotes.

43. This discussion of the causal stories is based on the framework developed in Deborah A. Stone, "Causal Stories and the Formation of Policy Agendas," *Political Science Quarterly* 104 (Summer 1989): 281–300. See also Stone, *Policy Paradox*, chap. 8.

44. Years later, those notions of microbehavior having unintended macrooutcomes, and of individually rational actions leading to collectively irrational outcomes, would be developed rigorously by Mancur Olson, *The Logic of Collective Action; Public Goods and the Theory of Groups* (Cambridge, MA: Harvard University Press, 1965) and Thomas C. Schelling, *Micromotives and Macrobehavior*, (New York: Norton, 1978).

45. Stone, "Causal Stories," p. 285.

46. President Lyndon B. Johnson, Remarks at the Holy Cross Commencement, Worcester, Massachusetts, June 10, 1964, Administrative History, Office of Science and Technology, box 8, folder OST, Vol II, Documentary Supplement, LBJL. Also available in *Public Papers of the President*.

47. At the time people often used the terms science and technology interchangeably, though from the context it is clear that they usually meant technology, the term I will use. Some people went further and used the term technology as if they were referring to an actor. I am aware of the pitfalls of such usage, but I quote it uncritically because my purpose is to understand how they were understanding their world and framing their problems.

48. *United Nations Scientific Conference*, 1949, Vol. 1, p. 2, speech of Secretary General Trygve Lie.

49. Ibid., Vol. 1, p. xvii.

50. Memorandum, Coombs to Staff, August 3, 1951, box 9, folder "memo to staff Aug. 3, 1951 from Mr. Coombs." President's Materials Policy Commission, HSTL.

51. The quotes are from PMPC, Vol. I, pp. 131 and 133, respectively. For the views of the executive director of the report, see Coombs to staff, August 3, 1951 and attached report, p. 17.

52. Federal Council for Science and Technology, "Research and Development on Natural Resources," May 1963, oversize attachments, near cover memo 6/21/63, WHCF, JFKL. Emphasis in original.

53. Trevor Pinch and Wiebe Bijker, "The Social Construction of Facts and Artifacts: Or how the Sociology of Science and the Sociology of Technology Might Benefit Each Other," in *The Social Construction of Technological Systems: New Directions in the Sociology and History of Technology*, Wiebe Bijker, Thomas P. Hughes, and Trevor Pinch, eds. (Cambridge, MA: The MIT Press, 1987), pp. 18–50.

54. Thomas P. Hughes, "The Evolution of Large Technological Systems," in *The Social Construction of Technological Systems: New Directions in the Sociology and History of Technology*, Wiebe Bijker, Thomas P. Hughes, and Trevor Pinch, eds. (Cambridge, MA: The MIT Press, 1987), pp. 51–82.

55. There are, of course, a few cases in which government agencies have themselves built systems, particularly in the areas of defense. As we will see in the next chapter, some government officials wanted the government to take a more aggressive role as a systems builder in the case of nuclear power. But for the cases analyzed here, policy makers' role was that of setting rules and allocating resources.

56. Stone discusses the importance of ambiguity in politics, that it makes possible coalitions that otherwise might fall apart. Thus ambiguity about parts of administration policy is not necessarily bad. See Stone, *Policy Paradox*, chap. 6.

CHAPTER 2

1. For a sampling of the literature on the development of nuclear energy, see Brian Balogh, *Chain Reaction: Expert Debate and Public Participation in American Commercial Nuclear Power, 1945–75* (Cambridge: Cambridge University Press, 1991); Joseph G. Morone and Edward J. Woodhouse, *The Demise of Nuclear Energy? Lessons for Democratic Control of Technology* (New Haven, CT: Yale University Press, 1989); and John L. Campbell, *Collapse of an Industry: Nuclear Power and the Contradictions of U.S. Policy* (Ithaca, NY: Cornell University Press, 1988).

2. See William D. Metz, "Oil Shale: A Huge Resource of Low-Grade Fuel," and Arthur M. Squires, "Clean Fuels from Coal Gasification," both in *Energy: Use, Conversion, and Supply*, Philip H. Abelson, ed. (Washington, DC: American Association for the Advancement of Science, 1974), and Richard H.K Vietor, *Energy Policy in America Since 1945: A Study of Business-Government Relations* (Cambridge: Cambridge University Press, 1984), pp. 45–46.

3. For an excellent, detailed history of the synfuels program, see Vietor, chap. 3.

4. Ibid, pp. 49–50.
5. President's Materials Policy Commission, *Resources for Freedom: Volume IV, The Promise of Technology* (Washington, DC: U.S. Government Printing Office, June 1952), pp. 171–178.
6. *New York Times*, January 14, 1948, p. 1, and January 28, 1948, p. 1.
7. *New York Times*, May 22, 1948, p. 28.
8. *New York Times*, May 9, 1949, p. 1.
9. Vietor, *Energy Policy*, pp. 51–61.
10. Press Release, The White House, July 30, 1954, folder 134-H Presidential Advisory Committee on Energy Supplies and Resources Policy, box 684, WHCF – Official Files, DDEL.
11. Executive Office of the President, Office of Defense Mobilization, *Report to the Cabinet Committee on Energy Supplies and Resources Policy*, November 24, 1954, esp. pp. IV-18 to IV-19 and V-3, folder Cabinet Committee on Energy Supplies and Resources Policy, box 10, WHCF – Confidential File, DDEL. Document declassified 11/7/84.
12. Federal Council for Science and Technology, *Research and Development on Natural Resources*, Report prepared by the Committee on Natural Resources, May 1963, WHCF – Oversize Attachments, near cover memo 6/21/63, JFKL.
13. For example, see the stories about Krug and quotes from him in the *New York Times*, "Oil From Coal and Shale Urged by Krug to Bar Crisis," 1/14/48, p. 1; "Strong Forces in Congress Urge Oil Export Embargo," 1/27/48, p. 1; "Oil-From-Coal Plant Dedicated by Krug," 5/22/48, p. 28; "Krug Backs Loans for Synthetic Oil," 2/2/49, p. 41; and "Expansion in Synthetic Fuels Called Vital to U.S. by Krug," 3/28/49, p. 1.
14. For the analysis of policy narratives, see Deborah Stone, *Policy Paradox and Political Reason* (Glenview, IL: Scott, Foresman, and Co., 1988), p. 116.
15. "Oil-From-Coal Plant Dedicated By Krug," *New York Times*, 5/22/48, p. 28.
16. Sometimes energy production was not even mentioned. For example, see statement by the President on the Atomic Energy Commission, August 1, 1949, folder Atomic Energy, box 12, Democratic National Committee Library Clippings, Subject File, HSTL. At other times it was, such as when Truman would claim that military applications would have civilian spinoffs, such as power reactors from the development of reactors for submarines. See *New York Times*, June 15, 1952, p. 56, which carries Truman's speech while dedicating the keel-laying of the Nautilus.
17. Energy Resources Group, "Use of Atomic Energy for Electric Power," Discussion paper, PMPC, July 16, 1951, pp. 1–4, folder Commodity – Energy, box 113, President's Materials Policy Commission: 1951–52, Record Group 220, HSTL.
18. President's Materials Policy Commission, *Resources for Freedom: Volume III, the Outlook for Energy Sources* (Washington, DC: U.S. Government Printing Office, June 1952). Quote is from p. 39.

19. Report of the General Advisory Committee of the Atomic Energy Commission to the President, June 14, 1952, p. 2, folder AEC – Gordon Dean, box 112, President's Secretary's Files – General File, HSTL.
20. For an account of the Atomic Energy Commission at this time, see Richard G. Hewlett and Francis Duncan, *Atomic Shield 1947/1952: Volume II of a History of the United States Atomic Energy Commission* (University Park, PA: The Pennsylvania State University Press 1969), esp. chap. 2.
21. Hewlett and Duncan, *Atomic Shield*, pp. 497–498.
22. Charles Moritz, ed., *Current Biography Yearbook 1965* (New York: W.H. Wilson Co, 1965), pp. 106–107. For more detail, see Olive Bell Daniels, *Farrington Daniels: Chemist and Prophet of the Solar Age* (Madison, WI: privately pub., 1978), chap. 9.
23. For discussions of the overall purposes of the speech, see Memorandum, James M. Lambie to General Cutler, July 29, 1953, folder Candor and United Nations Speech #1, box 12, Central Files – Subject Series, DDEL, and Memorandum, James M. Lambie, Jr., to Governor Adams, August 5, 1953, folder Candor and UN Speech #13, box 13, Central Files – Subject Series, DDEL.
24. Memorandum, Philip H. Watts to the Ad Hoc Committee on Armaments and American Policy, plus attached draft of speech, June 17, 1953, folder Candor and UN Speech #18, box 13, Central Files – Subject Series, DDEL.
25. Memorandum, C. D. Jackson to R. Gordon Arneson, September 2, 1953, plus attached speech draft, folder Candor and United Nations Speech #10, box 12, Central Files – Subject Series, DDEL.
26. U.S. President, *Public Papers of the Presidents of the United States* (Washington, DC: Office of the *Federal Register*, National Archives and Record Service, 1953) Dwight D. Eisenhower, 1953, pp. 813–822, quote from p. 820.
27. Morone and Woodhouse, *Demise of Nuclear Energy*, pp. 42–45.
28. Lewis Strauss to the President, 22 October 1957, folder Atomic Energy Commission #1 (1957), box 5, Administrations Series/Whitman Files, DDEL. Strauss, chairman of the AEC at the time, was unimpressed by the former officials' criticisms. See also Walter P. Reuther, *Atoms for Peace: A Separate Opinion on Certain Aspects of the Report of the Panel on the Peaceful Uses of Atomic Energy*, sent to the Joint Congressional Committee on Atomic Energy (n.p.: United Auto Workers, January 25, 1956), pp. 2–3.
29. For a basic history of the Kennedy nuclear policies, see William J. Barber, "Studied Inaction in the Kennedy Years," in *Energy Policy*, Goodwin, ed., pp. 324–330.
30. The President's letter is contained in the report itself. U.S. Atomic Energy Commission, *Civilian Nuclear Power: A Report to the President – 1962* (n.p.:n.p., November, 1962). The construction figures are on p. 12. The report is available as Appendix 12 of U.S. Congress, Joint Committee on Atomic Energy, *Development, Growth, and State of the Atomic Energy Industry*. 88th Cong., 1st. Sess., Feb. 20–21, 1963. The letter from the committee about the draft report is also attached as Appendix 15.

31. Memorandum, President Kennedy to Secretary of the Interior, et al., re. Interdepartmental Energy Study, February 15, 1963, folder NR 3-21-62, box 641, WHCF – Subject Files, JFKL.
32. Joint Committee, *Atomic Energy Industry*, 1963, esp. pp. 57–59 and 67–68.
33. Memorandum, Jerome Wiesner to Mr. Bundy, April 2, 1963, folder Office of Science and Technology, 3/63–11/63, box 284, National Security Files, Departments and Agencies, JFKL.
34. Barber, "The Kennedy Years," pp. 324–330.
35. Glenn T. Seaborg (AEC) to Mr. Douglass Cater (Special Asst. to the Pres.), May 21, 1964, plus attached analysis, folder AT 2, box 2, WHCF; Marguerite Owen (TVA) to Douglass Cater, May 25, 1964, folder AT 2, box 2, WHCF; Donald Hornig (OST) to George Reedy, June 19, 1964, folder AT 2 3/1/64–9/4/64, box 2, WHCF. All at the LBJL.
36. For a discussion of particular types of policy narratives, see Stone, *Policy Paradox*, chap. 6.
37. In addition to the sources previously cited, see Michael Smith, "Advertising the Atom," in *Government and Environmental Politics: Essays on Historical Developments Since World War Two*, Michael J. Lacey, ed. (Washington, DC and Baltimore, MD: The Woodrow Wilson Center Press and the Johns Hopkins University Press, 1989), pp. 232–262, for a discussion of the government's and nuclear industry's public relations campaign for civilian nuclear power. Brian Balogh depicts in detail the changing interpretation and importance of national security as a justification that the AEC used to promote civilian nuclear energy. See his *Chain Reaction*, chap. 4, especially pp. 95–110.
38. See Balogh, *Chain Reaction*, cited in footnote 37.
39. Merritt Roe Smith, "Technology, Industrialization, and the Idea of Progress," in *Responsible Science: The Impact of Technology on Society*, Kevin B. Byrne, ed., Nobel Conference XXI (San Francisco: Harper and Row, 1986), pp. 1–20. On technological choices, see Eric Schatzberg, "Ideology and Technical Choice: The Decline of Wooden Airplanes in the United States, 1920–1945," *Technology and Culture* 35 (January 1994): 34–69.
40. Langdon Winner, "Technological Frontiers and Human Integrity," in *Science, Technology, and Social Progress*, Steven L. Goldman, ed., Research in Technology Studies, Vol. 2 (Bethlehem, PA and London: Lehigh University Press and Associated University Presses, 1989), pp. 48–64.
41. David O. Woodbury, *Atoms for Peace* (New York: Dodd, Mead & Company, 1955). The quote is from p. 11.
42. Gordon Dean, *Report on the Atom: What You Should Know About the Atomic Energy Program of the United States* (New York: Alfred A. Knopf, 1953), p. 321. See also pp. 182–183 and 313–315.
43. Smith, "Advertising the Atom," esp. pp. 241–248.
44. AEC, *Civilian Nuclear Power*.
45. See Memorandum, Wiesner to Bundy, April 2, 1963; Wiesner's testimony in Joint Committee, *Atomic Energy Industry*, 1963; Memorandum, Kennedy to Secretary of the Interior, et al., February 15, 1963; U.S., Exec-

utive Office of the President, Office of Science and Technology, Federal Council for Science and Technology, *Research and Development on Natural Resources*, May 1963, esp. chaps. 1–2 and Appendix A.

46. Trevor J. Pinch and Wiebe E. Bijker, "The Social Construction of Facts and Artifacts: Or How the Sociology and Science and the Sociology of Technology Might Benefit Each other," in *The Social Construction of Technological Systems: New Directions in the Sociology and History of Technology*, Wiebe E. Bijker, Thomas P. Hughes, and Trevor Pinch, eds. (Cambridge, MA: The MIT Press, 1987), pp. 17–50. Note that this notion of shared meaning is slightly different from the one that Pinch and Bijker propound, which is based on different designs of the same technology.

47. See Morone and Woodhouse, *Demise*, and the arguments and sources cited in Part II.

48. *Proceedings of the United Nations Scientific Conference on the Conservation and Utilization of Resources*, 17 August–6 September, 1949, Lake Success, New York, volume I, Plenary Meetings (Lake Success, NY: United Nations Department of Economic Affairs, 1950), doc. E/CONF. 7/7, p. 7. Most of the rest were related to nonenergy resources.

49. A. M. Rosenthal, "U.S. Seeks to Harness Sun, May Ask Big Fund, Krug Says," *New York Times* 8/27/49, p. 1. Curiously, most of the article discusses his plans for synfuels, despite the headline.

50. Goodwin, "Truman Administration," p. 46. On the resignation, see the *New York Times*, November 11, 1949, p. 1. Krug disagreed with Truman about land reclamation policies.

51. Lamont C. Hempel, "The Politics of Sunshine: An Inquiry into the Origin, Growth, and Ideological Character of the Solar Energy Movement in America," Ph.D. dissertation, Claremont Graduate School, 1983, pp. 72–74.

52. The background on Krug's life comes from his obituary in the *New York Times*, March 28, 1970, p. 27. On his appointment as Secretary of the Interior and the laudatory piece about him, see *New York Times*, February 27, 1946, pp. 1 and 4.

53. See, for example, *New York Times*, June 18, 1947, p. 43; January 16, 1948, p. 1; and February 6, 1948, p. 1.

54. PMPC, Vol. I. Quotes are from pp. 14–15 and p. 129.

55. Some of the PMPC's internal studies and deliberations considered solar energy and concluded that only solar domestic heat and hot water could have any importance in the next twenty-five years. See Bertrand A. Landry and Russell W. Dayton, "Role of Technology in the Future of Unconventional Sources of Energy," report no. 6 of Group IV to the President's Materials Policy Commission, September 21, 1951, Battelle Memorial Institute, in folder Reports and Studies, Battelle Reports, box 36, President's Materials Policy Commission 1951–52, Record Group 220, HSTL. Draft chapter is in "Materials for a Free World – Possibilities of Solar Energy," folder Comments on Drafts of Report – General – Solar Energy, box 31, President's Materials Policy Commission, Executive Secretary, HSTL.

56. "The Possibilities of Solar Energy," chap. 15 in President's Materials Policy Commission, *Resources for Freedom: Vol. IV, The Promise of Technology* (Washington, DC: U.S. Government Printing Office, June 1952), pp. 213–220. The quote is from p. 217.
57. Task Force Report, 1954, p. III-15.
58. Orme Lewis to Nelson Rockefeller, Special Assistant to the President, August 18, 1955, plus attached speech by Spaght, folder 146-G Solar Energy, box 744, WHCF – Official Files, DDEL; Bernard M. Shanley, Secretary to the President, to Howard Pyle, Deputy Assistant to the President, September 6, 1955, plus attached letter, Pyle to Shanley, August 29, 1955, folder 146-G Solar Energy, box 744, WHCF – Official Files, DDEL.
59. Pyle to Shanley, August 29, 1955.
60. Bryce Harlow to General Parsons, n.d. but ca. September 9, 1955, with attached letter, folder 308 – World Symposium on Applied Solar Energy, box 929, WHCF – Official Files, DDEL.
61. Dwight D. Eisenhower to Lewis W. Douglas, October 26, 1955, folder 308 World symposium on Applied Solar Energy, box 929, WHCF – Official Files, DDEL.
62. FCST, *Research and Development on Natural Resources*, p. 33.
63. Ibid., pp. 47–50. Quote on p. 49.
64. PMPC, Vol. I, p. 169. For early internal discussions that frame the issue in this way, see Coombs to Staff, August 3, 1951, p. 7, and "Energy Resources, Major Problems and Issues," internal report, July 9, 1951, folder Energy Resources: Major Problems and Issues, box 11, President's Materials Policy Commission, 1951–52, HSTL.
65. PMPC, Vol. IV, p. 220.
66. Coombs to staff and attached report, August 3, 1951, p. 18.
67. PMPC, Vol. I, pp. 106 and 137. "Discussion of Energy Area Report – Second Draft – By Commission Members," p. 4 [meeting transcript], September 26, 1951, folder General File – Energy – Confidential, box 121, President's Materials Policy Commission 1951–52, HSTL. The early draft is "The Challenge of Energy," Chapter I, Volume I, Energy Section, Schwartz/Coombs, April 8, 1952, folder Previous Drafts Combined, Energy (Vol. I., April 1952), box 22, President's Materials Policy Commission, 1951–52, HSTL.
68. Halacy, *The Coming Age of Solar Energy*, pp. 66–67 and 85–98. Contracted research dates back at least before 1955. See D. Trivich, Paul A. Flinn, and H. J. Bowlden, "Photovoltaic Cells in Solar Energy Conversion," in *Solar Energy Research*, Farrington Daniels and John A. Duffie, eds. (Madison, WI: The University of Wisconsin Press, 1955), p. 149.
69. FCST, *Research and Development on Natural Resources*, p. 47.
70. For example, see figures cited below.
71. FCST, *Research and Development on Natural Resources*, p. 21 and Table 2, p. 30.
72. These data come from ibid., pp. 35–37. These tables are labeled "expenditures" which I assume refers to budget outlays, and I also assume, lacking evidence to the contrary, that the figures are in current dollars. I have been

unable to assemble a consistent, reliable time series of government R&D funding for solar energy going back into the 1940s, 1950s, and 1960s. The numbers floating around in the literature are contradictory and often without references to reliable primary sources. The available Bureau of the Budget (later Office of Management and Budget) documents do not disaggregate the budget in a way that is useful until the mid-1970s. The FCST study used here is better than other sources because it was an internal study, done by high-level officials in the agencies that were funding the research and development. The people involved in the study were the same people who prepared budget requests for their agencies and executed the budgets once they were passed by Congress. Unfortunately, the study only includes data from three fiscal years. The data presented here show that funding was much higher in the 1960s than the $100,000 many people quoted in the 1970s. For general descriptions of solar sources, see, for example, Eugene Ayres and Charles A. Scarlott, *Energy Sources: The Wealth of the World* (New York: McGraw-Hill, 1952) or William D. Metz and Allen L. Hammond, *Solar Energy in America* (Washington, DC: AAAS, 1978).

73. National Aeronautics and Space Administration, *Eighth Annual Report to Congress*, July 1–December 31, 1962, Washington, DC, pp. 91–92. Located in folder FG260 9-26-62, box 176, WHCF – Subject, JFKL.
74. FCST report, 1963, p. 37.

CHAPTER 3

1. For a detailed history of the uses of solar technologies dating back to the ancient Greeks, see Ken Butti and John Perlin, *A Golden Thread: 2500 Years of Solar Architecture and Technology* (New York: Van Nostrand Reinhold, 1980).
2. Palmer Coslett Putnam, *Power From The Wind* (New York: D. Van Nostrand Co., Inc., 1948). Putnam gives a history of the project in Chapter 1.
3. Ibid., and Foreword by Beauchamp E. Smith, pp. v–vi.
4. F. A. Brooks, "The Use of Solar Energy for Heating Water," in *Annual Report of the Smithsonian Institution: 1938* (Washington, DC: U.S. Government Printing Office, 1939), pp. 157 and 181.
5. Jerome E. Scott, Ronald W. Melicher, and Donald Sciglimpaglia, *Demand Analysis, Solar Heating and Cooling of Buildings, Phase I Report: Solar Water Heating in South Florida: 1923–1974*, Report No. NSF-RANN-74-190 (Washington, DC: U.S. Government Printing Office, 1974), pp. 3–6. See also Butti and Perlin, *A Golden Thread*, pp. 148–154.
6. Federal Public Housing Authority, "Public Housing Design: A Review of Experience in Low-Rent Housing," National Housing Agency, June, 1946, pp. 234–35.
7. Scott et al., *Solar Water Heating*, pp. 21–30, and Butti and Perlin, *Solar Architecture and Technology*, pp. 154–155.
8. Mary Davis Gillies, *McCall's Book of Modern Houses* (New York: Simon and Schuster, 1951), first ed., 1945. See the Foreword, examples of different homes, and p. 169.

9. Butti and Perlin, *A Golden Thread*, pp. 190–195.
10. Hoyt C. Hottel, "Artificial Converters of Solar Energy," in *Annual Report of the Board of Regents of the Smithsonian Institution, 1941* (Washington, DC: U.S. Government Printing Office, 1942), pp. 151–162. The quote is from p. 159.
11. Farrington Daniels, *Direct Use of the Sun's Energy* (New Haven, CT: Yale University Press, 1964; paperback ed., New York: Ballantine Pub., 1974). For a list of technologies, see his table of contents. On photovoltaics, see pp. 207 and 213.
12. Merritt L. Kastens, "The Economics of Solar Energy," in A. M. Zarem and Duane D. Erway, *Introduction to the Utilization of Solar Energy* (New York: McGraw-Hill Book Company, Inc., 1963), pp. 211–237. Kastens also claimed that the U.S. market for solar water heaters was still going up, from about 3 million units in 1954 to about 4.5 million units in 1960. Two-thirds of those units were replacements.
13. Trevor Pinch and Wiebe Bijker, "The Social Construction of Facts and Artifacts: Or How the Sociology of Science and the Sociology of Technology Might Benefit Each Other," in *The Social Construction of Technological Systems: New Directions in the Sociology and History of Technology*, Wiebe Bijker, Thomas P. Hughes, and Trevor Pinch, eds. (Cambridge, MA: The MIT Press, 1987), pp. 18–50.
14. See Frank N. Laird, "Constructing Future Technologies," under review.
15. Hottel, "Artificial Converters," p. 151.
16. For examples of analysis of the narratives that often underlie policy pronouncements, see Joseph R. Gusfield, *The Culture of Public Problems: Drinking, Driving and the Symbolic Order* (Chicago: University of Chicago Press, 1981), chap. 4; and Deborah A. Stone, *Policy Paradox and Political Reason* (Glenview, IL: Scott-Foresman and Co., 1988), chap. 6.
17. Hutchinson did research on passive solar houses, and concluded that they may be net money losers in terms of heating costs. See F. W. Hutchinson, "The Solar House: A Full-Scale Experimental Study," *Heating and Ventilating* 42 (September 1945): 96–97; idem, "The Solar House: A Research Progress Report," *Heating and Ventilating* 43 (March 1946): 54–56; idem, "The Solar House: A Second Research Progress Report," *Heating and Ventilating* 44 (March 1947): 55–59. One could critique Hutchinson's experiments in a number of ways. The point here is that he was a well-established, published researcher who belonged in the skeptical camp.
18. *Proceedings of the World Symposium on Applied Solar Energy*, Phoenix, Arizona, November 1–5, 1955 (Menlo Park CA: Stanford Research Institute, 1956), p. 26. The "Sun for Man's Use" Conference was held by the AFASE immediately prior to this symposium. It was a much more technical conference.
19. Jean Smith Jensen, "Harnessing the Sun Around the World," *The Sun At Work* 4 (March 1959): 3–7.
20. See Gusfield, *Culture of Public Problems*, pp. 10–11.
21. Ethan Barnaby Kapstein, "The Solar Cooker," *Technology and Culture* 22 (January 1981): 115. See also Olive Bell Daniels, *Farrington Daniels:*

Chemist and Prophet of the Solar Age (Madison, WI: priv. pub., 1978), esp. chap. 11 and p. 344 for the ACS and the NAS, respectively.

22. Farrington Daniels, "Solar Energy," *Science* 109 (January 21, 1949): 51–57. Quotation from p. 51. Emphasis in original.

23. Stone, *Policy Paradox*, pp. 109–113.

24. See Laird, "Constructing the Future," for a more detailed analysis of their views. For a sample of their writings, see Maria Telkes, "Future Uses of Solar Energy," *Bulletin of the Atomic Scientists* 7 (August 1951): 217–219; Eugene Ayres, "Power From the Sun," *Scientific American* 123 (August 1950): 16–21; and Palmer Coslett Putnam, *Energy in the Future* (Princeton, NJ: D. Van Nostrand Co., 1953). See his chap. 1 for an outline of the book.

25. Eugene Ayres and Charles A. Scarlott, *Energy Sources: The Wealth of the World* (New York: McGraw-Hill Book Company, Inc., 1952), p. 2.

26. See Donald Schön and Martin Rein, *Frame Reflection: Toward the Resolution of Intractable Policy Controversies* (New York: Basic Books, 1994) and Stone, *Policy Paradox*, chap. 6.

27. See Laird, "Constructing the Future," for details on their views.

28. For histories of the environmental movement, see Robert Gottlieb, *Forcing the Spring: The Transformation of the American Environmental Movement* (Washington, DC: Island Press, 1993), esp. chap. 1; Mark Dowie, *Losing Ground: American Environmentalism at the Close of the Twentieth Century* (Cambridge, MA: The MIT Press, 1995), esp. chaps. 1 and 2; and Samuel P. Hayes: *Beauty, Health, and Permanence: Environmental Politics in the United States, 1955–1985* (Cambridge: Cambridge University Press, 1987), chap. 1.

29. Lewis Herber, *Crisis in our Cities* (Englewood Cliffs, NJ: Prentice-Hall, Inc., 1965), chap. 11.

30. Farrington Daniels and John A. Duffie, eds., *Solar Energy Research* (Madison, WI: University of Wisconsin Press, 1955), p. vii.

31. Eventually, thirty-one people published papers in the volume that followed. See ibid., pp. v–vii. See Olive Daniels, *Farrington Daniels*, pp. 305–308, on the number of invitees.

32. Daniels, in Daniels and Duffie, p. 4.

33. Ibid., p. 251.

34. Resources For the Future, *The Nation Looks At its Resources* (Washington, DC: Resources for the Future, 1954), pp. 1–6.

35. Ibid., pp. 1–2.

36. Ibid., pp. 209–210 and 221–227.

37. Harvey Strum, "The Association for Applied Solar Energy/Solar Energy Society, 1954–1970," *Technology and Culture* 26 (3) (July 1985): 571–572. The quotation and some of the information is from *Proceedings of the World Symposium on Applied Solar Energy*, Phoenix, Arizona, November 1–5, 1955 (Menlo Park CA: Stanford Research Institute, 1956), p. 17.

38. *Proceedings of the World Symposium* , pp. 3 and 17. See also Strum, "The Association," 1985, p. 573.

39. *Proceedings of the World Symposium,* p. 15. For short biographical sketches of all the major participants, see pp. 301–304.
40. Ibid., p. 18.
41. D[aniel] S. Halacy, *The Coming Age of Solar Energy* (New York: Avon Books, 1975; first published 1963, Harper and Row Pub.) pp. 82–83. Halacy attributes the decline to the overoptimism of the popular reports that came out of the symposium.
42. For the AFASE publications, see Strum, "The Association," 1985, p. 574. For popular publications see Farrington Daniels, "A Limitless Resource: Solar Energy," *The New York Times Magazine,* March 18, 1956, pp. 26ff; Gordon Raisbeck, "The Solar Battery," *Scientific American* (December 1955): 102–110; Harry Tabor, "Progress in Solar Power," *Scientific American* (June 1956): 97–106; and William H. Stead, "The Sun and Foreign Policy," *Bulletin of the Atomic Scientists* 12 (3 March 1957): 86–90.
43. For lists of conferences, see Daniels, *Direct Use,* pp. 9–10; Halacy, *Solar Energy,* pp. 82–83; and Strum, "The Association," p. 577.
44. Strum, "The Association," pp. 576–577.
45. Ibid., pp. 577–578. For electricity prices, see Energy Information Administration, *Annual Energy Review,* DOE/EIA-0384(88) (Washington, DC: USGPO, 1988), pp. 212–213.
46. John W. Kingdon, *Agendas, Alternatives, and Public Policies,* 2nd ed. (New York: HarperCollins College Publishers, 1995).
47. Sheila Jasanoff, *The Fifth Branch: Science Advisors as Policy Makers* (Cambridge, MA: Harvard University Press, 1990), esp. chaps. 1, 5, and 11.

CHAPTER 4

1. For example, in promoting the Interstate Highway System, Eisenhower initially supported a plan to build $50 billion dollars worth of interstates, this when the entire annual federal budget was only $71 billion. Such a proposal makes current public works programs look timid indeed. T.A. Heppenheimer, "The Rise of the Interstates," *Invention and Technology* 7 (Fall 1991): 12.
2. Harvey Strum, "The Association for Applied Solar Energy/Solar Energy Society, 1954–1970," *Technology and Culture* 26 (3) (July 1985): 571–578, presents consumer economics as a central problem, but also includes others. See pp. 577–578.
3. Such political construction may not, in the long-term, succeed, and there is an extensive literature that tries to assess why nuclear power has failed. See John L. Campbell, *Collapse of an Industry: Nuclear Power and the Contradictions of U.S. Policy* (Ithaca, NY: Cornell University Press, 1988) and Joseph G. Morone and Edward J. Woodhouse, *The Demise of Nuclear Power? Lessons for Democratic Control of Technology* (New Haven, CT: Yale University Press, 1989) for two contrasting views of what went wrong.

4. For the history of nuclear power, see, in addition to Campbell, *Collapse*, and Morone and Woodhouse, *Demise*, Brian Balogh, *Chain Reaction: Expert Debate and Public Participation in American Commercial Nuclear Power, 1945–1975* (Cambridge: Cambridge University Press, 1991). Irvin C. Bupp and Jean-Claude Derian, *Light Water: How the Nuclear Dream Dissolved* (New York: Basic Books, 1978). For an example of the popular writing, see David O. Woodbury, *Atoms for Peace* (New York: Dodd, Mead, & Co., 1955) and for a discussion of the popular literature, see David E. Nye, *American Technological Sublime* (Cambridge, MA: The MIT Press, 1994), esp. p. 234.

5. "Atoms for Peace," *Public Papers of the Presidents of the United States: Dwight D. Eisenhower, 1953* (Washington, DC: USGPO, 1954), pp. 813–822, esp. pp. 820–822.

6. For a brief background of the "Atoms for Peace" speech, see Spenser Weart, *Nuclear Fear: A History of Images* (Cambridge, MA: Harvard University Press, 1988), pp. 158–160. See also my discussion in Chapter 3.

7. On Hosmer and Plowshare, see U.S. Congress, Joint Committee on Atomic Energy, "Development, Growth, and the State of the Atomic Energy Industry," Hearings, 88th Cong., 1st Sess., February 20–21, 1963, pp. 50–51. On the solar bills see Harvey Strum, "Eisenhower's Solar Energy Policy," *The Public Historian* 6 (2) (Spring 1984): 44–45.

8. On the fragmentation of energy policy making, and why we should expect that to be the case, see Charles O. Jones, "American Politics and the Organization of Energy Decision Making," in *Annual Review of Energy, Vol. 4*, Jack M. Hollander, ed. (Palo Alto, CA: Annual Reviews Inc, 1979), pp. 99–122.

9. Strum, "Eisenhower's Solar Energy Policy," 40.

10. Lewis to Rockefeller, August 18, 1955. Also, see letter, Howard Pyle to Bernard Shanley, August 29, 1955, attached to Shanley to Pyle, September 6, 1955, folder 146-G solar energy, box 744, WHCF – Official Files, DDEL. Pyle was a Deputy Assistant to the President, and was the person in the White House who seemed most positive towards the symposium. Lewis's participation in the conference is in a program attached to these letters.

11. Re. the skepticism, see note, B.N.H. [Bryce Harlow] to General Parsons, September 9, 1955, and for a copy of the message see letter, President Dwight D. Eisenhower to The Honorable Lewis W. Douglas, October 26, 1955, both in folder 308 – World Symposium, box 929, WHCF – Official Files, DDEL.

12. Strum, "Eisenhower's Solar Energy Policy," 41–42.

13. The changing relations between the White House and the conference organizers can be gleaned from internal and external White House correspondence. See letter, Albright to Eisenhower, September 26, 1952, and Eisenhower to Albright, October 2, 1952, both in folder OF-134-G (1), box 683, WHCF – Official Files, DDEL; Press Release, Horace M. Albright for Resources for the Future, November 13, 1952, folder OF-134-G(1), box 683, WHCF – Official Files, DDEL; Letter, Laurence F. Lee to Sherman

Adams, February 9, 1953, attached to Adams to Lee, February 18, 1953, and letter, Charles H. Sage to Sherman Adams, September 11, 1953, both in folder OF-134-G(1), box 683, WHCF – Official Files, DDEL; letter, Fairfield Osborne to General Eisenhower, September 26, 1952, plus attached lists, folder OF-134-G(1), box 683, WHCF – Official Files, DDEL; Memo, Gabriel Hauge to Governor Adams, February 14, 1953, attached to Hauge to Adams, February 18, 1953, folder OF-134-G(1), box 683, WHCF – Official File, DDEL; Memo, Bryce Harlow to Governor Adams, November 30, 1953, and attached notes, folder OF-134-G(1), box 683, WHCF – Official Files, DDEL.

14. Letter, Hauge to Gustavson, November 1, 1954, folder 134 OF-G(2), box 683, WHCF – Official Files, DDEL.
15. The separation between interests and values is often not as simple as one might think. See Ernst B. Haas, *When Knowledge Is Power: Three Models of Change in International Organizations* (Berkeley: University of California Press, 1990), p. 2.
16. Charles Lindblom and Edward J. Woodhouse, *The Policy Making Process*, 3rd. ed. (Engelwood Cliffs, NJ: Prentice Hall, 1993).
17. James McVeigh, Dallas Burtraw, Joel Darmstadter, and Karen Palmer, "Winner, Loser, or Innocent Victim? Has Renewable Energy Performed as Expected?" Renewable Energy Policy Project, Research Report No. 7 (Washington, DC: April 1999).
18. See Frank N. Laird, "Constructing the Future," under review, and Part II of this book.
19. The Interior Department did champion large-scale hydropower. This was a much more mature renewable energy technology than the other solar technologies and related to the Interior's traditional mission of water resources.
20. Julius Krug is clearly an exception to this pattern, as discussed in earlier chapters. See, for example, U.S. Department of the Interior, *Annual Report of the Secretary of the Interior: Fiscal Year Ending June 30, 1946* and other fiscal years for summaries of the program.
21. See Morone and Woodhouse, *Demise*, and Bupp and Derian, *Light Water*, for this background.
22. Weart, *Nuclear Fear*.
23. David O. Woodbury, *Atoms for Peace* (New York: Dodd, Mead, and Co., 1955). The quote is on pp. 3–4.
24. Michael Smith, "Advertising the Atom," in *Government and Environmental Politics: Essays on Historical Developments Since World War Two*, Michael J. Lacey, ed. (Washington DC and Baltimore, MD: The Wilson Center Press and The Johns Hopkins University Press, 1989), pp. 233–262. The quote is on p. 244.
25. See Balogh, *Chain Reaction*, pp. 104–106 for details.
26. On the budget cuts, see Morone and Woodhouse, *Demise*, pp. 42–43. For the aftermath to the speech, see Weart, *Nuclear Fear*, pp. 155–169, and Balogh, *Chain Reaction*, pp. 104–106. See Mark Hertsgaard, *Nuclear Inc.: The Men and Money Behind Nuclear Power* (New York: Pantheon Books, 1983), pp. 34–40; and Stephen Hilgartner, Richard C. Bell, and Rory O'Connor, *Nuke-*

speak: *The Selling of Nuclear Technology in America* (San Francisco: Sierra Club Books, 1982), pp. 41–53 for programs on nuclear ships, etc.

27. See Michael Smith, "Advertising the Atom," pp. 234–238, and Frank R. Baumgartner and Bryan D. Jones, *Agendas and Instabilities in American Politics* (Chicago: University of Chicago Press, 1993), p. 66.
28. U.S. Atomic energy Commission, *Civilian Nuclear Power: A Report to the President – 1962*, "Summary", pp. 7–15. Reprinted in U.S. Congress, Joint Committee on Atomic Energy, *Development, Growth, and State of the Atomic Energy Industry, Hearings*, 88th Cong., 1st sess., February 20–21, 1963.
29. U.S. Congress, JCAE, *Hearings*, part 1, February 20–21, 1963, p. 56.
30. Memo, Wiesner to Bundy, April 2, 1963, folder Office of Science and Technology, 3/63–11/63, box 284, National Security Files – Depts and Agencies, JFKL. The study to which Wiesner refers here is the Interdepartmental Energy Study discussed previously.
31. The FCST study that Wiesner supervised explicitly called for more R&D in nonnuclear energy sources, mentioning solar in particular. The report argued that the government's energy R&D program was out of balance in that it favored nuclear power too heavily. See Executive Office of the President, Office of Science and Technology, Federal Council for Science and Technology, *Research and Development on Natural Resources*, May 1963, esp. Appendix A.
32. Baumgartner and Jones, *Agendas and Instability*, chap. 4.
33. Smith, "Advertising the Atom," pp. 234–238.
34. See the discussion of the PMPC in chaps. 1 and 2.
35. Farrington Daniels, *Direct Use of the Sun's Energy* (New Haven, CT: Yale University Press, 1964; reprint ed., New York: Ballantine Press, 1974), pp. 1–2.
36. Ibid., chap. 1. Quote is from p. 3.
37. Federal Council for Science and Technology, Committee on Natural Resources, *Research and Development on Natural Resources*, May 1963. Data are on pp. 36–37.
38. *Energy R&D and National Progress*, Prepared for the Interdepartmental Energy Study by the Energy Study Group under the direction of Ali Bulent Cambel (Washington, DC: USGPO, 1964). See pp. 52–56 for a discussion of various economic goals and the superiority of optimal allocation. The quote is from p. xvii.
39. Ibid, pp. 29–32. The quotes are on pp. 29 and 30, respectively.
40. Trevor Pinch and Wiebe E. Bijker, "The Social Construction of Facts and Artifacts: Or How the Sociology of Science and the Sociology of Technology Might Benefit Each Other," in *The Social Construction of Technological Systems: New Directions in the Sociology and History of Technology*, Wiebe E. Bijker, Thomas P. Hughes, and Trevor Pinch, eds. (Cambridge, MA: The MIT Press, 1987), pp. 17–50.
41. *Energy R&D*, Table 1-26, between pp. 38 and 39.
42. Ibid.
43. Ibid.

44. Baumgartner and Jones, p. 22.
45. The quote is cited in Hilgartner et al., p. 44. See also Smith, "Advertising the Atom," for a discussion of advocates' enthusiasm for their technology. For the history of this controversy, see Balogh, *Chain Reaction*, Morone and Woodhouse, *Demise*, and Campbell, *Collapse of an Industry*. On the early decision to use light water reactors and to scale them up quickly, see Bupp and Derian, *Light Water*, and Freeman Dyson, *Disturbing the Universe* (New York: Harper and Row, 1979) chap. 9.
46. In his address to the Edison Electric Institute in 1968, Presidential Science Advisor Donald Hornig titled his talk "Future Energy Needs vs the Environment" and talked quite a bit about this conflict. Hornig address, June 4, 1968, folder "Vol. II – Documentary Supplement (2 of 3)," box 1, Administrative History, Office of Science and Technology, LBJL.

CHAPTER 5

1. Charles O. Jones, "American Politics and the Organization of Energy Decision Making," *Annual Review of Energy* 4 (1979); Frank R. Baumgartner and Bryan D. Jones, *Agendas and Instability in American Politics* (Chicago: Univeristy of Chicago Press, 1993); Deborah A. Stone, *Policy Paradox and Political Reason* (Glenview, IL: Scott, Foresman, and Co., 1988), chap. 10.
2. For more comprehensive details, see Neil de Marchi, "Energy Policy Under Nixon: Mainly Putting Out Fires," in *Energy Policy in Perspective: Today's Problems, Yesterday's Solutions*, Craufurd D. Goodwin, ed. (Washington, DC: The Brookings Institution, 1981), pp. 400–446. Richard H. K. Vietor, *Energy Policy in America Since 1945: A Study of Business-Government Relations* (Cambridge: Cambridge University Press, 1984), Part III. For a more extensive discussion of energy policy making within the EOP, see Frank N. Laird, "Energy Policy Institutions: Centralizing Policy in a Fragmented Polity," in preparation.
3. De Marchi, "Energy Policy Under Nixon," pp. 416–417. Executive Order number 11712, April 18, 1973, folder Ex FG 6-23 [3/21/73–7/27/73], box 1, WHCF – Sub – FG 6-23, NLNP.
4. Memo, Dick Fairbanks to Ken Cole, May 4, 1973, attached to Memo, Fairbanks to Gosden, May 18, 1973, folder Ex FG 6-23, National Energy Office [3/21/73–7/27/73], box 1, WHCF – Sub – FG 6-23, NLNP. Memo, Roy Ash to the President, May 24, 1973, folder [EX] UT 5/1/73–5/31/73, box 2, WHCF – Sub – UT, NLNP.
5. Statement by the President, Press Release, June 29, 1973, folder [EX] UT 6/1/73–6/30/73, box 2, WHCF – Sub – UT, NLNP, pp. 1 and 3. Davis, 1982, pp. 105–106; di Marchi, 1981, pp. 435–437. Letter, Richard Nixon to John Love, December 3, 1973, and Richard Nixon to Charles DiBona, December 3, 1973, both in "Ex FG 6-25/A[12/3/73]," box 3, WHCF – Sub – FG 6-25, NLNP. The EPO itself was not actually abolished until late March, 1974. See memo, Ken Cole to the President, March 20, 1974, plus attachment, "Ex FG 6-25 1/1/74-[7/31/74]" box 2, WHCF – Sub – FG 6-25, NLNP.

6. See di Marchi, 1981, pp. 418–419, for DiBona's articulation of these values.

7. Memo, Ash to the President, n.d. but early June 1973, "[EX] UT 6/1/73–6/30/73," box 2, WHCF – SUB – UT, NLNP, p. 1, and pp. 1–3 of attachment.

8. Memo, David N. Parker to John A. Love, October 8, 1973, folder Ex FG 999-46 1973–1974, box 16, WHCF – Sub – FG 999-46, NLNP, attachment.

9. di Marchi, 1981, pp. 404–409.

10. Memo, John Whitaker to John Ehrlichman, December 1, 1970, folder [EX] Utilities, box 1, WHCF – Sub – UT, NLNP.

11. Memo, John Whitaker to the President through John Ehrlichman, n.d., but early March 1971, folder March 1 thru 15, 1971, box 9, President's Office Files, Handwriting File, NLNP. See the attachments.

12. Memo, Will Kriegsman to John Ehrlichman through John Whitaker, April 16, 1971, folder [EX] UT 1/1/71 – [1 of 2], box 1, WHCF – Sub – UT, NLNP. The quotes are on pp. 1, 3, and 4.

13. Memo, Will Kriegsman to John Ehrlichman through John Whitaker, April 21, 1971, attached to John Whitaker to the President, April 21, 1971, folder CF UT [1 of 2] 1971–74, box 67, White House Special Files, Confidential Files, NLNP.

14. "Special Message to the Congress on Energy Resources, June 4, 1971, *Public Papers of the President of the United States. Richard Nixon, 1971* (Washington, DC: US Government Printing Office, 1972), pp. 703–714. di Marchi, 1981, p. 410. Letter, Chet Holifield to Richard Nixon, November 28, 1972, folder [EX] UT 1/1/71 – [2 of 2], box 1, WHCF – Sub – UT, NLNP.

15. Memo, Richard Fairbanks to John D. Ehrlichman, December 21, 1972, folder [EX] Utilities 1/1/73–2/28/73, box 1 WHCF – Sub – UT, NLNP. Quote is on p. 4. Memo, Peter Flanigan to the President, December 26, 1972, p. 2, folder [EX] UT 1/1/71 – [2 of 2], box 1, WHCF – Sub, NLNP. See di Marchi, 1981, pp. 412–415 and 420–421.

16. Memo, Roy Ash to the President, November 30, 1973, "Ex FG 999-45 [1973–1974]," box 16, WHCF – Sub, NLNP. See memo, Dick Fairbanks to Fred Malek, July 5, 1973, folder EX FG 999-46 1973–74, box 16, WHCF – Sub – FG 999-46; memo, William T. McCormack, Jr., to Chairman and Members of ERDA Working Group, July 18, 1973, folder Ex FG 999-46 1973–1974, box 16, WHCF – Sub – FG 999-46, NLNP; and memo, William T. McCormack, Jr., to Charles J. Dibona, July 19, 1973, folder Ex FG 999-46 1973–1974, box 16, WHCF – Sub – FG 999-46, NLNP. Memo, Bill McCormack to John Love, September 11, 1973, folder Ex FG 999-45 1973–1974, box 16, WHCF – Sub – FG 999-45, NLNP.

17. Memo, Roy Ash to the President, n.d. but early June 1973, folder [EX] UT 6/1/73–6/30/73, box 2, WHCF – Sub – UT, NLNP, p. 4 and attached charts. See also Press Release, June 29, 1973, pp. 3–4. For a detailed analysis to the proposed legislation, see the attachment to letter, Richard Nixon to Carl Albert, June 29, 1973, folder EX FG 999-45 [1973–1974], box 16, WHCF – Sub – FG 999-45, NLNP. See also di Marchi, 1981, p. 435.

18. Tom Alexander, "ERDA's Job Is to Throw Money at the Energy Crisis," *Fortune* (July 1976): 153; Davis, *Energy Politics*, pp. 232–233; Don E. Kash and Robert W. Rycroft, *U.S. Energy Policy: Crisis and Complacency* (Norman, OK: University of Oklahoma Press, 1984), pp. 241–242.
19. See E[lmer] E. Schattschneider, *The Semisovereign People: A Realist's View of Democracy in America.* (New York: Holt, Rinehart and Winson, 1960), pp. 2–4.
20. Press Release, White House, January 15, 1975, folder FG 383 1/1/75–1/20/75, box 200, WHCF – Sub, GRFL.
21. Vietor, *Energy Policy In America*, p. 322.
22. Briefing Book on ERDA and Congressional Relationships, November 15, 1974, Tab 3, folder Energy Res. and Dev. Admin, 1974, Activation and Congressional Relations, box 14, Glenn R. Schleede Files, GRFL.
23. Ibid., Tabs 3 and 8.
24. Cochrane, "Carter's Energy Policy," p. 548.
25. National Energy Plan, pp. 84–85.
26. See Vietor, *Energy Policy in America*, pp. 322–323, for this description and evaluation.
27. The events leading to and after the embargo, especially with regard to fossil fuels, are oft and well told. For example, see Neil de Marchi, "Energy Policy Under Nixon: Mainly Putting Out Fires," in *Energy Policy in Perspective: Today's Problems, Yesterday's Solutions*, Craufurd D. Goodwin, ed. (Washington, DC: The Brookings Institution, 1981), pp. 395–474; Richard B. Manke, *Squeaking By: U.S. Energy Policy Since the Embargo* (New York: Columbia University Press, 1976); Vietor, *Energy Policy in America*, part III; and David Howard Davis, *Energy Politics*, 3rd ed. (New York: St. Martins Press, 1982).
28. Richard F. Hirsh, *Technology and Transformation in the American Electric Utility Industry* (Cambridge: Cambridge University Press, 1989), p. 9, Fig. 7, for electricity prices. For fossil fuel prices, total energy consumption, and electricity data, see Department of Energy, Energy Information Administration, *1980 Annual Report to Congress: Volume Two: Data* (Washington, DC: Government Printing Office, 1981), pp. 6–7, 20–21, and 161–169. Population figures are from *The Statistical History of the United States From Colonial Times to the Present* (New York: Basic Books, 1976), p. 8.
29. Martin V. Melosi, *Coping with Abundance: Energy and Environment in Industrial America* (New York: Alfred A. Knopf, 1985) p. 209; de Marchi, "Energy Policy Under Nixon," pp. 398 and 406; Manke, *U.S. Energy Policy*, p. 14, discusses some of the reasons why the generating capacity was inadequate.
30. de Marchi, "Energy Policy Under Nixon," p. 406. These shortages were attributed to two different causes, each explanation reflecting obvious ideological roots. One argument claimed that government price and import controls stifled exploration, production, and efficient trade in these fuels. The other argued that the industry was manipulating supplies to create a shortage as a means for arguing that price controls should be lifted. For

the former see Manke, pp. 7–10, and for the latter see Robert Sherrill, "The Energy Industry's Fright Campaign," in *America's Energy*, Robert Engler, ed. (New York: Pantheon, 1980), pp. 273–277. Sherrill's article was originally published in 1972.

31. M. A. Adelman, "Is the Oil Shortage Real? Oil Companies as OPEC Tax-Collectors," *Foreign Policy* 9 (Winter 1972): pp. 82–83. See also Vietor, *Energy Policy*, p. 200.

32. See, for example, Gerald Garvey, *Energy, Ecology, Economy* (New York: W.W. Norton, 1972), esp. chap. 2; and Allen L Hammond, William D. Metz, and Thomas H. Maugh II, *Energy and the Future* (Washington, DC: American Association for the Advancement of Science, 1973), esp. pp. vi and 147.

33. "Utilities Face a Generation Gap," *Business Week* (August 2, 1969): 30–31.

34. *Business Week* (November 29, 1969): 48–62.

35. "Wintertime Mini-Crisis," *Newsweek* (February 15, 1971): 73.

36. Quoted in "Taking a Dim View," *Newsweek* (May 3, 1971): 81.

37. "The Great Oil Hunt," *Newsweek* (September 22, 1969); "The Desert Foxes," *Time* (February 15, 1971): 69–70.

38. See the *Washington Post* (September 4, 1973) and (September 6, 1973): C13.

39. Adelman, "Is the Oil Shortage Real?" pp. 69–107. A few economic analysts reached different conclusions and argued that, for the limited case of electricity, demand would not, contrary to conventional wisdom, continue increasing at the historical rate of roughly seven percent per year because increasing real prices for electricity would reduce future demand. This claim was, at the time, fairly heretical. Duane Chapman, Timothy Tyrrell, and Timothy Mount, "Electricity Demand Growth and the Energy Crisis," *Science* 178 (17 November 1972): 703–708.

40. Garvey, *Energy, Ecology, Economy*, 34–35. For an extended discussion see esp. chaps. 1 and 3.

41. Paul R. Ehrlich and Anne H. Ehrlich, *Population, Resources, Environment: Issues in Human Ecology* (San Francisco: W.H. Freeman and Company, 1970), p. 54.

42. On the official definition of policy problems, see Joseph R. Gusfield, *The Culture of Public Problems: Drinking-Driving and the Symbolic Order* (Chicago: University of Chicago Press, 1981), chap. 1. See also Stone, *Policy Paradox and Political Reason*, Part III. John W. Kingdon, *Agendas, Alternatives, and Public Policies* (New York: HarperCollins Publishers, 1984), chap. 1.

43. David E. Nye, *Consuming Power: A Social History of American Energies* (Cambridge, MA: The MIT Press, 1998), esp. chaps. 6–8.

44. Memo, John Whitaker to the President through John Ehrlichman, n.d., but early March 1971, folder March 1 thru 15, 1971, box 9, President's Office Files, Handwriting File, NLNP. Nixon annotated this memo indicating that he read it and approved of its contents.

45. American Petroleum Institute, "The Energy Supply Problem," December 1970, Oversize Attachment 6414, December 1970, WHCF – Subject – UT, NLNP.

46. Memo, Peter M. Flanigan to the President, n.d. but ca. early 1972, folder [EX] UT 1/1/71 – [2 of 2], box 1, WHCF – Sub, NLNP. The subject line of the memo reads "The Energy Crisis."

47. Meeting Notes, Ken Cole to the President, June 2, 1973, and attached fact sheet, folder [CF] UT 1 of 2, box 67, White House Special Files – Confidential Files, NLNP.

48. Letter, Frank Ikard to Peter Flanigan, June 23, 1973, folder [EX] UT 6/1/73–6/30/73, box 2, WHCF – Sub – UT, NLNP. Ikard was the President of the American Petroleum Institute, and signed his letter to Flanigan, a senior White House aide, just as "Frank." I do not know if this gesture of familiarity was real or affected.

49. Letter, John Love to David Link, September 5, 1973, folder [EX] UT 9/1/73–9/16/73, box 3, WHCF – Sub – UT, NLNP. David Link was the editor of a trade magazine for builders, and the letter accompanied an article that Love sent to the magazine.

50. See my discussion of this interpretive framework in the Introduction.

51. Memo, Love to the President, October 12, 1973, folder October 1973, box 23, President's Office Files – Handwriting File, NLNP.

52. "Special Message to the Congress on Energy Resources," June 4, 1971, *Public Papers of the President of the United States. Richard Nixon, 1971* (Washington, DC: US Government Printing Office, 1972), pp. 703–714.

53. Ibid., pp. 704–05.

54. Ibid., p. 706.

55. Ibid., p. 713.

56. di Marchi, "Energy Policy Under Nixon," p. 410.

57. "Special Message," pp. 711–712, quote on p. 711.

58. Ibid., pp. 713–714.

59. Meeting Notes, for meeting with John Love, September 7, 1973, plus attachments, folder [CF] UT [1 of 2] [1971–74], box 67, White House Special Files, Confidential Files, NLNP. The document is stamped "The President Has Seen . . ." The quotes are from pp. 1–2 of the attached draft presidential statement.

60. Memo, John Whitaker to the President through John Ehrlichman, n.d., but early March 1971, folder March 1 thru 15, 1971, box 9, President's Office Files, Handwriting File, NLNP. The first quote is on p. 1, the handwritten quote is on p. 2, with the emphasis in the original.

61. There was good reason to be sensitive to the politics of price deregulation. When the Federal Power Commission had attempted a very modest deregulatory step in 1970, it met with fierce opposition. President Nixon did, quietly and informally, relax import quotas up until the embargo. The oil import quota system has a very complicated history. See Vietor, *Energy Policy in America*, pp. 120–144 and 278–279.

62. Memo, Peter Flanigan to John Ehrlichman et al., July 7, 1972, attached to William Timmons to Bruce Kehrli, July 22, 1972, folder CF UT [1 of 2] 1971–74, box 67, White House Special Files, Confidential Files, NLNP. The discussion of the models is on pp. 3–5 and the quote is on pp. 6–7.

63. Letter, Peter Flanigan to Tom Paine, January 26, 1973, and attachments, folder [EX] Utilities 1/1/73–2/28/73, box 1, WHCF – Sub, NLNP. The Chairman of the Board of Gulf Oil sent a similar paper to Charles DiBona in May of 1973. DiBona at that time was the main Special Consultant to the President on energy. Letter, Charles J. DiBona to B. R. Dorsey, May 23, 1973, and attachments, folder [EX] UT 5/1/73–5/31/73, box 2, WHCF – Sub, NLNP.

64. Ikard to Flanigan, June 23, 1973, pp. 2–3 of the attachment.

65. Memo, Peter Flanigan to the President, December 26, 1972, p. 2, folder [EX] UT 1/1/71 – [2 of 2], box 1, WHCF – Sub, NLNP. A memo from Ken Cole to the President, n.d. but late December 1972, (folder Dec. 16–31, 1972, box 20, President's Office Files, Handwriting File, NLNP), which covered a number of domestic programs, including energy, echoed the same principles. The president saw both of these memos, albeit the first in a slightly modified form.

66. Don E. Kash and Robert W. Rycroft, *U.S. Energy Policy: Crisis and Complacency* (Norman, OK: University of Oklahoma Press, 1984), p. 208.

67. Meeting Notes, September 7, 1973, for Love energy meeting, September 8. The agenda item is on p. 3 of the notes and the estimate of passage is on p. 3 of the third attachment.

68. Melosi, 1985, pp. 297–98.

69. Memo, Robert L. Sansom to John Whitaker and Richard Fairbanks, July 31, 1972, plus attachment, folder [EX] UT 1/1/71 – [2 of 2], box 1, WHCF – Sub, NLNP.

70. For example, see Flanigan to President, 12/26/72, p. 2, and John D. Ehrlichman to the President, January 26, 1973, plus attached review, "[EX] Utilities 1/1/73–2/28/73," box 1, WHCF – SUB UT, NLNP, p. 2 of the review. Stamped "The President has seen . . ."

71. Frank R. Baumgartner and Bryan D. Jones, *Agendas and Instability in American Politics* (Chicago: University of Chicago Press, 1993).

72. The embargo began during October 19–21. *Facts on File*, July – December 1973, vol. 33, p. 880.

73. James O'Toole, *Energy and Social Change* (Cambridge: The MIT Press, 1976), pp. 73–75.

74. There is no need to review all of the twists and turns of federal and state energy policies during this period, which are related and analyzed elsewhere. Davis, *Energy Politics*; de Marchi, "Energy Policy Under Nixon"; idem, "The Ford Administration: Energy as a Political Good," in *Energy Policy in Perspective*, Goodwin, ed.; Don E. Kash and Robert W. Rycroft, *U.S. Energy Policy: Crisis and Complacency* (Norman, OK: University of Oklahoma Press, 1984); Melosi, *Coping with Abundance*; Vietor, *Energy Policy*.

75. John G. Clark, *The Political Economy of World Energy: A Twentieth Century Perspective* (Chapel Hill, NC: University of North Carolina Press, 1990), chap. 9.

76. Memo, Tom Korologos to the President through William E. Timmons, December 19, 1973, "December 16–31, 1973," box 24, President's Office Files, Handwriting File, NLNP.

77. Memo, William E. Simon to Heads of Agencies and Departments, January 9, 1974, "[EX] UT 1/1/74–1/15/74," box 5, WHCF – Sub – UT, NLNP, and memo, Richard Nixon to Heads of Departments and Agencies, January 17, 1974, "Ex FG 6-26 1/1/74–4/30/74," Box 1, WHCF – Sub – FG 6-26, NLNP.

78. Memo, Ken Cole to the President, January 19, 1974, "[EX] UT 1/16/74–1/20/74," box 5, WHCF – Sub – UT, NLNP. Memo is stamped "The President has seen . . ."

79. Memo, Roy Ash to the President, February 28, 1974, "February 1974," box 26, President's Office Files – Handwriting File, NLNP.

80. Memo, Glenn Schleede to list, August 20, 1974, folder UT 8/7/74–9/15/74, box 1, WHCF – Sub – UT, GRFL.

81. "Energy Scorecard," n.d. but 1976, folder Energy 1976 General, box 13, Glenn R. Schleede Files, GRFL.

82. Charles Mortiz, ed., *Current Biography Yearbook 1968* (New York: The W.H. Wilson Company, 1968), pp. 28–30.

83. For example, see memo, Roy Ash to Ken Cole et al., January 8, 1974, "[Ex] UT 1/1/74–1/15/74," box 5, WHCF – Sub, NLNP; Memo, Roy Ash to the President, January 16, 1974, attached to memo, Bruce Kehrli to Roy Ash, January 28, 1974, "January 16–31, 1974," box 25, President's Office Files, Handwriting File, NLNP; Memo, Al Haig to the President, January 24, 1974, "January 16–31, 1974," box 25, President's Office Files – Handwriting File, NLNP.

84. Memo, Roy Ash to the President, n.d., attached to memo, Bruce Kehrli to Roy Ash, February 11, 1974, "February 1974," box 26, President's Office Files – Handwriting File, NLNP.

85. Memo, Roy Ash to the President, January 16, 1974, "CF UT 2 of 2 1971–74," box 67, White House Special Files – Confidential Files, NLNP.

86. Memo, Al Haig to the President, November 6, 1973, plus attached speech draft, "November 1–15, 1973," box 23, President's Office Files – Handwriting File, NLNP.

87. Memo, Herbert Stein to the President, February 28, 1974, plus attached speech, "February 1974," box 26, President's Office Files – Handwriting Files, NLNP, and memo, Herbert Stein to the President, March 29, 1974, plus attached speech, "March 1974," box 26, President's Office Files – Handwriting File, NLNP. The former speech got the "Brilliant" annotation.

88. See especially Stein to President, February 28, 1974, pp. 8–9.

89. U.S. President, *Public Papers of the Presidents of the United States* (Washington, DC: Government Printing Office, 1975), Richard M. Nixon, 1973, pp. 918 and 919.

90. Ibid., pp. 916–918.

91. Ibid., p. 920.

92. Ibid., p. 925.

93. diMarchi, "Energy Policy Under Nixon,", pp. 458–465.

94. Federal Energy Administration, *Project Independence Report* (Washington, DC: Government Printing Office, November 1974), p. 17.

95. Federal Energy Administration, *Project Independence Blueprint Final Task Force Report: An Historical Perspective* (Washington, DC: Government Printing Office, November 1974), pp. 1–4.

96. Federal Energy Administration, *Project Independence Report*, p. i and, for quotation, pp. 18–19.

97. Ibid. p. 406 and esp. Figure VIII-1.

98. Rogers Morton also headed the Energy Resources Council, a group mandated by the same legislation that established the Energy Research and Development Agency (ERDA). Morton's Council had the authority to decide what part of the *Blueprint*, if anything, to recommend to the president for new policy.

99. Concerning Sawhill's firing, see David Howard Davis, *Energy Politics*, 3rd. ed. (New York: St. Martins Press, 1982) p. 107; The description of the Project Independence draft comes from Joel Havemann and James G. Phillips, "Energy Report/Independence Blueprint Weighs Various Options," *National Journal Reports* (November 2, 1974): 1635–1654.

100. The Ford administration repeated the need for price deregulation often in public, being more open about it than the Nixon White House. See Frank G. Zarb, Speech, October 16, 1975, Federal Energy Administration Press Release, folder SP 5/FG 240 to FG 383, box 86, WHCF – Sub, GRFL; White house Press Release, Statement by the President, December 22, 1975, folder Energy 1975: Presidential Statements, box 12, Glenn R. Schleede Files, GRFL; and Interview of Gerald R. Ford by Walter Cronkite, CBS News, February 3, 1976, folder Energy (2), box H36, President Ford Committee Records: Quotebooks, GRFL.

101. Letter, Senator Dewey F. Bartlett to the President, September 30, 1974, folder FG 383 ERDA 8/9/74–10/14/74, box 200, WHCF – Sub, GRFL.

102. The sometimes contradictory nature of U.S. energy policy goals is discussed by Mancke, *U.S. Energy Policy*, pp. 4–5.

103. Ken Cole, Briefing Notes on meeting on energy policy, December 19, 1974, plus attached briefing book, folder Util . . . Energy Policy Briefing 12/19/74, box 50, President's Office Files – Handwriting File, GRFL. See especially p. 2 of the briefing book.

104. Ibid., pp. 2–3.

105. Memo, Frank Zarb to the President through Rogers Morton, December 18, 1974, plus attachment, folder Utility: Energy Policy Briefing 12/19/74, box 50, President's Office Files – Handwriting File, GRFL. See p. 3 of the attachment, which is a decision memo for the President. On the decision memo, the President approved a 15% tax credit to homeowners for installing insulation but disapproved subsidies for low-income homeowners, even though the memo estimated that the tax credit would cost more than the subsidy.

106. See L. William Seidman to the President, December 31, 1974, folder Utilities – Energy (1), box 50, President's Office Files – Handwriting File, GRFL; Meeting Notes, February 18, 1975, folder UT 2/18/75–2/28/75, box 3, WHCF – Sub, GRFL; Meeting Notes, November 13, 1975, folder SP 2-4/1976 State of the Union 3/25/75–12/31/75, box 26, WHCF – Sub, GRFL;

Memo, Frank Zarb to the President, October 19, 1976, folder September 13, 1976 – Undated, box 10, Frank G. Zarb Files, GRFL.

107. Memo, Hugh Loweth to Roger Legassie, February 5, 1976, pp. 1–2, folder ENERGY 1976: Research and Development Plans, box 14, Glenn R. Schleede Files, GRFL.

108. Memo, Glenn Schleede to Jim Cannon, March 30, 1976, pp. 1–3 for the quotes, folder UT 3/8/76–4/25/76, box 6, WHCF – Sub, GRFL.

109. Energy Research and Development Administration, *A National Plan for Energy Research, Development and Demonstration: Creating Energy Choices for the Future*, Vol. 1: The Plan (Summary), ERDA 76-1 (Washington, DC: U.S. Government Printing Office, 1976), p. 3. See also Meeting Notes, June 26, 1975, folder BE 5 6/1/75–7/31/75, box 19, WHCF – Sub, GRFL.

110. Memo, Glenn Schleede to Eliska Hasek, March 23, 1976, folder Energy 1976, General, box 8, Glenn R. Schleede Files, GRFL. The same issue of public versus private sector came up over an ERDA report on solar energy. See memo, Glenn Schleede to Jack Blasy, July 10, 1975, folder Solar Energy, 1975, box 4, Glenn R. Schleede Files, GRFL.

111. ERDA, *National Plan*, 1976, p. 23.

112. Memo, Jim Mitchell to Russ Peterson, CEQ, August 30, 1976, folder CEQ 1976: Rpt on Eng. R&D, box 8, Glenn R. Schleede Files, GRFL.

113. Memo, Glenn Schleede to Jim Cannon, September 8, 1976, folder CEQ, 1976: Rpt on Eng. R&D, box 8, Glenn R. Schleede Papers, GRFL, pp. 1–2.

114. Press Release, September 13, 1976, and Press Release, September 24, 1976, both in folder Energy 1976 Presidential Statements, box 13, Glenn R. Schleede Files, GRFL.

115. Elliot Richardson and Frank G. Zarb, "Perspective on Energy Policy," December 16, 1976, pp. 4–5 and 10 (for the quote), pub. by the Energy Resources Council, folder Energy Resources Council, box 5, Frank G. Zarb Files, GRFL.

116. Neil de Marchi, "The Ford Administration: Energy as a Political Good," in *Energy Policy in Perspective*, Craufurd D. Goodwin, ed., pp. 542–543.

117. Oil prices declined slightly in constant dollars in 1977 and 1978, only to go up sharply in 1979 and 1980. Natural gas prices increased in constant dollars during the entire period. See Energy Information Administration, *Annual Energy Review 1988*, DOE/EIA – 0384(88) (Washington, DC: Government Printing Office, 1989), p. 65, Table 27. On the winter and energy studies, see James L. Cochrane, "Carter Energy Policy and the Ninety-fifth Congress," in *Energy Policy in Perspectives*, Goodwin, ed., pp. 550–551.

118. See Cochrane, "Carter Energy Policy," esp. pp. 564–584; Davis, *Energy Politics*, chaps. 3–4; for pre-Carter background on oil, John M. Blair, *The Control of Oil* (New York: Random House/Vintage, 1976); G. John Ikenberry, *Reasons of State: Oil Politics and the Capacities of American Government* (Ithaca, NY: Cornell University Press, 1988); Vietor, *Energy Policy*, chaps. 10–12.

119. Cochrane, "Carter Energy Policy," pp. 552–556.
120. Executive Office of the President, Energy Policy and Planning, *The National Energy Plan* (Washington, DC: Government Printing Office, 1977), p. 1. The major policy prescription was to eliminate waste and inefficiency. The plan was released nine days after the address to Congress. Despite the claims of simplicity, it was immensely complicated, with ten guiding principles and dozens of programs covering all forms of energy. *National Energy Plan*, esp. pp. 35–82.
121. Ibid., pp. 4–7.

CHAPTER 6

1. Hempel looks at ideological and value differences within the solar movement, but he takes a different approach than I do here, though he comes to similar conclusions. See Lamont Hempel, "The Politics of Sunshine: An Inquiry into the Origin, Growth, and Ideological Character of the Solar Energy Movement in America," Ph.D. dissertation, Claremont Graduate School, 1983, chap. 5.
2. For the conventional advoctates, see Paul Fannin, "Solar Energy: Overcoming the Barriers," *Arizona Business* 23 (August–September 1976): 2–9; and Bruce Anderson, *The Solar Home Book: Heating, Cooling, and Designing with the Sun* (Harrisville, NH: Cheshire Books, 1976), pp. 245–251. For an example from the ecological literature, see Amory B. Lovins, "Energy Strategy: The Road Not Taken," *Foreign Affairs* 55 (October 1976): 65–96, esp. p. 74.
3. On the MITRE study, see Edward Cowan, "Solar Heat Competitive with Electric, Agency Finds," *New York Times* (December 30, 1976): 1, and Victor K. McElheny, "Solar Energy Future: Optimism is Restrained," *New York Times* (December 31, 1976): 3. On the call for a study of solar electric technologies, see William D. Metz, "Solar Politics: Lame-Duck Officials Initiate a Major New Study," *Science* 194 (17 December 1976): 1256–1260. On the independent scientific studies, see William G. Pollard, "The Long-Range Prospects for Solar Energy," *American Scientist* 64 (July/August 1976): 424–429, who argued that solar electric technologies would never be economically feasible. Frederick H. Morse and Melvin K. Simmons, "Solar Energy," *Annual Review of Energy* 1 (1976): 131–158, claimed that solar would have little impact on the energy system by 1985, but that it had very extensive long-term potential. See especially pp. 153–154.
4. See, for example, *Sunpaper*, Journal and Newsletter of the New Mexico Solar Energy Association 2 (Winter 1976) or *AERO Sun-Times* 2 (January 1975): 2, both in NREL. "Shurcliff Throws in the Towel," *NESEA Newsletter* 3 (February 1977): 2–3. The NESEA is the New England Solar Energy Association, NREL.
5. *Encyclopedia of Associations*, 11th–14th eds. (Detroit, MI: Gale Research Co., 1977–1980) lists five in 1977 and fourteen in 1980 under solar, renewables, and alternative energy. This clearly understates the true numbers. The

burgeoning number of publications archived at the library of the National Renewable Energy Laboratory (NREL, formerly SERI) from the 1970s indicate, however imprecisely, the movement's growth.

6. For example, see "EPRI Executive Anticipates Solar Energy will Partially Fill the Gap between Supply and Demand in the Continuing Energy Crisis," *Solar Energy Report* 2 (7) (March 30, 1978), NREL; "Will the Solar Energy Industry Survive the New England Experiment?" *Solar Energy News* 1 (November 17, 1977), NREL; New York State Alliance to Save Energy, Inc., n.d. NREL; Southern Solar Energy Center Planning Project, Background Information and Presentation Materials, July 14, 1978, pp. 1–5, NREL; Solar Energy at Sandia Laboratories, Information Services Directorate, December 1977, p. 1, NREL; Florida Solar Energy Center, "FSEC Activities, Director's Report," December, 1978, p. 3, NREL; Charles Cox, "Solar as a Good Investment," *Sun Day Times*, pub. by Sun Day/Solar Action, May 1978, p. 6, NREL. Quote is from *Solar Utilization News* 3 (December 1978), p. 1, NREL.

7. "Passive Solar Project Needs Input," *Solar Utilization News* 3 (July 1978): 1, NREL; "Energy Boondoggles," *NESEA Newsletter* 4 (October 1978): 3, NREL; "Where the Sun is Hiding," *Sun☼Up* 2 (July 1978): 4, NREL. The statement by Congressman Jeffords is in James M. Jeffords, "Get Solar Energy Off the Ground," *Sun☼Up* 2 (July 1978): 10, NREL.

8. Peter E. Glaser, "Beyond Nuclear Power – The Large-Scale Use of Solar Energy," *Transactions of the New York Academy of Sciences* 31, Series 2 (December 1969): 951–967. Glaser had actually proposed the idea first in the journal *Solar Energy* in 1968, while he was president of the Solar Energy Society. See D[aniel] S. Halacy, *The Coming Age of Solar Energy* (New York: Avon Books, 1973), pp. 160–176.

9. See Halacy, *The Coming Age of Solar Energy*, pp. 204–221 for a description of the early announcement and of the entire system. The Meinels' own article is in Aden Baker Meinel and Marjorie Pettit Meinel, "Is it Time for a New Look at Solar Energy?" *Bulletin of the Atomic Scientists* 27 (October 1971): 32–37.

10. Meinel and Meinel, "New Look at Solar Energy?" p. 35.

11. For example, ibid., pp. 35–36. See also idem., "Physics Looks at Solar Energy," *Physics Today* 25 (February 1972): 44–50.

12. Norman C. Ford and Joseph W. Kane, "Solar Power," *Bulletin of the Atomic Scientists* (October 1971): 27–31.

13. See Allen L. Hammond, William D. Metz, and Thomas H. Maugh II, *Energy and the Future* (Washington, DC: AAAS, 1973), pp. 61 and 151. See also K. W. Böer, "The Solar House and Its Portent," *Chemtech* (July 1973): 394–400; Graham Chedd, "Brighter Outlook for Solar Power," *New Scientist* 58 (5 April 1973): 36–37; "Solar Energy May Achieve Wide Use by 1980s," *Chemical and Engineering News* 51 (January 29, 1973): 12–13. This last piece was a story about Dr. Böer's experimental solar house.

14. *Reader's Guide to Periodical Literature*, various years, s.v. solar, various phrases. The nontechnical articles totaled twelve in 1973

before the embargo. *New York Times Index*, various years, s.v. solar energy. The *Times* carried all of three articles in 1973 prior to the embargo.

15. For other examples of this conventional school, see Karl Keyerleber, "Clean Power From the Sun," *The Nation* 217 (October 29, 1973): 429–432; Colman McCarthy, "Letting the Sun Shine In," *Washington Post* (November 20, 1973): A18; "Sun Could Brighten Long-Term Energy Picture for U.S. Economy," *Commerce Today* 4 (March 18, 1974): 4–7; David Van Cleave, "Getting Bulk Power From Solar Energy," *Electric Light and Power* (September 1974): EG11–EG13; David G. Lee, "Tapping the Sun's Energy," *National Wildlife* 12 (August/September 1974): 18–21; and Fannin, "Solar Energy," 1976.

16. For example, see letter, George Löf to the President, January 25, 1975, attached to Letter, Warren S. Rustand to George O. G. Löf, February 4, 1975, plus attachments, in folder FG 1–2 (7/23/75), box 12, WHCF – Sub., GRFL.

17. See Fannin, "Solar Energy," 2–9.

18. "Utilities Deny Anti-Solar 'Cartel,'" *Solar Technology Report* 1 (October 1975): 1, NREL. "G. M. Plans Solar Power Hot Water System in Homes," *New York Times* (February 14, 1977): 31. See also Ray Reece, *The Sun Betrayed: A Report on the Corporate Seizure of U.S. Solar Energy Development* (Boston: The South End Press, 1979), pp. 166–179 and "Solar Heat Lights Up a New Industry," *Business Week* (May 16, 1977): 142–149.

19. Hawaii Natural Energy Institute, "Annual Report, 1977," (University of Hawaii – Manoa), p. 5, NREL; Doris E. Dissette, "Solar Energy for Small Clinic Buildings," *Health Services Management* (February 1977), NREL; Bill Strabala, "Sun-Generated Power Near Reality," *Denver Post* (May 8, 1977): 20. The last article quotes the director of product development for Martin Marietta extolling the virtues of solar. These articles also usually mentioned that solar was cleaner.

20. "Opinions on Capitol Hill: re. Solar: Humphrey," *AERO Sun-Times* 3 (May 1976): p. 8, NREL; "Opinions on Capitol Hill: re. ERDA: Abourezk," *Sun-Times* 3 (April 1976), p. 8, NREL; David S. Smits, "Housing Industry Holding Up Solar Homes," *Sun☼Up* 1 (May 1977): 1, NREL.

21. On the environmental movement generally, see Samuel P. Hayes, *Beauty, Health, and Permanence: Environmental Politics in the United States, 1955–1985* (Cambridge: Cambridge University Press, 1987); Lester W. Milbrath, *Environmentalists: Vanguard for a New Society* (Albany: State University of New York Press, 1984); Robert C. Paehlke, *Environmentalism and the Future of Progressive Politics* (New Haven, CT: Yale University Press, 1989); Robert Gottlieb, *Forcing the Spring: The Transformation of the American Environmental Movement* (Washington, DC: Island Press, 1993); and Mark Dowie, *Losing Ground: American Environmentalism at the Close of the Twentieth Century* (Cambridge, MA: The MIT Press, 1995).

22. Charles O. Jones, "American Politics and the Organization of Energy Decision Making," *Annual Review of Energy, Vol. 4*, ed. (1979), 104; David Howard Davis, *Energy Politics*, 3rd. ed. (New York: St. Martins Press, 1982), p. 276; and Martin V. Melosi, *Coping with Abundance: Energy and Environment in Industrial America* (New York: Alfred A. Knopf, 1985), pp. 297–298.

23. Aden Baker Meinel and Marjorie Pettit Meinel, "Is it Time for a New Look at Solar Energy?" *Bulletin of the Atomic Scientists* 27 (October 1971): 36–37.

24. Norman C. Ford and Joseph W. Kane, "Solar Power," *Bulletin of the Atomic Scientists* (October 1971): 27; "Chance for Solar Energy Conversion," *Chemical and Engineering News* 49 (December 20, 1971): 39; "Solar Energy May Achieve Wide Use by 1980s," *Chemical and Engineering News* 51 (January 29, 1973): 12.

25. Publications catering to alternative lifestyles also included solar as an important part of living ecologically. See *The Mother Earth News* 1 (January 1970): 2.

26. For example, see "Energy Policy," *Sierra Club Bulletin* 56 (June 1971): 3; "Defusing Old Smoky by Plugging into Nature," *Sierra Club Bulletin* 56 (September 1971): 24–27; "Consuming Energy in the Home," *Not Man Apart* 1 (August 1971): 29; and "The Great Mistakes Contest," *Not Man Apart* 2 (April 1972): 23.

27. "Cool Water, Wild Rivers, Clean Air, and Solar Power," *Audubon* (January 1970): 117.

28. For example, see Amory B. Lovins and John H. Price, *Non-Nuclear Futures: The Case for an Ethical Energy Strategy* (New York: Ballinger, 1975). See also the Foreword by David R. Brower.

29. For analyses of nuclear power controversies, see Henry F. Bedford, *Seabrook Station: Citizen Politics and Nuclear Power* (Amherst, MA: University of Massachusetts Press, 1990); John L. Campbell, *Collapse of an Industry: Nuclear Power and the Contradictions of U.S. Policy* (Ithaca, NY: Cornell University Press, 1988), chaps. 4 and 5; Joseph G. Morone and Edward J. Woodhouse, *The Demise of Nuclear Energy: Lessons for Democratic Control of Technology* (New Haven, CT: Yale University Press, 1989); Dorothy Nelkin, *Nuclear Power and Its Critics: The Cayuga Lake Controversy* (Ithaca, NY: Cornell University Press, 1971); and Spenser R. Weart, *Nuclear Fear: A History of Images* (Cambridge, MA: Harvard University Press, 1988), part IV.

30. "Attitude Studies Show Misunderstanding, Apathy," *Solar Technology Report* 2 (October 1976): 1–2, quote on p. 2, NREL.

31. Paul C. Yuen, in *Hawaii Natural Energy Institute Newsletter* 1 (December 1978): 1, NREL; Peter Harnik, "From Sun Day to the Solar Age," *Sun Day Times* (May 1978): 1, NREL; "Berkeley Solar," *Sun☼Up* 2 (July 1978): 17, NREL. The *Sun Day Times* was published by Solar Action, the group that organized Sun Day and that later became the core of the Solar Lobby.

32. Daniel P. Aiello, "Anticipatory Design & Humanistic Energy Systems," *Sunjournal*, the Aspen Energy Journal, 4 (Spring 1978): 3 (emphasis in

original), NREL. See also The "Declaration of Solar Independence," in AERO *Sun Times* 5 (February/March 1978): 10, NREL.

33. I have presented a simplified summary of this set of critical arguments, which of course had substantial variation and subtlety. For an introduction to some of these thinkers, see Murray Bookchin, "Ecology and Revolutionary Thought," in his *Post Scarcity Anarchism* (Berkeley, CA: Ramparts Press, 1971); Garrett De Bell, ed., *The Environmental Handbook* (New York: Ballentine Books, Inc., 1970); Editors of *Ramparts*, *Eco-Catastrophe* (New York: Harper and Row, 1970); and Paul Shepard and Daniel McKinley, eds., *The Subversive Science: Essays Toward an Ecology of Man* (Boston: Houghton Mifflin, 1969).

34. *A Time to Choose: America's Energy Future*, Final Report by the Energy Policy Project of the Ford Foundation, (Cambridge, MA: Ballinger, 1974). See also S. David Freeman, "Is There an Energy Crisis? An Overview," *Annals of the American Academy of Political Science* 410 (November 1973): 1–10.

35. David Brower, foreword to Amory B. Lovins and John H. Price, *Non-Nuclear Futures: The Case for an Ethical Energy Strategy* (New York: Ballinger, 1975).

36. Lovins and Price, *Non-Nuclear Futures*, p. xv.

37. On the use of metaphors in policy narratives, see Deborah A. Stone, *Policy Paradox and Political Reason* (Glenview, IL: Scott, Foresman, and Co., 1988), chap. 6.

38. See Weart, *Nuclear Fear*, part 4.

39. In addition to the works cited previously, see Egan O'Connor, "Solar Energy – How Soon?" *Chemtech* (May 1974): 264–267.

40. On technology as legislation, see Langdon Winner, *Autonomous Technology: Technics-Out-of-Control as a Theme in Political Thought* (Cambridge, MA: The MIT Press, 1977), pp. 317–324. See my introduction for a discussion of this interpretive framework.

41. Three major works that came out at this time were David Dickson, *Alternative Technology and the Politics of Technical Change* (Glasgow: Fontana/Collins, 1974); Ivan Illich, *Tools for Conviviality* (New York: Harper and Row, 1973); and E. F. Schumacher, *Small is Beautiful: Economics as if People Mattered* (New York: Harper and Row, 1973).

42. For a successful attempt to clarify one of the concepts, see Langdon Winner, "Decentralization Clarified," in his *The Whale and the Reactor* (Chicago: University of Chicago Press, 1986), pp. 85–97.

43. Tom Bender, *Sharing Smaller Pies*, quoted in *AERO Sun Times* (published by the organization AERO) 2 (February 1975): 8–9, NREL. Running through some of this literature is an implicit or explicit critique of capitalism as well, but that issue is not the most salient, even for those of obviously socialist orientation. Bender's article lists twelve desirable features of technologies, the last of which is that they "Permit ownership of the means of production by those who do the work" (p. 8). No self-respecting Marxist would put that item last.

44. See, for example, "Appropriate Technology," *AERO Sun-Times* 2 (February 1975): 8–9; "Appropriate Technology," *AERO Sun-Times* 2 (July 1975): 2–6; "Editor's Salutation," *UCAT News and Views* 3 (Spring 1980): 2; David Holzman, "Unions and Appropriate Technology: Conflict in the Solar Movement," *People and Energy* 4 (November/December 1978): 8–9; and Isao Fujimoto, "The Values of Appropriate Technology and Visions for a Saner World," pub. no. 010, National Center for Appropriate Technology, Butte, MT, n.d., but 1977. All of these sources are from the NREL.
45. Andrew Mackillop, "The Energy Equations: Technological Alternatives," *New Scientist* 60 (22 November 1973): 549 and 551. In addition to specific communities with these aims, there were national organizations, such as the Citizens' Energy Project in Washington, DC, founded in 1973. See undated pamphlet, Citizens' Energy Project, ca. 1979, NREL.
46. Harold E. Ketterer and John R. Schmidhauser, "Solar Energy: A Practical Alternative to Fossil and Nuclear Fuels," *Energy Sources* 1 (1974): 249–269. While rising energy prices could not be good for the poor, exactly how and the extent to which the energy crisis affected poverty was in some dispute. See James O'Toole, *Energy and Social Change* (Cambridge, MA: The MIT Press, 1976), pp. 63–65.
47. "Congress Boosts Solar Energy Funding," *Aviation Week and Space Technology* (August 23, 1976): 56; Victor K. McElheny, "Solar Energy Future: Optimism is Restrained," *New York Times* (December 31, 1976): 3.
48. Al Richman, "The Polls: Public Attitudes Toward the Energy Crisis," *Public Opinion Quarterly* 43 (1979): 576–585. The data cited are on pp. 580–582.
49. On the involvement of Friends of the Earth, see the discussion of Amory Lovins below. On the Public Interest Research Group, see Anita Gunn, "A Citizen's Handbook on Solar Energy," Public Interest Research Group, Washington, DC, n.d. but ca. 1977. On the growth of ISES chapters, see "NESEA Board Struggles with Growth & Organizational Change," (*New England Solar Energy Association Newsletter*) 2 (6) (December 1976): 1, NREL. For grassroots solar group, see "AERO's Aim and Origin," *AERO Sun-Times* 2 (January 1975): 2, NREL. AERO was the Alternative Energy Resources Organization, sponsored by the Northern Plains Resource Council, a group based in Montana.
50. Isao Fujimoto, "The Values of Appropriate Technology and Visions for a Saner World," National Center For Appropriate Technology, pub. no. 010, n.d. but ca. 1977, p. 3. The article is based on a talk delivered in February 1977. NCAT folder, NREL.
51. "Energy Strategies: The Road Not Taken," *Foreign Affairs* (October 1976): 65–96; *Soft Energy Paths: Toward a Durable Peace* (Cambridge, MA: FOE/Ballinger, 1977).
52. Lovins was not the only person to publish a major book on solar energy in this period, and these were not his first works on energy policy. The years 1977–1979 saw an explosion of work on energy policy, including solar policy. However, none of them had the impact of crystallizing support and

opposition to solar energy the way Lovins did, as well as providing a focus for a certain normative view of the proper role of energy in society. Whatever Lovins intended or thought of all this activity, he did become such a focus, and he reached a wide and influential audience by publishing in *Foreign Affairs*.

53. Lovins and Price, *Non-Nuclear Futures* contains many of the ideas in the later works, though not worked out as thoroughly.

54. These points are developed at length in Lovins, *Soft Energy Paths*, pp. 38–43. The claim that economic comparisons should be done differently was not unique to Lovins, as he acknowledged in his citations.

55. Ibid., chap. 2, esp. pp. 59–60.

56. Lovins, *Soft Energy Paths*, especially chaps. 2, 9, and 10; U.S. Senate, Joint Hearings, Select Committee on Small Business and Committee on Interior and Insular Affairs, "Alternative Long-Range Energy Strategies," December 9, 1976, 94th Congress, 2d Session, Interior Committee Serial (94-47), two volumes. See pp. 157–158, 167, and 171 and vol. 2, pp. 669 and 793 for examples. Quote is in Hearings, vol. 2, p. 682.

57. Senate Select Committee, "Alternative Energy Strategies," vol. 2, p. 707 and p. 682. Lovins often mentioned that the soft path could be undertaken as a series of "technical fixes" that would require no changes in institutions or lifestyles. See p. 701.

58. For a more detailed discussion of this split among solar advocates, see Hempel, *The Politics of Sunshine*, chap. 5.

59. Senate, Select Committee "Alternative Energy Strategies," two volumes.

60. Lovins, *Soft Energy Paths*, especially chaps. 6–8.

61. Senate Select Committee, "Alternative Energy Strategies," pp. 501, 503, and 507.

62. For analysis of policy narratives and causal stories, see Deborah A. Stone, *Policy Paradox and Political Reason*, (Glenview, IL: Scott Foresman, 1988).

63. Senate Select Committee, "Alternative Energy Strategies," vol. 1, p. 571.

64. "A Solar View of the Soft Path," in ibid., vol. 2, pp. 889–890.

65. "'Soft' Energy Paths – Reality and Illusion," in ibid., vol. 2, p. 938.

66. Letter, George L. Gleason to Catherine (sic) Schirmer, plus attachment, February 14, 1977, folder SC 3 1/20/77–1/20/82, box SC-4, WHCF, JCL, and William J. Lanouette, "A Latter-Day David Out to Slay the Goliaths of Energy," *National Journal* (October 1, 1977): 1532–1534.

67. B. J. Brinkworth, *Solar Energy for Man* (New York: John Wiley & Sons, 1972), p. 1. See also Halacy, *Age of Solar Energy*, pp. 146 and 229.

68. Halacy, *Age of Solar Energy*, p. 229.

69. The first quote is on page 14 of Wilson Clark, "How to Harness Sunpower and Avoid Pollution," *Smithsonian* 2 (November 1971): 14–21. The second quote is from Graham Chedd, "Brighter Outlook for Solar Power," *New Scientist* 58 (5 April 1973): 36. For the trade press, see "Chance for Solar

Energy Conversion," *Chemical and Engineering News* 49 (December 20, 1971): 39; Allen L. Hammond, "Solar Energy: The Largest Resource," *Science* 177 (September 22, 1972): 1088–1090; Idem., "Photovoltaic Cells: Direct conversion of Solar Energy," *Science* 178 (17 November 1972): 732–733.

70. Fannin, "Solar Energy," p. 3.

71. Fannin, "Solar Energy,"; Glaser, "Large-Scale Use of Solar Energy,"; Wilson Clark, "How to Harness Sunpower and Avoid Pollution," *Smithsonian* 2 (November 1971): 14–21; Donald F. Othmer and Oswald A. Roels, "Power, Fresh Water, and Food from Cold, Deep Sea Water," *Science* 182 (12 October 1973): 121–125.

72. Meinel and Meinel, "Physics Looks at Solar Energy," p. 44. But not all conventional advocates agreed. Aden Meinel criticized Glaser's solar satellite. See Bob Rankin, "Giant Solar Powered Electric Plants in the Sky Are Aerospace Industry's Newest Dream," *Congressional Quarterly Weekly Report* (April 22, 1978): 964–965.

73. Clarence Zener, "Solar Sea Power," *Bulletin of the Atomic Scientists* (January 1976): 17–24.

74. David Van Cleave, "Getting Bulk Power From Solar Energy," *Electric Light and Power* (December 1974): 11–13.

75. Fannin, "Solar Energy," p. 3. See also Mary Archer, "Science and the Sun," *New Scientist* 160 (29 November 1973): 636–638.

76. Fannin, "Solar Energy."

77. U.S. Energy Research and Development Administration, *A National Plan for Energy Research, Development & Demonstration: Creating Energy Choices for the Future*, ERDA-48, Vol. 1 (Washington, DC: Government Printing Office, June, 1975), p. II-5.

78. U.S. Department of Energy, *Solar Energy: A Status Report*, DOE/ET-0062 (Washington, DC: Government Printing Office, June 1978), p. 1.

79. Lewis J. Perelman, "Speculations on the Transition to Sustainable Energy," *Ethics* 90 (April 1980): 392.

80. Denis Hayes, "The Coming Energy Transition," *The Futurist* (October 1977): 303.

81. David W. Orr, "U.S. Energy Policy and the Political Economy of Participation," *The Journal of Politics* 41 (November 1979): 1028–1029.

82. See Orr, "U.S. Energy Policy,"; Hayes, "Energy Transition,"; Denis Hayes, *Rays of Hope: The Transition to a Post-Petroleum World* (New York: W. W. Norton and Co, 1977), chap. 12. See also the materials cited above.

83. These arguments are mainly drawn from Allen Hammond and William Metz, "Solar Energy Research: Making Solar After the Nuclear Model," *Science* 197 (July 15, 1977): 241–244, and William Metz, "Solar Thermal Electricity: Power Tower Dominates Research," *Science* 197 (22 July 1977): 353–356. These points are elaborated in Allen Hammond, "Photovoltaics: The Semiconductor Revolution Comes to Solar," *Science* 197 (July 29, 1977): 445–447, and William Metz, "Solar Thermal Energy: Bringing the Pieces Together," *Science* 197 (August 12, 1977): pp. 650–651.

84. Hammond and Metz, "Solar Energy Research," p. 241.
85. They also argued that the government's programs would fail to tap the economic potential of solar. Ibid., esp. p. 242.
86. Ibid., p. 243.

CHAPTER 7

1. Federal Energy Administration, *Project Independence Report* (Washington, DC: Government Printing Office, 1974), Appendices A-IX and A-X.
2. Executive Office of the President, Energy Policy and Planning, "The National Energy Plan: Summary of Public Participation," (Washington, DC: Government Printing Office, n.d. but 1977), p. 17.
3. Briefing paper by Stu Eizenstat and Kitty Schirmer, October 17, 1977, for meeting with Amory Lovins, and The Daily Diary of President Jimmy Carter, "10/18/77," both in 10/18/77, box PD-18, Presidential Diary, JCL. The briefing paper of the day before the meeting suggests the smaller, shorter meeting, while the diary entry presents what finally took place.
4. Lamont C. Hempel, "The Politics of Sunshine: An Inquiry into the Origin, Growth, and Ideological Character of the Solar Energy Movement in America," Ph.D. dissertation, Claremont Graduate Schools, 1983, pp. 155–156.
5. Briefing Paper, October 17, 1977.
6. Letter, Ian A. Forbes to Stuart E. Eizenstat, 10/26/77, folder Solar Energy [O/A 6239], box 278, Staff Office, Eizenstat, JCL.
7. President's Reorganization Project, "Decision Analysis Report," May 31, 1977, prepared by Sam Carradine, Robert Cunningham, Mac Destler, John Helmer, and Len Vernamonti, pp. 2–3, 7, and 10–11.
8. Frank N. Laird, "Technocracy Revisited: Knowledge, Power, and the Crisis in Energy Decision Making," *Industrial Crisis Quarterly* 4 (1990): 49–61, esp. p. 54 on the DPR's origins.
9. Letter, Katherine P. Schirmer to Leon Green, March 30, 1978, folder SC 3 1/20/77–1/20/81, box SC-4, WHCF – Sciences, JCL. See also Richard Corrigan, "Solar Energy – Will Federal Policy Work to Let the Sunshine In?" *National Journal* 10 (April 15, 1978): 592–593.
10. Memo, James R. Schlesinger and Charles Warren to Stuart Eizenstat, April 6, 1978, folder Solar Energy 1978 [O/A 7432] [1], box 279, Staff Offices – Eizenstat, JCL.
11. Corrigan, "Solar Energy," p. 594.
12. Stu Eizenstat and Kitty Schirmer to the President, May 9, 1978, folder Solar Energy 1978 [O/A 7432] [1], box 279, Staff Offices – Eizenstat, JCL. The memo was signed "Stu" and initialed by Carter.
13. Luther J. Carter, "Sun Day Seen as more Potent than Earth Day," *Science* 200 (April 14, 1978): 185–187. Sun Day was organized by Denis Hayes, the same person who organized the first Earth Day. Hayes embodied the growing linkage between the environmental movement and the solar movement. I discuss the administration's response to Sun Day in the next chapter.

14. On the process of analysis as a way of influencing policy and on redesigning the channels for interests, see Deborah A. Stone, *Policy Paradox and Political Reason* (Glenview, IL: Scott Foresman, 1988), parts II and III. On changing policy venues, see Frank R. Baumgartner and Bryan D. Jones, *Agendas and Instabilities in American Politics* (Chicago: University of Chicago Press, 1993), part one. On solar advocates in government, see Laird, "Technocracy Revisited," p. 54.

15. For a description of the DPR structure, see Allan R. Hoffman, "A National Strategy for Solar Energy: The Role of the Domestic Policy Review," in *The Solar Energy Transition: Implementation and Policy Implications*, AAAS Selected Symposium 74, Daniel Rich et al., eds. (Boulder, CO: Westview Press, 1983), pp. 36–37.

16. Ibid., p. 38.

17. Memo, Stuart Eizenstat to the Secretary of Energy et al., May 16, 1978, reprinted in Department of Energy, *Domestic Policy Review of Solar Energy*, Appendices, Final Report, Impacts Panel, October 1978, Vol. 2, TID-28835/2, pp. 1–4.

18. The study was supposed to be completed by mid-August. Ibid., p. 4.

19. "Primary energy" is a measure of the inputs into the energy system, such as the number of barrels of oil, tons of coal, and so on.

20. U.S. Department of Energy, *Solar Energy: A Status Report*, DOE/ET-0062, June 1978, pp. 6–8 and 11–12.

21. U.S. Congress, Office of Technology Assessment, *Application of Solar Technology to Today's Energy Needs*, Vol. 1 (Washington, DC: Government Printing Office, June 1978), p. 3.

22. Ibid., p. 11.

23. For description and analysis of the public participation programs, see Hoffman, "National Strategy," p. 39, and Laird, "Technocracy Revisited," pp. 54–55.

24. U.S. Department of Energy, Office of Consumer Affairs, *Summary Reports: Domestic Policy Review (DPR) Public Hearings on Solar Energy*, 2 vols., n.d. but ca. July 1978; *The Great Adventure: A Report on the 10 Regional Public Hearings On Solar Energy for the Domestic Policy Review*, HCP/U6354-01, prepared by the Franklin Institute and the Institute for Local Self-Reliance for the U.S. Department of Energy, Office of Consumer Affairs, October, 1978; Bernie Jones, et al., *Social Research on the 1978 Solar Domestic Policy Review*, August 18, 1978, prepared for the Solar Energy Research Institute.

25. For a detailed analysis of this aspect of the participation program, see Laird, "Technocracy Revisited," pp. 54–57.

26. *Status Report on Solar Energy Domestic Policy Review*, Public Review Copy, August 25, 1978, emphasis in original, reprinted in *Domestic Policy Review of Solar Energy*, TID-28835/2, Vol. 2, Appendices, Final Report, following p. D-20.

27. Ibid., section V, esp. p. V-7. The scenario assumed that oil would cost $25 per barrel in 2000. A quad (q) is a large unit of energy, a quadrillion Btu's. The scenario assumed a total American consumption of all energy

of 95 q in that year, so 18.1 q of solar was about 20% of the total energy demand.

28. *Status Report*, p. VI-1, Appendix D, following p. D-20.

29. During the Carter administration the United States used about 75 q of energy per year.

30. A presentation and analysis of the comments received on the draft are in *Domestic Policy Review of Solar Energy*, Appendices, Final Report, Vol. 2, Appendix D.

31. Walter S. Mossberg, "Solar Power Seen Meeting 20% of Needs By 2000; Carter May Seek Outlay Boost," *Wall Street Journal* (August 22, 1978): 4; Dick Kirschten, "Who Will Stop the Rain?" *National Journal* (September 23, 1978): 1521.

32. "Domestic Policy Review Fiasco," *People and Energy* (pub. by the Citizen's Energy Project) 4 (July/August 1978): 7, NREL; "Solar Policy Review: Feds Flunk," *People and Energy* 4 (September/October 1978): 11, NREL.

33. For a more extensive analysis of problems with the DPR participation process, see Laird, "Technocracy Revisited," pp. 54–58.

34. Domestic Policy Review of Solar Energy, "A Response Memorandum to the President," printed by the U.S. Department of Energy, TID 22834, February 1979.

35. Ibid., pp. ii–iii.

36. Ibid., p. vii and chapters III and IV.

37. Memo, Kitty Schirmer to Stu Eizenstat, December 13, 1978, folder SC 3 7/1/78–12/31/78, box SC-3, WHCF – Sciences, JCL.

38. The SEIA represented the conventional, more conservative wing of the solar movement. See the discussion of them in Chapter 6.

39. Meeting Notes, Stu Eizenstat to the President, February 23, 1979, 2/23/79 Backup Material in Box PD-48, Presidential Diary, JCL. The meeting, originally scheduled for 15 minutes, went for 45 minutes; see the Daily Diary of President Jimmy Carter, same location. The study was the *Blueprint for a Solar America*, discussed in Frank N. Laird, "Constructing the Future," under review.

40. Memo, Denis Hayes to Gerald Rafshoon and Greg Schneiders, n.d. but ca. December 15, 1978, folder SC 3 7/1/78–12/31/78, box SC-3, WHCF – Sciences, JCL; Letter, Denis Hayes et al., to the President, January 29, 1979, WHCF – Name File, JCL.

41. On the last point, see letter, Tom Tatum to Jack Watson, March 23, 1979, and attached memo, folder SC 3 3/1/79–5/31/79 letters/memos, box SC-3, WHCF – Sciences, JCL. For the other communications, see letter, James Blanchard et al. (116 signers) to President Jimmy Carter, February 4, 1979, folder SC 3 1/1/79–2/20/79, box SC-3, WHCF – Sciences; letter, Bill Bradley to the President, April 14, 1979, folder SC 33/1/79–5/31/79, box SC-3, WHCF – Sciences; letter, Jack H. Watson to Thomas P. O'Neill III, April 23, 1979, folder SC 3 3/1/79–5/31/79, box SC-3, WHCF – Sciences, all in JCL.

42. Al Richman, "The Polls: Public Attitudes Toward the Energy Crisis," *Public Opinion Quarterly* 43 (1979): 582. A poll cited in the *Blueprint*

gave even higher numbers for solar popularity. The absolute measures that one gets depends heavily on the precise working of the question, as well as other influences. Most interesting is that the ordering had been consistent over two years and solar had, if anything, been gaining in its ranking.

43. Memo, Jim Schlesinger to The President, February 6, 1979, pp. 1 and 3, folder Solar Energy [CF, O/A 731] [1], box 278, Staff Offices, Eizenstat, JCL.

44. Memo, Tom Lambrix to Stu Eizenstat, David Rubenstein, and Bert Carp, May 10, 1979, and attached decision memo draft, folder Solar Energy [CF O/A 731] [1], box 278, Staff Offices, Eizenstat, JCL.

45. See Ronald D. Brunner and Weston E. Vivian, "Citizen Viewpoints on Energy Policy," *Policy Sciences* 12 (1980): 147–174; Elizabeth Drew, "Phase: In Search of a Definition," *New Yorker* 55 (August 27, 1979): 45–73; Joseph A. Yager, "The Energy Battles of 1979," in *Energy Policy in Perspective: Today's Problems, Yesterday's Solutions*, Craufurd D. Goodwin, ed. (Washington, DC: The Brookings Institution, 1981), pp. 601–636.

46. Lambrix to Eisenstat, Rubenstein, and Carp, May 10, 1979, and attached draft decision memo.

47. Memo, Stu Eizenstat and Kitty Schirmer to The President, n.d. but ca. early June 1979, p. 19, no initials, folder "Solar Energy [CF O/A 731][2]," box 278, Staff Offices – Eizenstat, JCL.

48. Memo, Stu Eizenstat to the President (initialed by both), June 5, 1979, attached is Decision Memo, June 5, 1979, marked by president, folder Solar Energy [CF O/A 731] [2], box 278, Staff Offices – Eizenstat, JCL.

49. Solar Lobby, *Blueprint for a Solar America* (January 1979). See the studies cited in their footnote 18, particularly that by LaPorte. They may not have wanted to fight that particular battle in this document, but they were obviously aware of it and probably sympathetic to it. They also did not call their plan a soft energy path, though they cited Lovins in a number of places.

50. "Solar Hot Water for the White House," *Solar Utilization News* 3 (October 1978): 1, NREL. Anne Wexler, Stu Eizenstat, and Hugh Carter, Solar Energy Announcement, June 20, 1979, folder Solar Energy [CF O/A 731][2], box 278, Staff Offices – Eizenstat, JCL. Memo, Harry [a speech writer] to Kitty [Schirmer] and Tom [Lambrix], May 16, 1979, folder 6/20/79 remarks, Inauguration of West Wing Solar [energy] System [1], box 49, Staff Offices – Speech Writers – Chron File, JCL.

51. Letter, Gus Speth to Bernie [Aronson], 6/12/79, folder 6/20/79 – Remarks – Inauguration of West Wing Solar [Energy] System [1], box 49, Staff Offices – Speech Writers – Chron File, JCL.

52. Fact Sheet, The President's Message on Solar Energy, June 20, 1979, folder Solar Energy [CF O/A 731][2], box 278, Staff Offices – Eizenstat, JCL. Office of Media Liaison, White House Press Office, Background Report,

Solar Energy, June 22, 1979, folder SC 3 6/1/79–7/23/79, box SC-3, WHCF – Sciences, JCL.

53. Background Report, p. 4.
54. Eliot Marshall, "Carter Hails Solar Age in Presolstice Rite," *Science* 205 (6 July 1979): 21–24.
55. Memo, Gus Speth to the President, August 16, 1979, folder 8/16/79 [1], box 142, Staff Secretary – Handwriting File, JCL. Speth quote is on p. 2, emphasis in original. Solar advocates had gone public with their criticism, and the General Accounting Office, a part of Congress, had also issued a critique of a DOE solar program. See Neal R. Peirce and Jerry Hagstrom, "Solar Advocates Damn Carter, Brown with Faint Praise," *National Journal* 11 (August 4, 1979): 1289–1291; "GAO Rips DOE 'Solar in Federal Buildings' Program for Lacking Strategy," *Inside D.O.E.* (August 24, 1979): 8.
56. Memo, Gus Speth to Hamilton Jordan, August 16, 1979, folder 8/16/79 [1], box 142, Staff Secretary – Handwriting File, JCL.
57. Luther J. Carter, "Gus Speth, Planning the Conserver Society," *Science* 208 (30 May 1980): 1009–1012.
58. Anthony J. Parisi, "New Path for Solar Institute," *New York Times* (December 26, 1979): D1; Luther J. Carter, "Hayes Makes Sunshine At SERI," *Science* 210 (24 October 1980): 408–409.
59. Carter, "Gus Speth."
60. William Rice, "Federal Policy on Solar: Piecemeal," *Solar Age* 4 (November 1979): 26–29.
61. For a summary of legislation up to January 1975, see Federal Energy Administration, *General Facts on Energy*, prepared for Frank G. Zarb, Administrator, FEA by Communications and Public Affairs Research Branch, January 1975, pp. I-7 to I-10, folder General Facts on Energy (1), box 5, Frank G. Zarb Files, GRFL.
62. "The Congressional Program of Economic Recovery and Energy Sufficiency," February 1975, pp. 1–3, folder Energy 1975: Alt. Eng. Progs (2), box 11, Glenn R. Schleede Files, GRFL.
63. See memo, Mike Duval to Jim Cannon, March 10, 1975, folder UT 3/8/76–4/25/76, box 6, WHCF – Sub, GRFL, and memo, John Hill to Jim Lynn, n.d. but ca. March 1975, folder Energy 1975: Alt. Eng. Progs. (2), box 11, Glenn R. Schleede Files, GRFL.
64. Hempel, "The Politics of Sunshine," pp. 108–111.
65. Mike McCormack, *Congressional Record*, October 30, 1973, reprinted in U. S. House of Representatives, Committee on Science and Astronautics, Subcommittee on Energy, "H.R. 11864, Solar Heating and Cooling Demonstration Act of 1974," Background and Legislative History, Serial L, February, 1974, pp. 67–69. U.S. House of Representatives, Committee on Science and Technology, Subcommittee on Energy R,D&D, "Solar Heating and Cooling Demonstration Act of 1974," Oversight Hearings, 94th Cong., 1st Sess., May 13–15, 1975, pp. 1–2. See also the discussion of the act in James G. Phillips, "Energy Report: Solar Power Systems Receive $60 Million

Development Push," *National Journal Reports* (September 7, 1974): 1331–1339.

66. Comments of Mike McCormack, *Congressional Record* May 19, 1976, pp. 14413–14414.
67. U.S. House of Representatives, Committee on Science and Technology, Subcommittee on Energy R,D, &D, "Solar Heating and Cooling Demonstration Act of 1974," Oversight Hearings, 94th Cong., 1st Sess., May 13–15, 1975, pp. 34–36.
68. See Hempel, "The Politics of Sunshine," pp. 126–130, for a more detailed description of Ottinger's positions and how that affected McCormack.

CHAPTER 8

1. The Director of the OMB, Roy Ash, opposed trying to make the FY 1974 budget even larger at the last minute for several reasons, including that "it could be counterproductive because we never win in bidding contests in the Congress." Nixon agreed with Ash at the time to not to try to up the budget at the last minute. See Roy Ash to the President, April 16, 1973, folder April 1973, box 21, President's Office Files – Handwriting File, NLNP.
2. Statement by the President, Press Release, June 29, 1973, folder [EX] UT 6/1/73–6/30/73, box 2, WHCF – Sub – UT, NLNP. The quote is on p. 1, the other data are on pp. 4–5.
3. Memo, Glenn Schleede to Dick Fairbanks, October 11, 1973, plus attached Fact Sheet, folder [EX] UT 10/1/73–10/15/73, box 3, WHCF – Sub – UT, NLNP. The data are on pp. 3–6 of the Fact Sheet.
4. Elliot L. Richardson and Frank G. Zarb, "Perspective on Energy Policy," Report of the Energy Resources Council, p. 10, folder Energy Resources Council, box 5, Frank G. Zarb Files, GRFL. See also Frank G. Zarb to the President through Rogers C. B. Morton, December 18, 1974, and attachments, folder Utility – Energy: Energy Policy Briefing 12/19/74 (1), box 50, President's Handwriting File, GRFL. See also my discussion in Chapter 5.
5. David C. Mowery and Nathan Rosenberg, *Technology and the Pursuit of Economic Growth* (Cambridge: Cambridge University Press, 1991), especially chap. 1.
6. Alvin M. Weinberg, "Can Technology Replace Social Engineering?" in *Technology and the Future*, 5th ed., A. Teich, ed. (New York: St. Martins Press, 1990), pp. 29–38.
7. U.S., Executive Office of the President, Energy Policy and Planning, *The National Energy Plan* (Washington, DC: Government Printing Office, 1977), pp. x, 7, and 31–32.
8. *Public Papers of the Presidents of the United States: Richard M. Nixon, 1971* (Washington, DC: Government Printing Office, 1972), p. 708. Solar was the last in a list of "other," lower priority, R&D programs.

9. NASA/NSF Solar Energy Panel, *An Assessment of Solar Energy as a National Energy Resource* (Washington, DC: Government Printing Office, December 1972), p. 1.
10. Ibid. Figures are on p. 5 and quote is on p. 8.
11. On the split reaction to this report, see Lamont C. Hempel, "The Politics of Sunshine: An Inquiry into the Origin, Growth, and Ideological Character of the Solar Energy Movement in America," unpublished Ph.D. dissertation, Claremont Graduate School, 1983, pp. 103–108. A summary of the report's R&D recommendations are in NASA/NSF Solar Panel Report, p. 11.
12. NASA/NSF Solar Energy Panel, *Solar Energy*, p. 46.
13. Ibid., p. 11.
14. Memo, John Whitaker to the President through John Ehrlichman, n.d., but early March 1971, folder March 1 thru 15, 1971, box 9, President's Office Files – Handwriting File, NLNP. See the attachment to the memo.
15. For example, see Tod R. Hullin to Henry E. Cunningham, October 2, 1970, plus attachment, folder Gen SC6, box 5, WHCF – Sub – SC, NLNP. Hullin was the assistant to Ehrlichman, and the attachment is an issue of a newsletter put out by Kaiser Aluminum and Chemical Company, which discusses energy in general and is quite upbeat on solar.
16. Letter, Peter M. Flanigan to Allen F. Cordts, February 10, 1970, folder Gen SC6, box 5, WHCF – Sub – SC, NLNP.
17. U.S. House of Representatives, Committee on Science and Astronautics, *Solar Energy Research*, Staff report, 92d Congress, 2d Sess., Serial Z, December 1972, pp. 3–4 and 8–9. Note that these amounts are slightly different from those given in the administration documents cited in the previous chapter. There is no obvious way to resolve the differences.
18. U.S. Congress, House, Committee on Science and Astronautics, Subcommittee on Energy, *Solar Energy for the Terrestrial Generation of Electricity*, Hearings, 93d Congress, 1st Sess., June 5, 1973, p. 1.
19. Report, "A Longer Term Perspective: The Role of Research and Development," n.d. but ca. September 1974, pp. 21–22, folder Energy 1974: R&D – Gen'l (1), box 10, Glenn R. Schleede Files, GRFL; James G. Phillips, "Energy Report: Solar Power Systems Receive $60 Million Development Push," *National Journal Reports* (September 7, 1974): 1331–1339. Discussion of administration caution is on p. 1339. For an example of prosolar pressure from a Republican, see, Letter, Dean Burch to Jack M. Eckerd, October 3, 1974, plus attachment, folder SC 6 Physical Sciences 8/9/74–12/31/74, box 2, WHCF – Sub, GRFL; letter, Gerald Ford to Jack Eckerd, July 25, 1975, folder SC 6 1/1/75–7/31/75, box 2, WHCF – Sub, GRFL.
20. Federal Energy Administration, Project Independence Blueprint, "Solar Energy," Final Task Force Report, (Washington, DC: Government Printing Office, November 1974). The overview of solar is in Chapter I, and the list of possible incentives is in Appendix III. The estimates of maximum solar contributions are on p. I-7. The unit of energy q (quad) is one quadrillion

(10^{15}) Btu's, a very large unit. In the mid-1970s, the total primary energy consumed in the U.S. was about 75 q.

21. Elliot Richardson and Frank G. Zarb, "Perspective on Energy Policy," December 16, 1976, pp. 4–5 and 10 (for the quote), pub. by the Energy Resources Council, folder Energy Resources Council, box 5, Frank G. Zarb Files, GRFL.

22. D.H. Frieling et al., "A Critical Review and Analysis of the Advanced Research Implications of the Phase 0 Program Results on Solar Heating and Cooling of Buildings," Report to NSF and ERDA by Battelle Columbus Laboratories, RANN doc. no. NSF-RANN-75-017, March 1975, pp. 4–5.

23. None of these social research proposals came from the original three contractors, but instead had been added by the Battelle staff. Ibid., pp. 54–62.

24. Letter, Robert Seamans to the President, February 28, 1975, plus attached report, folder SC 6 1/1/75–7/31/75, box 2, WHCF – Sub, GRFL. Quote is on p. 6 of the attached report.

25. Interim Report, Interagency Task Force on Solar Energy, March 14, 1975, p. 2, folder Solar Heating and Cooling/Review of Reports on Solar, box 5, Andre M. Buckles Files, GRFL.

26. Davis, *Energy Politics*, p. 232.

27. Letter, Hubert H. Humphrey and Henry M. Jackson to the President, January 14, 1975, folder FG 383 1/1/75–1/20/75, box 200, WHCF – Sub, GRFL.

28. Letter, William T. Kendall to Hubert H. Humphrey, January 16, 1975, with identical letter to Henry Jackson attached, folder FG 383 1/1/75–1/20/75, box 200, WHCF – Sub, GRFL. It is interesting that someone as far down as a Deputy Assistant was chosen to reply to the senators. Perhaps there was a plausible deniability strategy at work.

29. Memo, Jerry Jones to Bill Walker, January 9, 1975, plus attachments, folder FG 383 1/1/75–1/20/75, box 200, WHCF – Sub, GRFL.

30. Memo, Jones to Walker, January 9, 1975, second attachment, pp. 2–3.

31. Memo, William Walker to the President through Donald Rumsfeld, May 19, 1975, folder FG 383 ERDA 4/1/75 – 5/31/75, box 201, WHCF – Sub, GRFL.

32. Douglas P. Bennett to the President through Richard B. Cheney, February 5, 1976, attached to James E. O'Connor to Douglas Bennett, February 12, 1976, folder FG 383 1/1/75–4/30/76, box 201, WHCF – Sub, GRFL.

33. Some of President Carter's appointments are discussed later.

34. U.S. Energy Research and Development Administration, "A National Plan for Energy Research, Development, and Demonstration: Creating Energy Choices for the Future," ERDA-48, vol. 1 (Washington, DC: Government Printing Office, June 1975), chap. 8.

35. Ibid., p. VI-1. See also, Memo, Glenn Schleede to Jack Blasy, July 10, 1975, folder Solar Energy, 1975, box 4, Glenn R. Schleede Files, GRFL, pp. 1–2. The White House – ERDA dispute over the roles of the private versus public sectors also figured prominently in this memo.

36. U.S. Congress Office of Technology Assessment, *An Analysis of the ERDA Plan and Program* (Washington, DC: Government Printing Office, October 1975), pp. 1–7 and chap. 4.
37. Ibid., pp. 126 and 243.
38. Memo, Glenn Schleede to Bill Nicholson, November 4, 1975, folder Solar Energy, 1975, box 41, Glenn R. Schleede Files, GRFL.
39. Note, Hugh Loweth to Glenn Schleede, January 14, 1976, plus attachment, folder Solar Energy 1976 Speech Material, box 41, Glenn R. Schleede Files, GRFL.
40. U.S. ERDA, *National Plan for Energy Research, Development, and Demonstration: Creating Energy Choices for the Future, 1976, Vol. 1: The Plan* (Washington, DC: Government Printing Office, April 1976), pp. 62–63 and 67–68 for solar.
41. Speech, Frank G. Zarb, October 9, 1976, folder Speeches – May–December-1976, box 8, Frank G. Zarb Files, GRFL. Quote is on p. 4.
42. Ibid., p. 7.
43. ERDA, Division of Solar Energy, "An Economic Analysis of Solar Water and Space Heating," November 1976, doc. DSE-2322-1 (Washington, DC: Government Printing Office, November 1976).
44. Memo, Wilfred Rommel (OMB) to the President, August 29, 1974, p. 4, attached to Staff Secretary to Michael Duval, et al., August 29, 1974, folder SC 6, Physical Sciences 8/9/74–12/31/74, box 2, WHCF – Sub, GRFL.
45. ERDA, *National Plan*, 1976, vol. 1, p. 16.
46. See letter, Peter Flanigan to Senator James Abourezk, March 6, 1973, plus attachments, "Ex SC 6 Physical Sciences 1/1/73," box 5, WHCF – Sub, NLNP, concerning the AEC report on solar and letter, Tom Korologos to Senator Carl T. Curtis, March 27, 1974, plus attachments, "Ex FG 6-26 1/1/74–4/30/74," box 1, WHCF – Sub, NLNP, about the R&D Advisory Committee meeting. For more detail, see Ray Reece, *The Sun Betrayed: A Report on the Corporate Seizure of U.S. Solar Energy Development* (Boston, MA: The South End Press, 1979).
47. This point will be elaborated later. Note here two pieces of evidence. One is a handwritten note in Michael Raoul-Duval's files that says "*Solar* fact (per Cong. Mike McCormack) if 1% total demand from solar must convert 10% old houses 7 million at cost of $70–105 billion" n.d. but probably 1975, folder Solar Energy, box 11, Michael Raoul-Duval Files, GRFL. The other concerns a solar initiative being put together by the FEA staff. An OMB official notes that "From all indications, FEA top management (Zarb, Hill, Zausner) has not taken a strong interest in this initiative,..." in memo, Henry Lum to James Mitchell, June 17, 1975, folder SC 6 1/1/75–7/31/75, box 2, WHCF – Sub, GRFL.
48. See President Ford's answers to questions, April 2, 1976, April 23, 1976, May 12, 1976, and May 22, 1976, all in folders Energy (1) and Energy (2), box H36, President Ford Committee Records, Quotebooks, GRFL.
49. Detailed Fact Sheet, President's Energy Message, February 26, 1976, folder Energy 1976: Pres. Eng. Mess., 2/26/76, Fact Sheet, box 13, Glenn R. Schleede Files, GRFL.

50. Budget authority is the amount of money that Congress puts into a specific activity, as opposed to obligations, which are the amounts that the agencies commit to spending in a fiscal year. See ERDA, *A National Plan for Energy Research, Development, and Demonstration: Creating Energy Choices for the Future* 1976, vol. 2: Program Implementation (Washington, DC: Government Printing Office, 1976): p. 76; and memo, Jim Connor to the President, February 27, 1976, plus attachment, folder Sciences, box 43, President's Office Files, Handwriting File, GRFL.
51. The figures are from ERDA, 1976, vol. 2, p. 76.
52. Dixie Lee Ray, *The Nation's Energy Future: A Report to Richard M. Nixon, President of the United States*, 1 December 1973, pp. 23–24, reprinted in Joint Committee on Atomic Energy, hearings, December 11, 1973, pp. 37–215.
53. ERDA, Division of Solar Energy, *Interim Report: National Program Plan for Research and Development in Solar Heating and Cooling*, ERDA 76-144 (Washington, DC: Government Printing Office, November 1976), p. 33.
54. See Reece, *The Sun Betrayed*, esp. chaps. 4 and 6.
55. Letter, Paul O'Neill to Senator Jacob K. Javits, September 21, 1976, plus attachment, folder SC6 8/1/76–1/20/77, box 30, WHCF – Sub, GRFL.
56. Memo, James Lynn to the President, July 9, 1976, esp. pp. 2–4 and 7, folder ERDA, 1976 Budget, box 15, Glenn R. Schleede Files, GRFL. Ford did not veto the bill, which became PL94-355.
57. Letter, James Lynn to Robert Seamans, July 10, 1975, folder SC6 1/1/75–7/31/75, box 2, WHCF – Sub, GRFL.
58. Letter, Robert W. Fri to James T. Lynn, September 30, 1975, plus attached briefing, folder ERDA 1975: Budget request estimates for FY1977, Box 15, Glenn R. Schleede Files, GRFL.
59. Press Guidance, re. Teem resignation, February 27, 1976, plus attached article, folder Solar Energy General 1976, box 41, Glenn R. Schleede files, GRFL.
60. *Public Papers of the Presidents of the United States: Jimmy Carter, 1977*, Book I, January 20 to June 24, 1977 (Washington, DC: Government Printing Office, 1977), Address to Congress, April 20, 1977, p. 670. In talking about new energy sources, the President said "The most promising, of course, is solar energy, . . ." Of course?
61. For a brief history of SERI, see Philip M. Boffey, "Solar Research Sweepstakes: States Vie for a Place in the Sun," *Science* 190 (10 October 1975): 128–130; Idem, "Solar Research Institute Starts Out in Partial Eclipse," *Science* 192 (2 April 1976): 36; Idem, "Solar Energy Research Institute: Grumbles About a Change in Plans," *Science* 196 (15 April 1977): 278–280; Burt Solomon, "Big SERI Loses Ground to Little SERIs," *The Energy Daily* 6 (March 9, 1978): 1–2.
62. Energy Policy and Planning, *The National Energy Plan*, pp. 75–77.
63. Allen Hammond and William Metz, "Solar Energy Research: Making Solar After the Nuclear Model," *Science* 197 (July 15, 1977): 241.

64. Richard Corrigan, "Solar Energy – Will Federal Policy Work to Let the Sunshine In?" *National Journal* 10 (April 15, 1978): 592–595, esp. pp. 592–594.

65. Memo, Charlie Schultze to the President, May 1, 1978, folder [1978 Energy Supply Initiatives] 5/2/78, box 84, Office of the Staff Secretary, JCL. The quote is from p. 3, emphasis in original.

66. Memo, James McIntyre to the President, n.d. but ca. 5/2/78, folder [1978 Energy Supply Initiative] 5/3/78 [1], box 84, Office of the Staff Secretary, JCL. See also the memos from Press and Schlesinger cited later.

67. Memo, Charles Warren and Gus Speth to the President, April 28, 1978, folder [1978 Energy Supply Initiatives] 5/2/78, box 84, Office of the Staff Secretary, JCL.

68. Ibid., p. 2 for all of the quotes. Emphasis in original.

69. Memo, Frank Press to the President, n.d. but ca. 5/1/78, folder Energy Policies 4/24/77–11/5/79, box 6, Staff Offices – Press, JCL. Analysis section of the memo is unpaginated, but quote is from second page of analysis.

70. Memo, Jim Schlesinger to the President, n.d. but ca. 5/1/78, folder [1978 Energy Supply Initiative] 5/2/78, box 84, Office of the Staff Secretary, JCL. Schlesinger was trained as an economist and held economic rationality as a very important value. See James L. Cochrane, "Carter Energy Policy and the Ninety-fifth Congress," in *Energy Policy in Perspective: Today's Problems, Yesterday's Solutions*, Craufurd D. Goodwin, ed. (Washington, DC: The Brookings Institution, 1981), pp. 552–554.

71. On last minute changes, see memo, Jim Fallows to the President, May 2, 1978, folder 5/3/78 – Sun Day Speech, Denver, CO, box 23, Speech Writers – Chron File, JCL.

72. The text of the speech is in *Public Papers of the Presidents, Jimmy Carter 1978*, Vol. I (Washington, DC: Government Printing Office, 1979), pp. 824–826.

73. Pamela G. Hollie, "Energy Plea on Sun Day: Convert Dream to Reality," *New York Times* (May 4, 1978): A1; Martin Tolchin, "Carter Orders a Rise for Solar Research," *New York Times* (May 4, 1978): A42; David S. Broder, "25,000 Here Join Sun Day Celebration," *Washington Post* (May 4, 1978): A1.

74. Luther J. Carter, "A Bright Solar Prospect Seen by CEQ and OTA," *Science* 200 (12 May 1978): 627–630.

75. Stuart Eizenstat and Kitty Schirmer to the President, October 31, 1978, "11/6/78," Box 108, Office of the Staff Secretary – Handwriting File, JCL.

76. Frank Press to the President, n.d. but 1978, "Energy Policies 4/24/77–11/5/79," box 6, Staff Offices – Sci/Tech Advisor to the President – Press, JCL.

77. Jim Schlesinger to the President, n.d. but 5/2/78, pp. 7–8, "1978 Energy Supply Initiative 5/2/78," box 84, Office of the Staff Secretary – Handwriting File, JCL. Emphasis in original.

78. Charles Warren and Gus Speth to the President, 4/28/78, "1978 Energy Supply Initiative, 5/2/78," Box 84, Office of the Staff Secretary – Handwriting File, JCL.

79. Joseph A. Yager, "The Energy Battles of 1979," in *Energy Policy*, Goodwin, ed., pp. 620–628. Elizabeth Drew, "Phase: In Search of a Definition," *New Yorker* 55 (August 27, 1979): 45–73. For a partial list of who went to Camp David see "Camp David Advisers: Who Met Carter," *Congressional Quarterly Weekly Report* 37 (July 14, 1979): 1393. Solar advocates are conspicuous by their absence, with the exception of S. David Freeman.

80. "Energy and National Goals," July 15, 1979, *Public Papers of the President, Jimmy Carter, 1979*, Vol. II, (Washington, DC: Government Printing, 1980), pp. 1235–1241.

81. Ibid., pp. 1239–1240. Quote is on p. 1240.

82. Yager, "Energy Battles," pp. 624–628, and much greater detail in Drew, "Phase."

83. Memo, Patrick H. Caddell to the President, August 7, 1979, folder 8/16/79 [1], box 142, Staff Secretary Handwriting File, JCL. The list is on p. 4.

84. Memo, Jack Watson to the President, August 14, 1979, folder 8/16/79 [1], box 142, Staff Secretary Handwriting File, JCL. Carter's note is on the first page of the memo, and the double underlining is in the original.

85. Letter, Jimmy Carter to Thomas P. O'Neill, Jr., July 27, 1979, folder FG 999-20, box FG 237, WHCF – Subject, JCL.

86. Memo, Harry Schwartz to Stu Eizenstat, July 24, 1979, folder SC 3 7/24/79 – 1/20/81, box SC-3, WHCF – Sciences, JCL.

87. Yager, "The Energy Battles," pp. 631–634.

88. Memo, Charles W. Duncan, Jr., January 15, 1980, and memo, Gus Speth to the President, July 18, 1980, attached to memo, Jack Watson to Stu Eizenstat and John White, July 22, 1980, both in folder SC-3 7/24/79–1/20/81, box SC-3, WHCF – Sciences, JCL.

89. Steve Lohr, "Duncan Memo Asks Cut in Solar Energy Funds" *New York Times* (May 24, 1980): A29; idem, "No Cuts in U.S. Solar Goals Cited" *New York Times* (May 29, 1980): D1.

90. Speth to the President, July 18, 1980. The covering memo on Speth's memo suggests that his idea was initially brushed off. For the formation of the task force, see memo, Stu Eizenstat to Charles Duncan, Frank Press, Jim McIntyre, and Gus Speth, September 24, 1980, folder SC 3 7/24/79–1/20/81, box SC-3, WHCF – Sciences, JCL.

91. James T. McIntyre Jr. to the President, n.d. but 5/3/78, "[1978 Energy Supply Initiative] 5/3/78 [1]," box 84, Office of the Staff Secretary – Handwriting File, JCL.

92. Ibid. McIntyre worked for the OMB, and so had access to some of the best budget data.

93. U.S. Department of Energy, *National Energy Plan II* (Washington, DC: Government Printing Office, May 1979), p. 34. When the administration

proposed cuts in solar programs, Congress frequently put the money back in the budget.

94. Fact Sheet, Presidential Message on Solar Energy, 6/20/79, esp. p. 6, "SP-2-3-125," box SP-13, WHCF – Subject – Speeches, JCL.

95. U.S. Department of Energy, *Congressional Budget Request FY1981*, vol. 2, January 1980, pp. 27 and 45.

96. U.S. Senate, Committee on Governmental Affairs, Subcommittee on Energy, Nuclear Proliferation, and Federal Services, "The Department of Energy's Fiscal Year 1981 Budget Request," July 16, 1980, pp. 4–5.

CHAPTER 9

1. For a discussion of the ways that partisans in policy disputes can contest the boundaries between normative and empirical claims, see Sheila Jasanoff, *The Fifth Branch: Science Advisers as Policymakers* (Cambridge, MA: Harvard University Press, 1990), chap. 11.

2. Handwritten note, n.d. but 1975, folder Solar Energy, box 11, Michael Raoul-Duval flies, GRFL.

3. For a blatant example, see Letter, John Love to David Link, September 5, 1973, folder [EX] UT 9/1/73–9/16/73, box 3, WHCF – Sub – UT, NLNP.

4. For an analysis of the values held by various members of the environmental movement, see Lester W. Milbrath, *Environmentalists: Vanguard for a New Society* (Albany: State University of New York Press, 1984), which includes a three-nation attitudinal survey.

5. Langdon Winner, *Autonomous Technology: Technics-out-of-Control as a Theme in Political Thought* (Cambridge, MA: The MIT Press, 1977), chap. 8.

6. Trevor Pinch and Wiebe E. Bijker, "The Social Construction of Facts and Artifacts: Or How the Sociology of Science and the Sociology of Technology Might Benefit Each Other," in *The Social Construction of Technological Systems: New Directions in the Sociology and History of Technology*, Wiebe E. Bijker, Thomas P. Hughes, and Trevor Pinch, eds. (Cambridge, MA: MIT Press, 1987), pp. 17–50.

7. David B. Truman, *The Governmental Process: Political Interest and Public Opinion* (New York: Alfred A. Knopf, 1951); Robert A. Dahl, *A Preface to Democratic Theory* (Chicago: University of Chicago Press, 1956); idem, *Dilemmas of Pluralist Democracy: Autonomy Versus Control* (New Haven, CT: Yale University Press, 1982).

8. On the public support, see the survey data cited in Al Richman, "The Polls: Public Attitudes Toward the Energy Crisis," *Public Opinion Quarterly* 43 (1979): 576–585, and the data in Lamont C. Hempel, "The Politics of Sunshine: An Inquiry into the Origin, Growth, and Ideological Character of the Solar Energy Movement in America," Ph.D. Dissertation, Claremont Graduate School, 1983, p. 198.

9. Avraham Shama and Ken Jacobs, "Solar Energy: Where Policy-Makers and Conservationists Disagree," *Long Range Planning* 15 (1982): 63–75.

They do a content analysis of solar publications of the period and show that policy makers put much more emphasis on economics and national security than did advocates. Their results do show, however, that economics was the most frequently discussed value cluster even among advocates.

10. Barbara C. Farhar, Charles T. Unseld, Rebecca Vories, and Robin Crews, "Public Opinion About Energy," *Annual Review of Energy* 5 (1980): 141–172, esp. p. 147. This is a massive review article that summarizes hundreds of surveys taken on energy in the 1970s.

11. Ibid., p. 143.

12. On the attentive public in energy issues, see Jon D. Miller, "A Conceptual Framework for Understanding Public Attitudes Toward Conservation and Energy Issues," in *Energy and Material Resources: Attitudes, Values, and Public Policy*, AAAS Selected Symposium 75, W. David Conn, ed. (Boulder, CO: Westview Press, 1983), pp. 61–78.

13. For a study comparing solar advocates to nuclear advocates and to the general public in the state of Washington, see Riley E. Dunlap and Marvin E. Olsen, "Hard-Path Versus Soft-Path Advocates: A Study of Energy Activists," *Policy Studies Journal* 13 (December 1984): 413–428. For a similar study in Great Britain, see Stephen Cotgrove and Andrew Duff, "Environmentalism, Middle-Class Radicalism, and Politics," *Sociological Review* 28 (1980): 333–351.

14. See Joseph R. Gusfield, *The Culture of Public Problems: Drinking-Driving and the Symbolic Order* (Chicago: University of Chicago Press, 1981), esp. chap. 1.

15. Frank R. Baumgartner and Bryan D. Jones, *Agendas and Instability in American Politics* (Chicago: University of Chicago Press, 1993), esp. chaps. 1–3.

16. For a critique of the way DOE's nuclear past influenced the way it ran solar programs, see William D. Metz and Allen L. Hammond, *Solar Energy in America* (Washington, DC: The American Association for the Advancement of Science, 1978).

17. See Baumgartner and Jones, *Agendas and Instabilities*.

18. For more critique of the DPR participation program, see Frank N. Laird, "Technocracy Revisited: Knowledge, Power, and the Crisis of Energy Decision Making," *Industrial Crisis Quarterly* 4 (1990): 49–61. For a more detailed discussion of the relationship between democratic theory and forms of participation in technology policy, see Frank N. Laird, "Participatory Analysis, Democracy, and Technological Decision Making," *Science, Technology, and Human Values* 18 (Summer 1993): 341–361, and Frank Laird, "Participating in the Tension: A Response to Guston," *Social Epistemology* 7 (January 1993): 35–46.

19. Edward J. Woodhouse, "Sophisticated Trial and Error in Decision Making About Risk," in *Technology and Politics*, Michael E. Kraft and Norman J. Vig, eds., (Durham, NC: Duke University Press, 1988), pp. 208–226; Joseph G. Morone and Edward J. Woodhouse, *The Demise of Nuclear Energy? Lessons for Democratic Control of Technology* (New Haven, CT: Yale University Press, 1989).

20. Langdon Winner, "Citizen Virtues in a Technological Order," *Inquiry* 35 (Fall 1992): 341–361. The quote is from p. 343.
21. For example, see Langdon Winner, "Decentralization Clarified," chap. 5 in his *The Whale and the Reactor: A Search for Limits in an Age of High Technology* (Chicago: University of Chicago Press, 1986).

Index